THE GRAND PROCESSION OF PTOLEMY PHILADELPHUS

E. E. RICE

OXFORD UNIVERSITY PRESS
1983

Oxford University Press, Walton Street, Oxford OX2 6DP
London Glasgow New York Toronto
Delhi Bombay Calcutta Madras Karachi
Kuala Lumpur Singapore Hong Kong Tokyo
Nairobi Dar es Salaam Cape Town
Melbourne Auckland
and associated companies in
Beirut Berlin Ibadan Mexico City Nicosia

Oxford is a trade mark of Oxford University Press

Published in the United States
by Oxford University Press, New York

© E. E. Rice 1983

British Library Cataloguing in Publication Data
Kallixeinos of Rhodes.
The grand procession of Ptolemy Philadelphus.—
(Oxford classical and philosophical manuscripts)
I. Title   II. Rice, E. E.
888'.0108   PA3946.C55
ISBN 0-19-814720-1

Library of Congress Cataloging in Publication Data
Rice, E. E.
The grand procession of Ptolemy Philadelphus.
(Oxford classical and philosophical monographs)
Includes text in Greek, with translation in English
of: Megalē pompē Ptolemaiou tou Philadelphou /
Kallixeinos.
1. Egypt—History—Greco-Roman period, 332 B.C.–640.
2. Processions—Egypt—Alexandria. 3. Ptolemy II
Philadelphus, King of Egypt. 4. Kallixeinos of Rhodes.
Megalē pompē Ptolemaiou tou Philadelphou. I. Kal-
lixeinos, of Rhodes. Megalē pompē Ptolemaiou tou
Philadelphou. 1983. II. Title. III. Series.
DT92.R52 1983   932'.02   83-2387
ISBN 0-19-814720-1

Set by Hope Services, Abingdon
and printed in Great Britain
by Hazell Watson & Viney Ltd, Aylesbury, Bucks

Acknowledgements

I owe much to many for the completion of this manuscript, and the depth of my gratitude is belied by the brevity of these acknowledgements: Mount Holyoke College, Somerville College Oxford (with its Katharine and Leonard Woolley Travelling Fellowship), the Dr M. Aylwin Cotton Foundation, and Wolfson College Oxford have maintained me; Martin Robertson, John Boardman, J. J. Coulton, and Dorothy J. Thompson, *inter alios*, have advised me; the Editorial Committee of the Oxford Classical and Philosophical Monographs and the Delegates of Oxford University Press have accepted this manuscript for publication. I am especially grateful to Mr P. M. Fraser, who has endured innumerable readings of both thesis and manuscript and who has, characteristically, improved both. Finally, I cannot adequately express my thanks to my parents, to whom this book is dedicated.

Wolfson College
Oxford
March 1983

E. E. RICE

Addendum

I was able to consult *Alexandre et Dionysos*, vol. II of P. Goukowsky, *Essai sur les origines du mythe d'Alexandre* (Nancy, 1978-81), only when this manuscript was in proof. Goukowsky's work traces the link between Alexander and Dionysus, which the author sees as culminating in the Grand Procession of Ptolemy Philadelphus. Nothing in Goukowsky's presentation of the evidence changes the general conclusions which I have presented in this study about the Alexander-Dionysus link. However, I may comment briefly upon a few specific points which he makes concerning the Grand Procession. On pp. 81 ff., Goukowsky states that the Grand Procession is a celebration of the Ptolemaieia festival held in 271-70 BC, and cites the nature of the fragmentary, excerpted text as the explanation for the lack of emphasis on Ptolemy Soter. It will be discussed in Chapter 5 below why this argument and the connection of the Grand Procession with the Ptolemaieia are unacceptable. In note 16 to his chapter, Goukowsky claims that the figure of Penteteris in the Grand Procession can only be explained if the festival was part of the isolympic (i.e. penteteric) Ptolemaieia. He is apparently unaware that various festivals were called 'the Penteteris' in informal contexts (see pp. 186-7 below); apart from the papyrological references to various 'Penteterides' (noted ibid.), this is quite clear from Kallixeinos' phrase (197D) αἱ τῶν Πεντετηρίδων (N.B. not τῆς Πεντετηρίδος) γραφαί.

Contents

Abbreviations

The abbreviations used are the standard ones for epigraphical, papyrological, and periodical publications. This list includes only those works to which frequent reference is made, and those which are not sufficiently clear in themselves. Other works which deal primarily with Kallixeinos are discussed in Chapter 1.

Caspari, 'Nilschiff'	F. Caspari, 'Das Nilschiff Ptolemaios IV', *JDAI* xxxi (1916), 1 ff.
Caspari, 'Studien'	F. Caspari, 'Studien zur dem Kallixeinosfragment Athenaios 5, 197C–203B', *Hermes* lxviii (1933), 400 ff.
Franzmeyer	W. Franzmeyer, *Kallixenos' Bericht über das Prachtzelt und den Festzug Ptolemaeus II* (Diss. Strassburg, 1904)
Köster	A. Köster, *Studien zur Geschichte des Antiken Seewesens*, *Klio* Beiheft xxxii (1934), 20–53
Ptol. Alex.	P. M. Fraser, *Ptolemaic Alexandria* (3 vols., Oxford, 1972)
Studniczka	Franz Studniczka, *Das Symposion Ptolemaios II*, *Sächs. Abh.* xxx (2) (1914)

1. Introduction

In the fifth book of the *Deipnosophistai* of Athenaeus of Naucratis, the detailed account of the Grand Procession of Ptolemy Philadelphus (197C–203B = *FGrH* 627 F 2) is excerpted from a larger work by Kallixeinos of Rhodes called *About Alexandria*. The fragmentary text is divorced from its original context, and its interpretation is hampered by lacunae, textual confusion, and an abrupt ending. The quotation comprises the description of a huge civic procession composed of several smaller processions in honour of gods, deified mortals, and two personifications from nature. The smaller procession recorded in the most detail is that of Dionysus, which occupies about 75 per cent of the text (197E–202A). The occasion, purpose, and date of the Grand Procession are not stated in the fragment, and, in his preface to the quotation, Athenaeus says only that the event occurred in Alexandria during the reign and under the auspices of Ptolemy II Philadelphus (196A). Little is known about Kallixeinos, whose fragments appear only in Athenaeus: his date is indeterminate, he probably wrote in Alexandria, and he may be referred to in other ancient sources.

The description of the Grand Procession appears as the culmination of a catalogue of wonders which surpass each other in luxury and ostentation. Although the account verges on the incredible in terms of the prodigious size of the objects involved, the scale and scope of the event, and the unremitting emphasis on wealth and extravagance, not only common sense, but also an examination of the text and a consideration of the procession's possible context suggest that the description by Kallixeinos has an historical basis. The ultimate reliability of his account could only be corroborated by independent information about the procession, which has yet to be found, but no detail recorded in the text can be disproved finally, given current knowledge of ancient art and technology; on the contrary, many details can be supported by archaeological, epigraphical, and literary material. Moreover, Kallixeinos appears to be a trustworthy source of information in three other fragments which describe Alexandrian marvels of similarly overwhelming conception. Kallixeinos' literary account may be considered in itself an important primary source for the cultural history of Alexandria in the early third century BC.

The scope of the Grand Procession touches on many aspects of Ptolemaic studies. Kallixeinos describes an event, not an object or a structure like other writers of Hellenistic ecphrases. A study of the text therefore entails a consideration of related matters—date, context, occasion, and purpose—

all of which have significant historical implications in this case. Economic questions arise from the amazing wealth seen throughout the procession, which has often been adduced to discredit the accuracy of Kallixeinos despite the fact that Ptolemaic riches were legendary in contemporary sources. The objects in the procession which are not native to Egypt must have been brought as a result of the trading contacts with the rest of the Hellenistic world and beyond. Politically, the procession sheds light on the complex national and international issues of the time; certain measures of propaganda extol the legitimacy and glory of the royal family at home and abroad, and the striking display of military force at the end of the procession must be seen in terms of the contemporary power struggle among the newly-founded Hellenistic states. Processions staged by later Hellenistic kings may have been intended to rival this one, and these used comparable opportunities for political propaganda in other situations.

In terms of religion, this unique text is the earliest detailed literary account of a Greek religious procession, which in any case guarantees its importance, but the specific information provided about the cult of Dionysus (who figures most prominently) offers the fullest picture of his worship in third-century Alexandria. Much of the religious iconography seen in the procession illustrates the types of change which occurred when the religion of the Macedonians was transferred from its native, civic context to a foreign setting.

Finally, the procession provides information about the artistic culture of Alexandria, of which there are lamentably few remains. The literary description of various objects supplements material finds and helps to clarify the archaeological record.

As a document which incorporates many features of contemporary society, the account of the procession serves as a useful focus for their study since its diverse information appears in a specific, unified context and can in turn be extrapolated to illuminate other problems of the period. An examination of the internal elements of the text and a consideration of its wider implications are necessary because the only studies of the former were never exhaustive and are now outdated, and because, in the latter case, assumptions have often been made without a proper examination of their foundations.

Analyses of the Grand Procession have been few. The earliest monograph is the essay by Joseph Kamp, *De Ptolemaei Philadelphi Pompa Bacchica* (Bonn, 1864), dealing only with the sectional procession of Dionysus within the Grand Procession. His work contains a partial text (notable for some bizarre emendations), and a commentary consisting mainly of a paraphrase of the text with some mythological observations. Few artistic parallels are given, and historical discussion is confined to a multiplication of literary references to Bacchic beliefs and to processions and worship held by Alexander the Great's army. Kamp's work suffers from the paucity of historical and archaeological information available at the time to the author, and to his deliberate limitation of the topic.

The short essay by P. Thomas Kramer, *Die Gelehrte Tischgesellschaft des Athenäus V Buch, Cap. 1–45* (Augsburg, 1872), gives a description of the *Deipnosophistai*, a history of its editions, and a translation of 185A–209A. A series of highly selective notes elucidates the text (notes 126–148 concern the procession). Kramer limits his observations to mythological subjects, proposed textual emendations, and specific problems of interpretation arising from the text, such as the identification of some animals and vase-shapes. His references to analogous material are taken only from ancient literary sources, and he offers no historical interpretation of the procession, nor any analysis of its various elements.

The only monograph of this century to deal with the procession is *Kallixenos' Bericht über das Prachtzelt und den Festzug Ptolemaeus II* by W. Franzmeyer (Diss. Strassburg, 1904). Franzmeyer discusses each feature of the procession (and of the ornamental pavilion whose description in Athenaeus precedes that of the procession), which makes his work the most comprehensive to date, but he concentrates on analogies for the objects and discussions of the mythical characters rather than on the reasons for the inclusion of either. His references to archaeological and historical material are brief, superficial, and now outdated, and if occasional comments are sensible, they are not especially enlightening. Franzmeyer accepted the view that the procession celebrated the cult of the Theoi Soteres in connection with the cult of Alexander, occurring in 275/4 as part of the first grand festival after the marriage of Philadelphus and Arsinoe II, and he gives no further historical discussion. Since this assumption is dubious, there is despite Franzmeyer's work a need for a detailed historical investigation of the procession's context, and for a re-examination of the text from many angles.

A short article by F. Caspari briefly examines the procession *as a procession* (*Hermes* lxviii (1933), 400 ff.). After a few general observations on processions in Greek religious festivals, and a partial catalogue of festivals with their processions from the time of Alexander, he includes a few comments on the technical aspects of this procession, such as the question of its duration and the logistical problems involved in the march-past of the troops. Although useful, the article considers only a fraction of the issues raised in the text.

The reader may find studies dealing with the other fragments of Kallixeinos useful for discussions of the date and general credibility of the author, and for artistic comparisons between the procession and the subjects of his other descriptions. The ornamental pavilion of Ptolemy II, described by Kallixeinos immediately before the procession (196A–197C = Appendix I, F 2) and treated in a cursory fashion by Franzmeyer, was examined in great detail by Franz Studniczka, *Das Symposion Ptolemaios II*.[1] Kallixeinos' account of the '40' (Tessarakontērēs), a huge warship constructed for Ptolemy IV whose description is quoted by Athenaeus after the procession (203E–204D = Appendix I, F 1), has been given tentative interpretations in studies of ancient warships, notably by Casson,[2] Morrison and Williams,[3] and Landels,[4] although the problems surrounding the form of this ship have not been entirely solved. The description of Ptolemy IV's Nile Barge, the Thalamegos, is the final quotation of Kallixeinos by Athenaeus (204D–206C = Appendix I, F 1, 204D ff.). It has been discussed and reconstructed by Caspari,[5] and with less detail and success, by Köster.[6] (These other descriptions and their relevant studies are briefly considered in Chapter 4B.) A more general reference work on Kallixeinos is the article by Jacoby,[7] who unfortunately never wrote his commentary on the text (*FGrH* 627).

The account of the procession has been variously used as evidence for problems in early third-century Ptolemaic history. The date and occasion of the procession were considered by historians of the last century, whose opinions were divided into three main schools of thought.[8] It was considered as the celebration either of Philadelphus' coronation (whether before or after the death of Soter), or of the marriage of Philadelphus and Arsinoe II, or of the deification of Ptolemy I. Interpretations of the procession changed drastically after the publication of the decree from Amorgos of the Nesiotic League (*SIG*[3] 390; first published in *R. Ph.* 1890), which records the establishment by Philadelphus of the Ptolemaieia festival in honour of his father. Since the elements of the festival seen in the decree have much in common superficially with certain features of the procession, it has been frequently assumed that Kallixeinos describes one specific celebration of the Ptolemaieia. Much ingenuity has been expended in this century to identify the date of the particular celebration, with different

---

[1] *Sächs. Abh.* xxx (2) (1914).

[2] L. Casson, *Ships and Seamanship in the Ancient World* (Princeton, 1971), 108 ff. and *passim*.

[3] J. S. Morrison and R. T. Williams, *Greek Oared Ships 900–322* (Cambridge, (1968), 296; J. S. Morrison, *IJNA* i (1972), 232.

[4] J. G. Landels, *Engineering in the Ancient World* (London, 1978), 152 ff.

[5] *JDAI* xxxi (1916), 1 ff.

[6] *Studien zur Geschichte des Antiken Seewesens, Klio* Beiheft xxxii (1934), 20–53.

[7] *RE* s.v. Kallixeinos.

[8] For a classification of these opinions see A. Bouché-Leclerq, *Histoire des Lagides* (4 vols., Paris. 1903–7), i. 156–7 n. 1.

interpretations of the text being used to produce datable criteria (e.g. the marital status of Philadelphus and the progress of the Carian and First Syrian Wars).[9] Opinions have varied, and the views have been stated and re-stated not without some vehemence. The most generous of these opinions is that the procession belongs to an indeterminate celebration of the Ptolemaieia within the decade 279 to 270 BC. P. M. Fraser has, on the other hand, recently maintained that the procession formed no part of any Ptolemaieia.[10]

The lack of any satisfactory examination of the procession as a self-contained literary account of artistic objects and mythical scenes, and the disagreement among those who use the text primarily as a piece of historical evidence, now make a reconsideration of the description of the Grand Procession by Kallixeinos desirable.

The text presented here is based on the Teubner edition of Kaibel (which, with a few changes, was subsequently adopted by Jacoby in *FGrH* 627), with occasional readings taken from other editions of Athenaeus. There has been no special study of the text of the procession, and the latest editions of the *Deipnosophistai* have not been completed as far as Book V, where the fragments of Kallixeinos occur. The translation is based on the text printed here. (The line numbers quoted throughout this volume refer only to the text as it is printed in Chapter 2 and are therefore given along-side the standard numerical divisions of the text of Athenaeus.) Quotations from other fragments of Kallixeinos are taken from the text of Jacoby, which has been reprinted in Appendix I. The commentary which follows is not a line-by-line examination of the text, but a discussion of the proces-sion, which has been divided into the consecutive thematic sections which seem to occur naturally (see the diagram of these divisions on p. 28). Al-though the commentary seeks to establish the credibility of Kallixeinos' account by furnishing literary and archaeological analogies for some of the objects and tableaux which appear in the procession, it is not its purpose to list all the relevant material which might illustrate specific details. It concentrates only on certain points of special historical, mythological, or artistic interest, and textual points are discussed in detail only when

[9] Ibid., i. 156 ff.; H. von Prott, *RhM* n.F. liii (1898), 460 ff.; J. P. Mahaffy, *A History of Egypt under the Ptolemaic Dynasty* (2nd ed., London, 1914), 70; W. Otto, *Priester und Tempel im hellenistischen Agypten* (2 vols., Leipzig and Berlin, 1905), i. 147; id., *Philologus* lxxxvi (1931), 405 n. 10; 414–15 n. 27; id., *Beiträge zur Seleukidengeschichte, Bay. Abh.* xxxiv (1) (1928), 5 ff.; E. Bevan, *A History of Egypt under the Ptolemaic Dynasty* (London, 1927), 127–8; *CAH* vii. 703 n. 1; W. W. Tarn, *Antigonos Gonatas* (Oxford, 1913), 261 n. 10; id., *Hermes* lxv (1930), 447 n. 2; id., *JHS* liii (1933), 59 ff.; Caspari, *Hermes* lxviii (1933), 400.
[10] *BCH* lxxviii (1954), 57 n. 3; *Ptol. Alex.* i. 231–2; ii. 381 n. 335.

they affect the understanding of the fragment. The various parts of the procession will therefore necessarily receive an uneven treatment, extending from a cursory discussion of familiar or obvious items to a detailed examination of anomalous subjects and those crucial to the interpretation of the text.

The commentary is followed by two chapters of discussion: the first examines Kallixeinos of Rhodes as an author and historical personality, the second the historical interpretations of the procession. The text, translation, and commentary appear first so that relevant questions, and some introductory discussion of them, will be familar to the reader before the chapters of interpretation, whose arguments follow directly from the text. As a result, some problems introduced in the commentary remain unresolved until the last chapters.

I have made no attempt at consistency in the English spelling of Greek names, but have used those versions most familar in academic works, i.e. Kallixeinos, but Athenaeus.

2. Text and Translation

Manuscripts of Athenaeus

A *Venetus Marcianus* 447 (tenth century AD) Main manuscript containing Books III–XV (74A–702C) of the *Deipnosophistai*; this redaction reflects the second abridgement of the text of Athenaeus (see below, p. 137).

C *Parisinus Suppl. gr.* 841

E *Laurentianus* (Florence)
Manuscripts C and E both date from the fifteenth to sixteenth centuries AD and contain Books I–III (as far as 73E) and the rest of the fifteen books as they were abbreviated in the so-called *Epitome* (the third abridgement of the *Deipnosophistai*; see below, p. 137).

Selected Editions

Schweighäuser   *Athenaei Naucratitae Deipnosophistarum Libri Quindecim*, ed. Johannes Schweighäuser (Strassburg, 1801–7)

Dindorf   Athenaeus, ed. W. Dindorf (Leipzig, 1827)

Meineke   *Athenaei Deipnosophistae*, ed. A. Meineke (Leipzig, Teubner, 1858–67)

Kaibel   *Athenaei Naucratitae Dipnosophistarum* libr. xv rec. Georg. Kaibel (Leipzig, Teubner, 1887–90) (with emendations by Wilamowitz)

Gulick   *The Deipnosophists*, ed. C. B. Gulick (Loeb, London and Cambridge, Mass., 1927–41)

Jacoby   *Die Fragmente der griechischen Historiker*, ed. F. Jacoby (Berlin and Leiden, 1923–58), 627

Selected Critical Studies

Cobet, C. G., *Oratio de Arte Interpretandi Grammatices et Critices Fundamentis Innixa Primario Philologi Officio* (Leiden, 1847)

Meineke, A., *Philologicarum Exercitationum in Athenaei Deipnosophistas Specimen Secundum* (Berlin, 1846)

Meyer, J., *Emendationes et Observationes in Athenaei novissimam editionem* (Regensburg, 1897)

Peppink, S. P., *Observationes in Athenaei Deipnosophistas* (Leiden, 1936)

197 C   "Ἡμεῖς δὲ ἐπειδὴ τὰ κατὰ τὴν σκηνὴν διεληλύθαμεν, ποι
ησόμεθα καὶ τὴν τῆς πομπῆς ἐξήγησιν· ἤγετο γὰρ διὰ τοῦ κατὰ
197 D   τὴν πόλιν σταδίου. πρώτη δ' ἐβάδιζεν ⟨ἡ⟩ Ἑωσφόρου· καὶ γὰρ
ἀρχὴν εἶχεν ἡ πομπὴ καθ' ὃν ὁ προειρημένος ἀστὴρ φαίνεται χρόνον·
ἔπειθ' ἡ τοῖς τῶν βασιλέων γονεῦσι κατωνομασμένη. μετὰ δὲ   5
ταύτας αἱ τῶν θεῶν ἁπάντων, οἰκείαν ἔχουσαι τῆς περὶ ἕκαστον
αὐτῶν ἱστορίας διασκευήν. τὴν δὲ τελευταίαν Ἑσπέρου συν
έβαινεν εἶναι, τῆς ὥρας εἰς τοῦτο συναγούσης τὸν καιρόν. τὰ
δὲ κατὰ μέρος αὐτῶν εἴ τις εἰδέναι βούλεται, τὰς τῶν Πεντε
τηρίδων γραφὰς λαμβάνων ἐπισκοπείτω.   10
197 E   "Τῆς δὲ Διονυσιακῆς πομπῆς πρῶτοι μὲν προῇεσαν οἱ
τὸν ὄχλον ἀνείργοντες Σιληνοί, πορφυρᾶς χλαμύδας, οἱ δὲ
φοινικίδας ἠμφιεσμένοι. τούτοις δ' ἐπηκολούθουν Σάτυροι καθ'
ἕκαστον τοῦ σταδίου μέρος εἴκοσι, λαμπάδας φέροντες κισσίνας
διαχρύσους· μεθ' οὓς Νῖκαι χρυσᾶς ἔχουσαι πτέρυγας. ἔφερον   15
δ' αὗται θυμιατήρια ἐξαπήχη κισσίνοις διαχρύσοις κλωσὶ δια
κεκοσμημένα, ζῳωτοὺς ἐνδεδυκυῖαι χιτῶνας, αὐταὶ δὲ πολὺν
197 F   κόσμον χρυσοῦν περικείμεναι. μετὰ δὲ ταύτας εἴπετο βωμὸς
ἐξάπηχυς διπλοῦς κισσίνη φυλλάδι διαχρύσῳ πεπυκασμένος, ἔχων
ἀμπέλινον χρυσοῦν στέφανον μεσολεύκοις μίτραις κατειλημμένον.   20
ἐπηκολούθουν δ' αὐτῷ παῖδες ἐν χιτῶσι πορφυροῖς, λιβανωτὸν καὶ
σμύρναν, ἔτι δὲ κρόκον ἐπὶ χρυσῶν μαζονόμων φέροντες ἑκατὸν
εἴκοσι· μεθ' οὓς Σάτυροι τεσσαράκοντα ἐστεφανωμένοι κισσίνοις
χρυσοῖς στεφάνοις. τὰ δὲ σώματα οἱ μὲν ἐκέχριντο ὀστρείῳ,
198 A   τινὲς δὲ μίλτῳ καὶ χρώμασιν ἑτέροις. ἔφερον δὲ καὶ οὗτοι   25
στέφανον χρυσοῦν ἐξ ἀμπέλου καὶ κισσοῦ εἰργασμένον·
"Μεθ' οὓς Σιληνοὶ δύο ἐν πορφυραῖς χλαμύσι καὶ κρη
πῖσι λευκαῖς. εἶχε δ' αὐτῶν ὁ μὲν πέτασον καὶ κηρύκειον
χρυσοῦν, ὁ δὲ σάλπιγγα. μέσος δὲ τούτων ἐβάδιζεν ἀνὴρ μείζων
τετράπηχυς ἐν τραγικῇ διαθέσει καὶ προσώπῳ, φέρων χρυσοῦν   30
Ἀμαλθείας κέρας, ὃς προσηγορεύετο Ἐνιαυτός, ᾧ γυνὴ περι
καλλεστάτη κατὰ ⟨ταὐτὸ⟩ τὸ μέγεθος εἵπετο πολλῷ χρυσῷ καὶ

3 ⟨ἡ⟩ Kaibel   5 ἐπωνομασμένη superscripsit κατω- C   6 ἕκαστον
Wilamowitz: ἐκάστων A   8 εἰς τοῦτον Kaibel   10 ⟨ἀνα⟩γραφὰς?
Jacoby   12 σιληνοὶ C: σειληνοὶ A   χλαμύδας Dindorf (v. 27):
χλανίδας AC   13–14 καθ'ἑκάτερον? Kaibel   μέρος Musurus: μέρους
A   [κισσίνας]? Kaibel   15 Νῖκαι...(numerale)? Kaibel: Νῖκαι ⟨ί⟩?
Jacoby   16 διαχρύσοις Kaibel: καὶ χρυσοῖς A   κλωσὶ Adam: καιωσι
A   17 αὐταὶ Schweighäuser: αὗται A   20 κατειλημμένον AC: διειλημμένον Kaibel
24 ἐκέχριντο C: ἐκέχρηντο A   26 κισσου Schweighäuser: καὶ χρυσοῦ A
27 χλαμύσι A: χλανίσι C   28 κηρύκειον C: κηρύκιον A   29–30 μείζων
⟨ἢ⟩ τετράπηχυς Kaibel   30 προσώπῳ AC: προσωπείῳ Cobet   31 Ἀμαλθείας

'Since we have considered the subject of the pavilion in detail, we will also describe the Grand Procession. It was led through the city stadium. First of all marched the sectional procession of the Morning Star, because the Grand Procession began at the time when that aforementioned star appeared. Next came the sectional procession named after the parents of the kings. After these processions came those of all the gods, having the attributes which were appropriate to the traditions of each of them. It happened that the procession of the Evening Star came last of all, since the season brought the time of day to the point when that star appeared. If anyone wishes to know the details of all of these processions, let him take and study the records of the Penteteric festivals.

'In the procession of Dionysus, Silenoi were sent forth first to restrain the crowds; some of them wore purple cloaks, others crimson ones. Satyrs followed them, twenty along each part of the stadium, carrying gilded torches of ivy leaves. After them came Nikai with golden wings; they carried thymiateria nine feet tall which were adorned with gilded ivy leaves. The women had on chitons embroidered with figures, and wore much gold jewelry. A double altar nine feet long followed them, thickly covered with gilded ivy foliage and having a golden crown of vine leaves which was entwined with white-striped ribbons. Boys in purple chitons followed it, carrying frankincense and myrrh and also saffron on 120 golden trenchers. After them came forty Satyrs crowned with golden ivy crowns; the bodies of some of them were smeared with purple dye, others with vermilion and other colours. They carried a gold crown made of vine and ivy.

'After them came two Silenoi in purple cloaks and white sandals, one of them had a petasos and a golden herald's staff, and the other a trumpet. Between them walked a taller man, six feet tall, in a tragic costume and mask, who carried the golden horn of Amaltheia. He was called Eniautos. A very beautiful woman of the same height followed him, adorned with

---

C: Ἀμαλθίας A   32 κατὰ ⟨ταὐτὸ⟩ τὸ μέγεθος Jacoby: κατὰ ταὐτὸ μέγεθος
Rohde: κατ'⟨ἐκεῖνον⟩ τὸ μέγεθος Wilam.: ⟨καὶ ἴση⟩ κατὰ τὸ μέγεθος Meyer

198 B διαπρεπεῖ . . . κεκοσμημένη, φέρουσα τῇ μὲν μιᾷ τῶν χειρῶν
στέφανον περσαίας, τῇ δ᾿ ἑτέρᾳ ῥάβδον φοίνικος. ἐκαλεῖτο δὲ
αὕτη Πεντετηρίς. ταύτῃ δ᾿ ἐπηκολούθουν Ὧραι τέσσαρες διεσ-   35
κευασμέναι, καὶ ἑκάστη φέρουσα τοὺς ἰδίους καρπούς· ἐχόμενα
τούτων θυμιατήρια δύο κίσσινα ἐκ χρυσοῦ ἐξαπήχη καὶ βωμὸς ἀνὰ
μέσον τούτων τετράγωνος χρυσοῦ· καὶ πάλιν Σάτυροι στεφάνους
ἔχοντες κισσίνους χρυσοῦς, φοινικίδας περιβεβλημένοι. ἔφερον δ᾿ οἱ μὲν
οἰνοχόην χρυσῆν, οἱ δὲ καρχήσιον· μεθ᾿ οὓς ἐπορεύετο Φίλικος   40
198 C ὁ ποιητής, ἱερεὺς ὢν Διονύσου, καὶ πάντες οἱ περὶ τὸν Διόνυσον
τεχνῖται. τούτων δ᾿ ἐφεξῆς ἐφέροντο Δελφικοὶ τρίποδες, ἆθλα
τοῖς τῶν αὐλητῶν χορηγοῖς, ὁ μὲν παιδικὸς ἐννέα πηχῶν τὸ ὕψος,
ὁ δὲ πηχῶν δώδεκα ὁ τῶν ἀνδρῶν.

   Μετὰ τούτους τετράκυκλος πηχῶν • τεσσαρεσκαίδεκα,   45
ὀκτὼ δὲ τὸ πλάτος, ἤγετο ὑπὸ ἀνδρῶν ὀγδοήκοντα καὶ ἑκατόν.
ἐπὶ δὲ ταύτης ἐπῆν ἄγαλμα Διονύσου δεκάπηχυ σπένδον ἐκ καρ-
χησίου χρυσοῦ, χιτῶνα πορφυροῦν ἔχον διάπεζον καὶ ἐπ᾿ αὐτοῦ
κροκωτὸν διαφανῆ. περιεβέβλητο δὲ ἱμάτιον πορφυροῦν χρυσο-
198 D ποίκιλον. προέκειτο δ᾿ αὐτοῦ κρατὴρ Λακωνικὸς χρυσοῦς   50
μετρητῶν δεκαπέντε καὶ τρίπους χρυσοῦς, ἐφ᾿ οὗ θυμιατήριον
χρυσοῦν καὶ φιάλαι δύο χρυσαῖ κασσίας μεσταὶ καὶ κρόκου.
περιέκειτο δ᾿ αὐτῷ καὶ σκιὰς ἐκ κισσοῦ καὶ ἀμπέλου καὶ τῆς
λοιπῆς ὀπώρας κεκοσμημένη. προσήρτηντο δὲ καὶ στέφανοι καὶ
ταινίαι καὶ θύρσοι καὶ τύμπανα καὶ μίτραι πρόσωπά τε σατ-   55
198 E υρικὰ καὶ κωμικὰ καὶ τραγικά. τῇ δὲ τετρακύκλῳ . . . ἱερεῖς
καὶ ἱέρειαι καὶ †περσειστελεταὶ† καὶ θίασοι παντοδαποὶ καὶ
⟨αἱ⟩ τὰ λῖκνα φέρουσαι. μετὰ δὲ ταύτας Μακέται αἱ καλούμεναι
Μιμαλλόνες καὶ Βασσάραι καὶ Λυδαί, κατακεχυμέναι τὰς τρίχας
καὶ ἐστεφανωμέναι τινὲς μὲν ὄφεσιν, αἱ δὲ μίλακι καὶ ἀμπέλῳ   60
καὶ κισσῷ. κατεῖχον δὲ ταῖς χερσὶν αἱ μὲν ἐγχειρίδια, αἱ
δὲ ὄφεις.
198 F   Μετὰ δὲ ταύτας ἤγετο τετράκυκλος . . . πηχῶν ὀκτὼ

33 διαπρεπεῖ ⟨ἐσθῆτι⟩ Meineke: ⟨ἱματίῳ⟩, ⟨χιτῶνι⟩ Meyer   34 περσαίας A:
περσέας C   35 ⟨αἱ⟩ τέσσαρες Kaibel   38 χρυσοῦς Schweighäuser,
Cobet   40 Φίλικος Fraser, Ptol. Alex. ii. 859, n. 407: Φιλίσκος AC   43 αὐλητῶν L. Robert, Ét. Épig. et Phil. (Paris, 1938), 31 ff.: ἀθλητῶν A   παιδικὸς Kaibel: παιδίσκος A: παιδίσκων Müller, FHG, iii. 60, alii   45 μετὰ ⟨δὲ⟩? μῆκος
πηχῶν C   47 Διονύσου C: Διονυσίου A   52 κασσίας AC: κασίας
Kaibel   56 ⟨ἐπηκολούθουν⟩, ⟨εἵποντο⟩ Schweighäuser   57 περσεισ-
τελεταὶ A: ἱεροστολισταὶ Rohde: πέρυσι τελεσταὶ Schweighäuser: ἱεροπρεπεῖς
τελεσταὶ Meineke: Ὀρφεοτελεσταὶ Casaubon: περὶ τὰς τελετάς? Preller, ed.
Polemon p. 178 adnot.   58 ⟨αἱ⟩ Wilam.   ταύτας Kaibel: ταῦτα
AC   ⟨βάκχαι⟩ Μακετίδες? Kaibel: ⟨καὶ⟩ αἱ καλούμεναι vel ⟨αἱ⟩ Μακέται καλ.
⟨καὶ⟩ Μιμαλλόνες Schweighäuser   59 Ληναὶ Wilam., Kl. Schr. iv. 154 no. 83
60 μίλακι Kaibel: μίλαξι AC   63 τετράκυκλος ⟨longitudinis nota⟩ πηχῶν Schweighäuser: †πηχῶν Jacoby: 'octo ulnarum fuit longitudo'? Kaibel

much gold jewelry and a magnificent ⟨costume⟩; in one hand she carried a crown of persea, in the other a palm branch. She was called Penteteris. Four Horai followed her, elaborately dressed and each carrying her own fruits. Following them were two golden thymiateria of ivy, nine feet tall, and between them was a square altar of gold. Once again came Satyrs, having golden ivy crowns and dressed in scarlet; some of them carried a golden oinochoe, and others a karchesion. After them marched the poet Philikos, who was the priest of Dionysus, and all the Guild of the Artists of Dionysus. Delphic tripods were carried right after them as prizes for the choregoi of the flautists. The one for the choregos of the boys' class was $13\frac{1}{2}$ feet tall, and the one for the choregos of the men was 18 feet tall.

'After them a four-wheeled cart, 21 feet long by 12 feet wide, was drawn by 180 men. In it was a fifteen-foot statue of Dionysus pouring a libation from a golden karchesion. He wore a purple chiton reaching to his feet and a transparent, saffron-coloured robe on top of that. The statue also wore a purple himation woven with gold. Before the figure lay a golden Laconian krater of fifteen measures, and also a three-legged, golden table on which lay a golden thymiaterion and two gold phialai full of cassia and saffron. The statue was covered by a canopy decorated with ivy, vine, and other fruits, and fastened to it were crowns, fillets, thyrsoi, drums, headbands, and satyric, comic, and tragic masks. There ⟨followed⟩ behind the cart priests, priestesses, many different thiasoi, and female likna-bearers. After them came Macedonian women called Mimallones, Bassarai, and Lydai, who had hair streaming loose and were crowned, some with snakes, others with smilax, vine, and ivy. Some of them held daggers in their hands, others snakes.

'After them a four-wheeled cart was led along by sixty men . . . 12 feet

πλάτος ὑπὸ ἀνδρῶν ἑξήκοντα, ἐφ᾽ ἧς ἄγαλμα Νύσης ὀκτάπηχυ
καθήμενον, ἐνδεδυκὸς μὲν θάψινον χιτῶνα χρυσοποίκιλον, 65
ἱμάτιον δὲ ἠμφίεστο Λακωνικόν. ἀνίστατο δὲ τοῦτο μηχανι-
κῶς οὐδενὸς τὰς χεῖρας προσάγοντος, καὶ σπεῖσαν ἐκ χρυσῆς
φιάλης γάλα πάλιν ἐκάθητο. εἶχε δὲ ἐν τῇ ἀριστερᾷ θύρσον
ἐστεμμένον μίτραις. αὕτη δ᾽ ἐστεφάνωτο κισσίνῳ χρυσῷ καὶ
βότρυσι διαλίθοις πολυτελέσιν. εἶχε δὲ σκιάδα καὶ ἐπὶ τῶν 70
γωνιῶν τῆς τετρακύκλου κατεπεπήγεσαν λαμπάδες διάχρυσοι
τέτταρες.

199 A   "Εξῆς εἵλκετο ἄλλη τετράκυκλος μῆκος πηχῶν εἴκοσι,
πλάτος ἐκκαίδεκα, ὑπὸ ἀνδρῶν τριακοσίων, ἐφ᾽ ἧς κατεσκεύαστο
ληνὸς πηχῶν εἴκοσι τεσσάρων, πλάτος πεντεκαίδεκα, πλήρης 75
σταφυλῆς. ἐπάτουν δὲ ἑξήκοντα Σάτυροι πρὸς αὐλὸν ᾄδοντες
μέλος ἐπιλήνιον. ἐφειστήκει δ᾽ αὐτοῖς Σιληνός· καὶ δι᾽ ὅλης
τῆς ὁδοῦ τὸ γλεῦκος ἔρρει.

"Εξῆς ἐφέρετο τετράκυκλος μῆκος πηχῶν εἴκοσι πέντε,
πλάτος τεσσαρεσκαίδεκα. ἤγετο δὲ ὑπὸ ἀνδρῶν ἑξακοσίων· ἐφ᾽ 80
ἧς ἦν ἀσκὸς τρισχιλίους ἔχων μετρητάς, ἐκ παρδαλῶν [δερμάτων]
199 B   ἐρραμμένος. ἔρρει δὲ καὶ οὗτος κατὰ μικρὸν ἀνιέμενος κατὰ
πᾶσαν τὴν ὁδόν.

"Ηκολούθουν δ᾽ αὐτῷ Σάτυροι καὶ Σιληνοὶ ἑκατὸν εἴκοσι
ἐστεφανωμένοι, φέροντες οἱ μὲν οἰνοχόας, οἱ δὲ φιάλας, οἱ 85
δὲ θηρικλείους μεγάλας, πάντα χρυσᾶ· ἐχόμενος ἤγετο κρατὴρ
ἀργυροῦς ἑξακοσίους χωρῶν μετρητάς, ἐπὶ τετρακύκλου ἑλκομένης
ὑπὸ ἀνδρῶν ἑξακοσίων. εἶχε δὲ ὑπὸ τὰ χείλη καὶ τὰ ὦτα καὶ
199 C   ἐπὶ τὴν βάσιν ζῷα τετορευμένα, καὶ διὰ μέσου ἐστεφάνωτο στεφάνῳ χρυσῷ διαλίθῳ. ἑξῆς ἐφέρετο κυλικεῖα 90
ἀργυρᾶ δωδεκαπήχη δύο, ὕψος πηχῶν ἕξ. ταῦτα δ᾽ εἶχεν ἄνω
τε ἀκρωτήρια καὶ ἐν ταῖς γάστραις κύκλῳ καὶ ἐπὶ τῶν ποδῶν
ζῷα τριημιπήχη καὶ πηχυαῖα πλήθει πολλά· καὶ λουτῆρες
μεγάλοι δέκα καὶ κρατῆρες ἐκκαίδεκα, ὧν οἱ μείζους ἐχώρουν
μετρητὰς τριάκοντα, οἱ δ᾽ ἐλάχιστοι πέντε. εἶτα λέβητες 95
ἕξ, βανωτοὶ εἴκοσι τέσσαρες ἐπ᾽ ἐγγυθήκαις πάντες, καὶ ληνοὶ

64 ἑξακοσίων? Jacoby   66 ἀνίστατο δὲ Schweighäuser: ἀνίστατο δὴ A
73 εἴκοσι ... ('minimum εἴκοσι πέντε') Kaibel   74 ἐφ᾽ ἧς C: ἐφεξῆς A
77 ἐφειστήκει C: ἐφεστήκει A   80 'latitudinis nota fortasse corrupta'
Kaibel: κδ´ alii   81 [δερμάτων] Meineke: 'aut παρδαλείων scribendum aut δερ-
μάτων delendum' Cobet: παρδαλεῖων alii   86 ἐχομένως alii   87 ἑλκομένης Meineke: ἐλκόμενος A   89 ἐπὶ Rice: ὑπὸ AC   τετορευμένα Salmasius:
τετορνευμένα A   90 'ἐπεφέρετο A   κυλικεῖα Villebrun: κυλίκια AC
93 τριημιπήχη Schweighäuser: τρία ἡμιπήχη A   94 μέγιστοι?
96 [ἕξ] Kaibel   βα⟨λα⟩νωτοὶ Jahn   πάντες Kaibel: πέντε A

wide, on which there was a seated statue of Nysa twelve feet tall, wearing a yellow chiton woven with gold thread, and wrapped in a Laconian himation. This statue stood up mechanically without anyone laying a hand on it, and it sat back down again after pouring a libation of milk from a gold phiale. It held in its left hand a thyrsos bound with fillets. The figure was crowned with golden ivy leaves and with grapes made of very precious jewels. The statue had a canopy, and four gilded torches were fastened to the corners of the cart.

'Next, another four-wheeled cart, 30 feet long by 24 feet wide, was pulled by 300 men, on which there was set up a wine-press 36 feet long by $22\frac{1}{2}$ feet wide, full of ripe grapes. Sixty Satyrs trampled them as they sang a vintage song to the flute, and a Silenos superintended them. The grape juice flowed through the whole street.

'Next there came a four-wheeled cart, $37\frac{1}{2}$ feet long by 21 feet wide, which was pulled by 600 men. On it was an askos made of leopard skins which held 3,000 measures. As the wine was released little by little, it also flowed over the whole street.

'One hundred and twenty crowned Satyrs and Silenoi followed it, some carrying oinochoai, others phialai, and others large therikleioi—all of gold. Next a silver krater holding 600 measures was led along on a four-wheeled cart drawn by 600 men. Under the rim and handles and on the foot it had figures of chased metal, and it was wreathed in the middle with a gold crown studded with jewels. Next were carried two silver cup-stands, 18 feet by 9 feet. These had finial ornaments on top, and around their curving sides and on their feet they had figures $2\frac{1}{4}$ and $1\frac{1}{2}$ feet tall, many in number. There were ten large basins and sixteen kraters, of which the larger ones held thirty measures, and the smallest, five measures. Next there were six cauldrons, twenty-four banotoi, all on stands, and two silver

199 D ἀργυραῖ δύο, ἐφ᾽ ὧν ἦσαν βῖκοι εἴκοσι τέσσαρες, τράπεζά τε
ὀλάργυρος δωδεκάπηχυς καὶ ἄλλαι ἑξαπήχεις τριάκοντα· πρὸς
δὲ τούτοις τρίποδες τέσσαρες, ὧν εἷς μὲν εἶχε τὴν περίμετρον
πηχῶν ἑκκαίδεκα, κατάργυρος ὢν ὅλος, οἱ δὲ τρεῖς ἐλάττονες 100
ὄντες διάλιθοι κατὰ μέσον ὑπῆρχον. μετὰ τούτους ἐφέροντο
Δελφικοὶ τρίποδες ἀργυροῖ ὀγδοήκοντα τὸν ἀριθμόν, ἐλάττους
τῶν προειρημένων, ὧν αἱ γωνίαι . . ., τετραμέτηρτοι ὑδρίαι
εἴκοσι καὶ ἕξ, ἀμφορεῖς Παναθηναικοὶ δεκαέξ, ψυκτῆρες ἑκατὸν
199 E ἑξήκοντα· τούτων ὁ μέγιστος ἦν μετρητῶν ἕξ, ὁ δὲ ἐλάχ- 105
ιστος δύο. ταῦτα μὲν οὖν ἦν ἅπαντα ἀργυρᾶ.
   "᾽Εχόμενοι δὲ τούτων ἐπόμπευον οἱ τὰ χρυσώματα
φέροντες, κρατῆρας Λακωνικοὺς τέτταρας ἔχοντας στεφάνους
ἀμπελίνους . . . τετραμέτρητοι, ἕτεροι Κορινθιουργεῖς δύο—
οὗτοι δ᾽ εἶχον ἄνωθεν καθήμενα περιφανῆ τετορευμένα ζῷα 110
καὶ ἐν τῷ τραχήλῳ καὶ ἐν ταῖς γάστραις πρόστυπα ἐπιμελῶς
πεποιημένα. ἐχώρει δ᾽ ἕκαστος μετρητὰς ὀκτώ— ἐπ᾽ ἐγγυθή-
199 F καις· καὶ ληνός, ἐν ᾗ ἦσαν βῖκοι δέκα, ὁλκεῖα δύο, ἑκάτερον
χωροῦν μετρητὰς πέντε, κώθωνες διμέτρητοι δύο, ψυκτῆρες
εἴκοσι δύο, ὧν ὁ μέγιστος ἐχώρει μετρητὰς τριάκοντα, ὁ 115
δ᾽ ἐλάχιστος μετρητήν. ἐπόμπευσαν δὲ τρίποδες χρυσοῖ μεγάλοι
τέτταρες, καὶ χρυσωματοθήκη χρυσῆ διάλιθος πηχῶν δέκα ὕψος,
ἔχουσα βασμοὺς ἕξ, ἐν οἷς καὶ ζῷα τετραπάλαιστα ἐπιμελῶς
πεποιημένα, πολλὰ τὸν ἀριθμόν, καὶ κυλικεῖα δύο, καὶ ὑάλινα
200 A διάχρυσα δύο· ἐγγυθῆκαι χρυσαῖ τετραπήχεις δύο, ἄλλαι ἐλάτ- 120
τους τρεῖς, ὑδρίαι δέκα, βωμὸς τρίπηχυς, μαζονόμια εἴκοσι
πέντε. μετὰ δὲ ταῦτα ἐπορεύοντο παῖδες χίλιοι καὶ ἑξακόσιοι
ἐνδεδυκότες χιτῶνας λευκούς, ἐστεφανωμένοι οἱ μὲν κισσῷ, οἱ
δὲ πίτυι, ὧν διακόσιοι μὲν καὶ πεντήκοντα χοεῖς εἶχον χρυσοῦς,
τετρακόσιοι δὲ ἀργυροῦς, ἕτεροι δὲ τριακόσιοι καὶ εἴκοσι 125
ψυκτήρια ἔφερον χρυσᾶ, οἱ δὲ ἀργυρᾶ·
   "Μεθ᾽ οὓς ἄλλοι παῖδες ἔφερον κεράμια πρὸς τὴν τοῦ
γλυκισμοῦ χρείαν ὧν εἴκοσι μὲν ἦν χρυσᾶ, πεντήκοντα δὲ ἀργυρᾶ,
200 B τριακόσια δὲ κεκηρογραφημένα χρώμασι παντοίοις· καὶ κερασθέντων ἐν ταῖς ὑδρίαις καὶ πίθοις πάντες κοσμίως ἐγλυκίσθη- 130
σαν οἱ ἐν τῷ σταδίῳ."

---

101 μετὰ ⟨δὲ⟩?   103 ⟨ζῷα εἶχον τετορευμένα⟩ Dobree   τετραμέτρητοι Meineke:
τετράμετροι AC   ὑδρεῖαι A   107 ἐχόμενοι Schweighäuser: ἐχόμενα A
109 ἀμπελίνους alii: ἀμπελίους A   ⟨διαχρύσους sim.⟩ Kaibel: ἀμπελίνους,
τετραμετρήτους. ἕτεροι Κορ. Schweighäuser   112 ⟨ἐκεῖτο δ᾽⟩ ἐπ᾽ ἐγγ. Meineke   114 κώθωνες C: κωθῶναι A   117 'etiam latitudo videtur
indicata fuisse' Kaibel   119 κυλικεῖα Schweighäuser: κυλίκια A   121 μαζονόμια Casaubon: μαζονομίαι A: μαζονομεῖα Cobet   124 πίτυι, ὧν

wine-presses on which were twenty-four bikoi, a solid silver table 18 feet long, and thirty others 9 feet long. In addition to these were four three-legged tables, of which one, being plated in silver all over, had a circumference of 24 feet, while the three other smaller ones were encrusted with jewels in the middle. After these were carried Delphic tripods of silver, eighty in number, smaller than those mentioned before, whose angles . . . of four measures, twenty-six hydriae, sixteen Panathenaic amphorae, and 160 psykters. The largest of these held six measures, and the smallest two. All of these vessels were silver.

'Right after these marched those carrying the gold plate, four Laconian kraters with crowns of vine . . . holding four measures, two others of Corinthian workmanship on stands. (These had figures in the round of beaten metal on their upper part, and on the necks and bellies carefully executed figures in low relief. Each of them held eight measures.) Then there appeared a wine-press, on which were ten bikoi, two bowls each of five measures, two Laconian cups of two measures, twenty-two psykters, of which the largest held thirty measures, and the smallest one measure. Next in the procession were four large three-legged tables of gold, and a golden jewel-encrusted chest for gold objects, 15 feet high, which had six shelves holding carefully made figures four spans high, many in number; two cup-stands, two gilded glass vessels, two golden stands for vessels which were six feet high and three smaller ones, ten hydriai, an altar of $4\frac{1}{2}$ feet, and twenty-five trenchers. After these marched 1,600 boys wearing white chitons, some wreathed in ivy, others with pine; 250 of them had golden choes, 400 had silver choes, and 320 others carried gold psykters, others silver ones.

'After these boys, other boys carried jars to be used for sweet wine, of which twenty were gold, fifty were silver, and 300 were decorated with encaustic painting in many colours. And when the liquid was mixed in hydriai and pithoi, all those in the stadium received their due portion of sweet wine.'

Schweighäuser: πιτνίωι A   130–1 ἐγλυκίσθησαν Rice: ἐγλυκάσθησαν A: ἐγλυκάνθησαν Cobet

Ἑξῆς τούτοις καταλέγει τετραπήχεις τραπέζας ἐφ' ὧν
πολλὰ θέας ἄξια πολυτελῶς κατεσκευασμένα περιήγετο θεάματα,
ἐν οἷς καὶ ὁ τῆς Σεμέλης θάλαμος ἐν ᾧ ἔχουσι χιτῶνας τινὲς
διαχρύσους καὶ λιθοκολλήτους τῶν πολυτιμήτων.   135
Οὐκ ἄξιον δ' ἦν παραλιπεῖν τήνδε τὴν τετράκυκλον
μῆκος οὖσαν πηχῶν εἴκοσι δύο, πλάτος δεκατεσσάρων, ὑπὸ
200 C ἀνδρῶν ἑλκομένην πεντακοσίων, ἐφ' ἧς ἄντρον ἦν βαθὺ καθ'
ὑπερβολὴν κισσῷ καὶ μίλῳ· ἐκ τούτου περιστεραὶ καὶ φάσ-
σαι καὶ τρυγόνες καθ' ὅλην ἐξίπταντο τὴν ὁδόν, λημνίσκοις 140
τοὺς πόδας δεδεμέναι πρὸς τὸ ῥᾳδίως ὑπὸ τῶν θεωμένων
ἁρπάζεσθαι. ἀνέβλυζον δὲ ἐξ αὐτοῦ καὶ κρουνοὶ δύο, ὁ μὲν
γάλακτος, ὁ δὲ οἴνου. πᾶσαι δ' αἱ περὶ αὐτὸν Νύμφαι στεφάνους εἶχον χρυσοῦς, ὁ δὲ Ἑρμῆς καὶ κηρύκειον χρυσοῦν, ἐσθῆ-
τας δὲ πολυτελεῖς.   145
"Ἐπὶ δὲ ἄλλης τετρακύκλου, ἣ περιεῖχε τὴν ἐξ
200 D Ἰνδῶν κάθοδον Διονύσου, Διόνυσος ἦν δωδεκάπηχυς ἐπ' ἐλέφαντος κατακείμενος, ἠμφιεσμένος πορφυρίδα καὶ στέφανον κίσσου καὶ
ἀμπέλου χρυσοῦν ἔχων. εἶχε δ' ἐν ταῖς χερσὶ θυρσόλογχον
χρυσοῦν, ὑπεδέδετο δ' ἐμβάδας χρυσοβαφεῖς. προεκάθητο 150
δ' αὐτοῦ ἐπὶ τῷ τραχήλῳ τοῦ ἐλέφαντος Σατυρίσκος πεντά-
πηχυς ἐστεφανωμένος πίτυος στεφάνῳ χρυσῷ, τῇ δεξιᾷ χειρὶ
αἰγείῳ κέρατι χρυσῷ σημαίνων. ὁ δὲ ἐλέφας σκευὴν εἶχε χρυσῆν καὶ περὶ τῷ τραχήλῳ κίσσινον χρυσοῦν στέφανον.
200 E "Ἠκολούθουν δὲ τούτῳ παιδίσκαι πεντακόσιαι κεκοσ- 155
μημέναι χιτῶσι πορφυροῖς, χρυσῷ διεζωσμέναι. ἐστεφάνωντο
δὲ αἱ μὲν ἡγούμεναι ἑκατὸν εἴκοσι χρυσοῖς πιτυΐνοις
στεφάνοις. ἠκολούθουν δ' αὐταῖς Σάτυροι ἑκατὸν εἴκοσι,
πανοπλίας οἱ μὲν ἀργυρᾶς, οἱ δὲ χαλκᾶς ἔχοντες. μετὰ
δὲ τούτους ἐπορεύοντο ὄνων ἴλαι πέντε ἐφ' ὧν ἦσαν Σιληνοὶ 160
καὶ Σάτυροι ἐστεφανωμένοι. τῶν δὲ ὄνων οἱ μὲν χρυσᾶς,
οἱ δὲ ἀργυρᾶς προμετωπίδας καὶ σκευασίας εἶχον. μετὰ
200 F δὲ τούτους ἐλεφάντων ἅρματα ἀφείθη εἴκοσι τέτταρα καὶ
συνωρίδες τράγων ἑξήκοντα, κόλων δεκαδύο, ὀρύγων ἑπτά,

132 τραπέζας ... ('intercidit plaustrorum τετρακύκλων mentio') Kaibel   134 εἶχον?
139 μίλῳ Schweighäuser: μίλτῳ AC   ⟨ἐσκιασμένον sim.⟩ Meineke   140 λι-
νίσκοις C   143 'αὐτὸν Mercurium intellego Bacchum puerum ad Nymphas
Nisaeas deferentem; oratio non integra' Kaibel: περὶ αὐτὸ Cobet: περὶ δὲ ταύτην
νύμφαι C   144 'post χρυσοῦν plenius incidendum, ut ἐσθ. δ. πολ. ad Nymph-
arum ornatum pertineat' Meineke   149 εἶχε δ' Schweighäuser: εἶχεν AC
150 χρυσοβαφεῖς Casaubon: χρυσογραφεῖς AC: χρυσορραφεῖς Wilamowitz   152 [χει-
ρι] alii   159 οἱ μὲν ⟨χρυσᾶς, οἱ δὲ⟩ ἀργυρᾶς, οἱ δὲ χαλκᾶς Kaibel: ὡπλισμένοι
ἀργυραῖς καὶ χρυσαῖς πανοπλίαις καὶ χαλκαῖς E: οἱ μὲν ἀργυρᾶς, οἱ δὲ χρυσᾶς? Jacoby
164 κόλων Gesner: κώλων A

After these things he told at length of six-foot long tables on which the many tableaux, extravagantly arranged and worthy of view, were led around; among these was the Chamber of Semele, in which some figures wore chitons which were embroidered with gold and set with gems of the highest value.

It would not be right to pass over the four-wheeled cart, 33 feet long by 21 feet wide, drawn by 500 men, on which there was a deep cave profusely shaded with ivy and yew. All along the route there flew out from it pigeons, ring-doves, and turtle-doves whose feet were fastened with ribbons so that they could be easily caught by the spectators. Two springs gushed forth from the cave, one of milk and one of wine. All the Nymphs round about him had golden crowns, and Hermes had a golden herald's staff, and very rich clothing.

'On another four-wheeled cart, which contained the "Return of Dionysus from India", an 18-foot statue of Dionysus, having a purple cloak and a golden crown of ivy and vine, lay upon an elephant. He held in his hands a golden thyrsos-lance, and his feet were shod with felt slippers embroidered with gold. In front of him on the neck of the elephant there sat a young Satyr seven feet tall, wreathed with a golden crown of pine, signalling with a golden goat-horn in his right hand. The elephant had gold trappings and a golden ivy crown about its neck.

'Five hundred little girls followed him, dressed in purple chitons and golden girdles. The first 120 girls were wreathed with golden pine crowns. One hundred and twenty Satyrs followed them, some wearing silver armour, others bronze. After them marched five troops of asses on which rode crowned Silenoi and Satyrs. Some of the asses had frontlets and harnesses of gold, others of silver. After them marched twenty-four elephant quadrigae, sixty bigae of goats, twelve of saiga antelopes, seven of

βουβάλων δεκαπέντε, στρουθῶν συνωρίδες ὀκτώ, ὀνελάφων 165
ἑπτά, καὶ συνωρίδες δ' ὄνων ἀγρίων, ἄρματα τέσσαρα.
ἐπὶ δὲ πάντων τούτων ἀνεβεβήκει παιδάρια χιτῶνας ἔχοντα ἡνιοχικοὺς καὶ πετάσους. παρανεβεβήκει δὲ παιδισκάρια διεσκευασμένα πελταρίοις καὶ θυρσολόγχοις, κεκοσμημένα ἱματίοις διαχρύσοις. ἐστεφάνωτο δὲ τὰ μὲν ἡνιο- 170
χοῦντα παιδάρια πίτυι, τὰ δὲ παιδισκάρια κισσῷ. ἐπῆσαν
δὲ καὶ συνωρίδες καμήλων ⟨ἕξ⟩, ἐξ ἑκατέρου μέρους τρεῖς,
αἷς ἐπηκολούθουν ἀπῆναι ὑφ' ἡμιόνων ἀγόμεναι. αὗται δ' εἶχον
201 Α σκηνὰς βαρβαρικὰς ὑφ' ὧν ἐκάθηντο γυναῖκες Ἰνδαί, καὶ
ἕτεραι κεκοσμημέναι ὡς αἰχμάλωτοι. κάμηλοι δ' αἱ μὲν 175
ἔφερον λιβανωτοῦ μνᾶς τριακοσίας, σμύρνης τριακοσίας,
κρόκου καὶ κασσίας καὶ κινναμώμου καὶ ἴριδος καὶ τῶν
λοιπῶν ἀρωμάτων διακοσίας· ἐχόμενοι τούτων ἦσαν Αἰθίοπες
δωροφόροι, ὦν οἱ μὲν ἔφερον ὀδόντας ἐξακοσίους, ἕτεροι δὲ
ἐβένου κορμοὺς δισχιλίους, ἄλλοι χρυσίου καὶ ἀργυρίου 180
201 Β κρατῆρας ἑξήκοντα καὶ ψήγματα χρυσοῦ· μεθ' οὓς ἐπόμπευσαν
κυνηγοὶ †β' ἔχοντες σιβύνας ἐπιχρύσους. ἤγοντο δὲ καὶ
κύνες δισχίλιοι τετρακόσιοι, οἳ μὲν Ἰνδοί, οἱ λοιποὶ δὲ
Ὑρκανοὶ καὶ Μολοσσοὶ καὶ ἑτέρων γενῶν. ἐξῆς ἄνδρες ἑκατὸν
πεντήκοντα φέροντες δένδρα ἐξ ὧν ἀνήρτητο θηρία παντοδαπὰ 185
καὶ ὄρνεα. εἶτ' ἐφέροντο ἐν ἀγγείοις ψιττακοὶ καὶ ταὼ καὶ
μελεαγρίδες καὶ φασιανοὶ καὶ ὄρνιθες Αἰθιοπικοί, πλήθει
πολλοί." εἰπὼν δὲ καὶ ἄλλα πλεῖστα καὶ καταλέξας ζῴων
ἀγέλας ἐπιφέρει· "πρόβατα Αἰθιοπικὰ ἑκατὸν τριάκοντα,
201 C Ἀράβια τριακόσια, Εὐβοϊκὰ εἴκοσι, ὀλόλευκοι βόες Ἰν- 190
δικοὶ εἴκοσι ἕξ, Αἰθιοπικοὶ ὀκτώ, ἄρκτος λευκὴ μεγάλη μία,
παρδάλεις ιδ', πάνθηροι ις', λυγκία δ', ἄρκηλοι γ', καμη-
λοπάρδαλις μία, ῥινόκερως Αἰθιοπικὸς α'.
"Ἑξῆς ἐπὶ τετρακύκλου Διόνυσος πρὸς τὸν τῆς Ῥέας
βωμὸν καταπεφευγώς, ὅτε ὑπὸ Ἥρας ἐδιώκετο, στέφανον ἔχων 195

167–68 ἀνεβεβήκει—παρανεβεβήκει Kaibel: ἀναβεβήκει—παραναβεβήκει AC   δὲ
A: δὲ καὶ C   170 διαχρύσοις Meineke: καὶ χρυσίοις A   171 ἐπῆσαν
Meineke: ἐπῆσαν AC   172 ⟨ἕξ⟩ Kaibel   173 ὑφ'ὦν Meineke: ἐφ'ὦν
A   177 κασσίας A: κασίας C   ἴριδος C: εἴριδος A   178 ἦσαν
Jacoby: ἦσαν A   179 ⟨ἐλεφάντων⟩ ὀδόντας Meineke   180 χρυσίου Kaibel: χρυσοῦ
A: χρυσέους καὶ ἀργυρέους C   181 χρυσοῦ Wilam: χρυσίου A   182 β' numerum
iusto minorem esse vidit Schweighäuser β' Mue.: κ' Meineke: ρ' vel ν' Kaibel   186 ταὼ
Schweighäuser: ταοὶ AC   187–8 καὶ φασιανοὶ καὶ ὄρνιθες Αἰθιοπικοί, πλήθει
πολλοί cf. Ath. 387D: καὶ φασιανοὶ ὄρνιθες καὶ ἄλλοι Αἰθιοπικοί, πλήθει πολλοί AC
188 εἰπὼν δὲ καὶ: (lemma in A) ΤΩΝ ΕΙΣ Λ ΤΕΛΟΣ ΤΟΤ Θ ΑΡΧΗ ΤΟΤ ΔΕΚ-
ΑΤΟΥ ('quae non suo loco posita sunt,' Kaibel)   189 ἀγέλας ⟨πολλὰς⟩?
Jacoby   190 εἴκοσι ('vix verum,' Kaibel)   ὀλόλευκοι Dindorf:
καὶ ὀλόλευκοι Kaibel: κολοιλευκοι A   192 πάνθηρες C   194 πρὸς Kaibel:
περὶ AC: ἐπι? Kaibel, Meyer

oryxes, fifteen of hartebeest, eight bigae of ostriches, seven of onelaphoi, four bigae of onagers, and four quadrigae of horses. Little boys were mounted on all of these, wearing the chitons of charioteers and petasoi; beside them were mounted little girls wearing himatia woven with gold, and armed with light shields and thyrsos-lances. The boy charioteers were crowned with pine, and the girls with ivy. In addition to these, there were six bigae of camels, three on either side, which were followed by carts drawn by mules. These contained foreign tents under which sat Indian women and others dressed as prisoners. More camels carried 300 minae of frankincense, 300 of myrrh, and 200 of saffron, cassia, cinnamon, orris, and other spices. Ethiopian tribute-bearers followed right after them; some of them carried 600 elephant tusks, others 2,000 logs of ebony, and others sixty kraters full of pieces of gold and silver and gold dust. After them came two kynegoi with gilded hunting spears. Two thousand four hundred dogs were also led along, some Indian, the others Hyrcanian, Molossian, and other breeds. Right after them came 150 men carrying trees from which were suspended different kinds of animals and birds. Then there were borne along in cages parrots, peacocks, guinea fowl, pheasants, and Ethiopian birds, many in number.' Telling also of many other things, and enumerating herds of animals, he included, 'One hundred and thirty Ethiopian, three hundred Arabian, and twenty Eubocan sheep, twenty-six all-white Indian cows plus twenty Ethiopian ones, one large white bear, fourteen leopards, sixteen cheetahs, four caracals, three cheetah cubs, one giraffe, and one Ethiopian rhinoceros.

'Next in a four-wheeled cart appeared Dionysus, having fled to the Altar of Rhea when he was pursued by Hera; Dionysus had a golden crown,

χρυσοῦν, Πριάπου αὐτῷ παρεστῶτος ἐστεφανωμένου χρυσῷ κισσίνῳ. τὸ δὲ τῆς Ἥρας ἄγαλμα στεφάνην εἶχε χρυσῆν.
201 D   "... Ἀλεξάνδρου δὲ καὶ Πτολεμαίου ἀγάλματα,
ἐστεφανωμένα στεφάνοις κισσίνοις ἐκ χρυσοῦ. τὸ δὲ τῆς
Ἀρετῆς ἄγαλμα τὸ παρεστὸς τῷ Πτολεμαίῳ στέφανον εἶχεν 200
ἐλαίας χρυσοῦν· καὶ Πρίαπος δ᾽ αὐτοῖς συμπαρῆν, ἔχων
στέφανον κίσσινον ἐκ χρυσοῦ. Κόρινθος δ᾽ ἡ πόλις παρεστῶσα τῷ Πτολεμαίῳ ἐστεφάνωτο διαδήματι χρυσῷ. παρέκειντο
δὲ πᾶσι τούτοις κυλικεῖον μεστὸν χρυσωμάτων κρατήρ τε χρυσοῦς μετρητῶν πέντε. τῇ δὲ τετρακύκλῳ ταύτῃ ἠκολούθουν 205
201 E γυναῖκες, ἔχουσαι ἱμάτια πολυτελῆ καὶ κόσμον. προσηγορεύοντο δὲ πόλεις, αἵ τε ἀπ᾽ Ἰωνίας καὶ ⟨αἱ⟩ λοιπαὶ Ἑλλην-
ίδες, ὅσαι τὴν Ἀσίαν καὶ τὰς νήσους κατοικοῦσαι ὑπὸ τοὺς
Πέρσας ἐτάχθησαν. ἐφόρουν δὲ πᾶσαι στεφάνους χρυσοῦς.

"Ἐφέρετο καὶ ἐπ᾽ ἄλλων τετρακύκλων θύρσος ἐνενη- 210
κοντάπηχυς χρυσοῦς καὶ λόγχη ἀργυρᾶ ἑξηκοντάπηχυς, καὶ ἐν
ἄλλῃ φαλλὸς χρυσοῦς πηχῶν ρκ᾽ διαγεγραμμένος καὶ διαδεδεμένος
στέμμασι διαχρύσοις, ἔχων ἐπ᾽ ἄκρου ἀστέρα χρυσοῦν, οὗ ἦν ἡ
περίμετρος ς᾽.

"Πολλῶν οὖν καὶ ποικίλων εἰρημένων ἐν ταῖς πομ- 215
201 F παῖς ταύταις μόνα ἐξελεξάμεθα ἐν οἷς ἦν χρυσὸς καὶ ἄργυρος·
καὶ γὰρ διαθέσεις πολλαὶ ἀκοῆς ἦσαν ἄξιαι καὶ θηρίων πλήθη
καὶ ἵππων καὶ λέοντες παμμεγέθεις εἴκοσι καὶ τέσσαρες. ἦσαν
δὲ καὶ ἄλλαι τετράκυκλοι οὐ μόνον εἰκόνας βασιλέων φέρουσαι,
ἀλλὰ καὶ θεῶν πολλάς· μεθ᾽ ἃς χορὸς ἐπόμπευσεν ἀνδρῶν ἑξα- 220
κοσίων, ἐν οἷς κιθαρισταὶ συνεφώνουν τριακόσιοι, ἐπιχρύσους
202 A ἔχοντες ὅλας κιθάρας καὶ στεφάνους χρυσοῦς· μεθ᾽ οὓς ταῦροι διῆλθον
δισχίλιοι ὁμοιοχρώματοι χρυσόκερῳ, προμετωπίδας χρυσᾶς καὶ
ἀνὰ μέσον στεφάνους ὅρμους τε καὶ αἰγίδας πρὸ τῶν στηθῶν
ἔχοντες. ἦν δὲ ἅπαντα ταῦτα χρυσᾶ. 225

"Καὶ μετὰ ταῦτα Διὸς ἤγετο πομπὴ καὶ ἄλλων παμπόλλων θεῶν, καὶ ἐπὶ πᾶσιν Ἀλεξάνδρου, ὃς ἐφ᾽ ἅρματος
ἐλεφάντων ἀληθινῶν ἐφέρετο χρυσοῦς, Νίκην καὶ Ἀθηνᾶν
ἐξ ἑκατέρου μέρους ἔχων. ἐπόμπευσαν δὲ καὶ θρόνοι πολλοὶ

198 ... Ἀλεξάνδρου, κτλ. ('oratio mutila' Kaibel): ⟨μετὰ δὲ ταύτην εἴπετο ἄλλη τετράκυκλος . . . (the size), ἐφ᾽ ἧς ἦν⟩ Ἀλεξάνδρου Ehrenberg, *Alexander and the
Greeks* (Oxford, 1938), 6 (cf. p. 99 *infra*)   202 κίσσινον Casaubon: κισσὸν Α
203 τῷ Ἀλεξάνδρῳ Wilamowitz, alii   204 κυλικεῖον Casaubon: κυλίκιον Α
206 κόσμον ⟨χρυσοῦν⟩? Kaibel: κ. ⟨πολύν⟩? Jacoby   207 ⟨αἱ⟩ Rohde
213 ἐπ᾽ ἄκρου Ε: ἐπ᾽ ἄκρον Α   215 εὑρημένων Wilamowitz: παρηγμένων?
Kaibel: περιηγμένων Meyer   220 πολλάς Ε, Kaibel: πολλαί Α
μεθ᾽ἃς Α: μεθ᾽ἃ C

and Priapus stood beside him crowned with a golden ivy crown. The statue of Hera had a golden stephanē.

'. . . statues of Alexander and Ptolemy wreathed with ivy crowns of gold. The statue of Arete beside Ptolemy had a golden crown of olive. Priapus, having an ivy crown of gold, was also present with them. The city of Corinth standing by Ptolemy was crowned with a golden diadem. Adjacent to all these figures were a cup-stand full of gold vessels and a golden krater of five measures. This cart was followed by women wearing very costly himatia and jewelry. They were called by the names of cities of Ionia and the rest of the Greek cities which, situated in Asia and the Islands, had been subdued by the Persians. All wore golden crowns.

'There were carried in other carts a golden thyrsos which was 135 feet long, and a ninety-foot long silver spear. In another cart was borne a golden phallos, measuring 180 feet in length, painted all over and bound with golden fillets, having at the end a gold star whose circumference was 9 feet.

'Although many and various things have been said about these processions, we have chosen only those things in them which were silver and gold. For there were also many representations worthy of report, and a great number of beasts and horses, and twenty-four extremely large lions. There were also other four-wheeled carts carrying statues not only of kings, but also many of gods. After them a chorus of 600 men marched in procession, among whom were 300 kitharistai playing in concert, who had kitharas gilded all over and gold crowns. After them came 2,000 golden-horned bulls all of the same colour, having golden frontlets and crowns in the middle, and necklaces and aegises on their chests. All of this was of gold.

'And after these things came the processions of Zeus and of all the other gods, and after all of them, the procession of Alexander, whose golden statue was borne upon a quadriga of real elephants with Nike and Athena on either side. In the procession were also led along many thrones

202 B ἐξ ἐλέφαντος καὶ χρυσοῦ κατεσκευασμένοι, ὧν ἐφ᾿ ἑνὸς μὲν 230
ἔκειτο στεφάνη χρυσῆ, ἐπ᾿ ἄλλου δὲ κέρας χρυσοῦν, ἐπ᾿
ἄλλου δὲ ἦν στέφανος χρυσοῦς, καὶ ἐπ᾿ ἄλλου δὲ κέρας
ὁλόχρυσον. ἐπὶ δὲ τὸν Πτολεμαίου τοῦ Σωτῆρος θρόνον στέφανος ἐπέκειτο ἐκ μυρίων κατεσκευασμένος χρυσῶν. ἐπόμπευσε δὲ καὶ θυμιατήρια χρυσᾶ τριακόσια καὶ πεντήκοντα, 235
καὶ βωμοὶ δὲ ἐπίχρυσοι ἐστεφανωμένοι χρυσοῖς στεφάνοις,
ὧν ἑνὶ παρεπεπήγεσαν δᾷδες χρυσαῖ δεκαπήχεις τέσσαρες.
ἐπόμπευσαν δὲ καὶ ἐσχάραι ἐπίχρυσοι β΄, ὧν ἡ μὲν δωδεκάπηχυς τῇ περιμέτρῳ, τεσσαρακοντάπηχυς ὕψει, ἡ δὲ πηχῶν πεν-
202 C τεκαίδεκα. ἐπόμπευσαν δὲ καὶ Δελφικοὶ τρίποδες χρυσοῖ ἐν- 240
νέα ἐκ πηχῶν τεσσάρων, ἄλλοι ὀκτὼ ⟨ἐκ⟩ πηχῶν ἕξ, ἄλλος πηχῶν τριάκοντα, ἐφ᾿ οὗ ἦν ζῷα χρυσᾶ πενταπήχη καὶ στέφανος
κύκλῳ χρυσοῦς ἀμπέλινος. παρῆλθον δὲ καὶ φοίνικες ἐπίχρυσοι ὀκταπήχεις ἑπτά, καὶ κηρύκειον ἐπίχρυσον πηχῶν τεσσαράκοντα πέντε, καὶ κεραυνὸς ἐπίχρυσος πηχῶν τεσσαράκοντα, 245
ναός τε ἐπίχρυσος, οὗ ἡ περίμετρος πηχῶν μ΄· δίκερας
πρὸς τούτοις ὀκτάπηχυ. πολὺ δὲ καὶ ζῴων πλῆθος ἐπιχρύσων
202 D συνεπόμπευεν, ὧν ἦν τὰ πολλὰ δωδεκαπήχη· καὶ θηρία ὑπερ-
άγοντα τοῖς μεγέθεσι καὶ ἀετοὶ πηχῶν εἴκοσι· στέφανοί τε
χρυσοῖ ἐπόμπευσαν τρισχίλιοι διακόσιοι, ἕτερός τε μυστικὸς 250
χρυσοῦς λίθοις πολυτελέσι κεκοσμημένος ὀγδοηκοντάπηχυς.
οὗτος δὲ περιτίθετο τῷ τοῦ Βερενικείου θυρώματι· αἰγίς τε
ὁμοίως χρυσῆ. ἐπόμπευσαν δὲ καὶ στεφάναι χρυσαῖ πάνυ πολλαί, ἃς ἔφερον παιδίσκαι πολυτελῶς κεκοσμημέναι· ὧν μία δί-
πηχυς εἰς ὕψος, τὴν δὲ περίμετρον ἔχουσα ἑκκαίδεκα πηχῶν. 255
202 E ἐπόμπευσε δὲ καὶ θώραξ χρυσοῦς πηχῶν δώδεκα καὶ ἕτερος
ἀργυροῦς πηχῶν †ιη΄ ἐννέα†, ἔχων ἐφ᾿ ἑαυτοῦ κεραυνοὺς χρυσοῦς
δεκαπήχεις δύο καὶ στέφανον δρυὸς διάλιθον· ἀσπίδες χρυσαῖ
εἴκοσι, πανοπλίαι χρυσαῖ ξδ΄, κνημῖδες χρυσαῖ τριπήχεις β΄,
λεκάναι χρυσαῖ δεκαδύο, φιάλαι πολλαὶ πάνυ τὸν ἀριθμόν, 260
οἰνοχόαι τριάκοντα, ἐξάλειπτρα μεγάλα δέκα, ὑδρίαι δεκαδύο, μαζονόμια πεντήκοντα, τράπεζαι διάφοροι, κυλικεῖα χρυ-
202 F σωμάτων πέντε, κέρας ὁλόχρυσον πηχῶν λ΄. ταῦτα δὲ τὰ χρυσώματα ἐκτὸς ἦν τῶν ἐν τῇ Διονύσου πομπῇ διενεχθέντων· εἶτ᾿

230–231 ἐφ᾿ ἑνὸς μὲν – ἐπ᾿ ἄλλου κέρας C: ἐφ᾿ ἑνος – ἐπ᾿ ἄλλου δίκερας A: ᾽1. δὲ κέρας
pro δίκερας᾽ Kaibel   234–5 ἐπόμπευσαν C   236 δὲ A: δ΄ Schweighäuser: δ᾿ ε΄Meineke: †δὲ Jac.   237 παρεπεπήγεσαν C: παραπεπήγεσαν A
241 ⟨ἐκ⟩ Kaibel   250 μύρτινος? Kaibel   252 βερενικίου A
257 [ἐννέα] Musurus: πηχῶν ἐννεακαίδεκα? Kaibel   ἐφ᾿ἑαυτοῦ alii:
ἐφ᾿ ἑαυτὸν A   259 β΄ ᾽corruptum,᾽ Kaibel   261 ἐξάλειπτρα Hem-
sterhuys: ἐξ ἄλειπτρα A   262 κυλικεῖα C: κυλίκια A

constructed from ivory and gold; on one of these lay a golden stephanē, on another a gold horn, on another a golden crown, and on still another a horn of pure gold. On the throne of Ptolemy Soter lay a crown made from 10,000 pieces of gold. There also appeared in the procession 350 golden thymiateria, and gilded altars crowned with gold crowns. Four torches fifteen feet long were affixed to one of them. In the procession were also two gilded escharai, of which one was 18 feet in circumference, and 60 feet in height, while the other measured $22\frac{1}{2}$ feet. Golden Delphic tripods also appeared in the procession; nine of them were 6 feet tall, eight others 9 feet tall, and one other, 45 feet tall, on which there were golden figures $7\frac{1}{2}$ feet high and a golden vine wreath which encircled it. There passed by seven gilded palm trees 12 feet high, a gilded herald's staff $67\frac{1}{2}$ feet long, a gilded thunderbolt 60 feet long, and a gilded shrine whose circumference was 60 feet. In addition to all of these was a dikeras 12 feet tall. A very great number of gilded figures appeared in the procession along with everything else, of which many were 18 feet high. There were also beasts of an extraordinary size, and eagles 30 feet high. Golden crowns, numbering 3,200, also appeared in the procession, and one other mystic crown of gold, decorated with very precious jewels and measuring 120 feet. This crown was put around the door of the Berenikeion. There was likewise a golden aegis. Very many golden stephanai also appeared in the procession, which richly dressed little girls carried; one of these was 3 feet tall and had a circumference of 24 feet. Also in the procession was a golden breastplate 18 feet long and another silver one 27 feet long which had on it two golden thunderbolts 15 feet long and an oak crown studded with jewels. There were twenty gold shields, sixty-four golden panoplies, two golden greaves $4\frac{1}{2}$ feet in length, twelve golden dishes, a very large number of phialai, thirty oinochoai, ten large unguent-boxes, twelve hydriai, fifty trenchers, various tables, five cup-stands for gold vessels, and a pure gold horn 45 feet long. This gold plate was in addition to that carried in the procession of Dionysus.

ἀργυρωμάτων ἄμαξαι τετρακόσιαι καὶ χρυσωμάτων εἴκοσι, ἀρω- 265
μάτων δὲ ὀκτακόσιαι.

"Ἐπὶ δὲ πᾶσιν ἐπόμπευσαν αἱ δυνάμεις αἱ ἱππικαὶ καὶ
πεζικαί, πᾶσαι καθωπλισμέναι θαυμασίως· πεζοὶ μὲν εἰς πέντε
203 A μυριάδας καὶ ἑπτακισχιλίους καὶ ἑξακοσίους, ἱππεῖς δὲ δισμύρ-
ιοι τρισχίλιοι διακόσιοι. πάντες δ᾽ οὗτοι ἐπόμπευσαν, τὴν 270
ἁρμόζουσαν ἑκάστῳ ἠμφιεσμένοι στολὴν καὶ τὰς προσηκούσας
ἔχοντες πανοπλίας." ἐκτὸς δ᾽ ὧν πάντες οὗτοι εἶχον πανοπλιῶν
καὶ ἄλλαι πλεῖσται ἦσαν ἀποκείμεναι, ὧν οὐδὲ τὸν ἀριθμὸν ἀνα-
γράψαι ῥάδιον. κατέλεξε δ᾽ αὐτὸν ὁ Καλλίξεινος.

"Ἐστεφανώθησαν δ᾽ ἐν τῷ ἀγῶνι καὶ στεφάνοις χρυσοῖς 275
εἴκοσι. Πτολεμαῖος δὲ ὁ πρῶτος καὶ Βερενίκη εἰκόσι τρισὶν
ἐφ᾽ ἁρμάτων χρυσῶν καὶ τεμένεσιν ἐν Δωδώνῃ. καὶ ἐγένετο τὸ
203 B δαπάνημα τοῦ νομίσματος τάλαντα δισχίλια διακόσια τριάκοντα
ἐννέα, μναῖ πεντήκοντα. καὶ ταῦτ᾽ ἠριθμήθη πάντα τοῖς οἰκονό-
μοις διὰ τὴν τῶν στεφανούντων προθυμίαν πρὸ τοῦ τὰς θέας 280
παρελθεῖν. ὁ δὲ Φιλάδελφος Πτολεμαῖος, ⟨ὁ⟩ υἱὸς αὐτῶν, εἰκόσι χρυσαῖς δυσὶ μὲν ἐφ᾽ ἁρμάτων χρυσῶν, ἐπὶ δὲ κιόνων ἐξαπήχει μιᾷ,
πενταπήχεσι πέντε, τετραπήχεσι ἕξ."

275–6 χρυσοῖς εἴκοσι A: ⟨καὶ⟩ εἰκόσι Kaibel   276 Βερενίκη εἰκόσι τρισὶν
Cobet: Βερ. εἴκοσι τρ. A   276 ff. Πτολεμαῖος μὲν ὁ πρῶτος–Δωδώνῃ. ὁ δὲ
Φιλάδελφος–τετραπήχεσι ἕξ. καὶ ἐγένετο–παρελθεῖν Wilam.   278 δα-
πάνημα ἡμεδαποῦ (vel ῾Ροδίου) νομίσματος? Kaibel: [τοῦ νομίσματος]?   281 ⟨ὁ⟩
Rice, vel υἱὸς ⟨ὢν⟩ αὐτῶν   εἰκόσι Cobet: εἴκοσι A

Then there were 400 cartloads of silver plate, 20 of gold, and 800 of spices.

'At the very end, the infantry and cavalry forces marched in procession, all of them fully armed in a marvellous fashion. The foot numbered 57,600, and the horse 23,200. All these marched along dressed in the uniform appropriate to each, and having the proper panoply.' Besides the armour worn by all these troops, there were also many other panoplies kept in reserve, whose number is not easy to record, but Kallixeinos gave the full count.

'In the competition they were crowned with twenty gold crowns. Ptolemy I and Berenike ⟨were honoured⟩ with three statues in golden chariots and with precincts in Dodona. And the cost in coin was 2,239 talents and 50 minae; all this was counted out by the oikonomoi before the spectacle was over through the eagerness of those giving the crowns. Their son Ptolemy Philadelphus ⟨was honoured⟩ with two golden statues on golden chariots, and with others on columns, one of 9 feet, five of 7½ feet, and six of 6 feet.'

3. The Grand Procession

THE GRAND PROCESSION

The procession was an important part of worship in Greek religion. Greek religious festivals consisted invariably of four main parts:[1] (1) a procession of the statue or ritual objects of the honoured god on a prescribed route around the city, often stopping at certain points for specific acts of ritual, heading toward the god's temple or sacred precinct; (2) the sacrifice before the temple; (3) the public feast upon the sacrificial offerings, and (4) athletic or artistic competitions. Although the importance of each of these elements varied among different festivals, the procession remained a standard feature of most of them. It was the climax of the Athenian Panathenaia, but was also an important part of the City Dionysia, in which the dramatic competition was the main focus of the festival.[2] At the Olympic festival whose games were the apex of Greek athletic endeavour, the morning of the third day was occupied with religious rites culminating in a great procession from the Magistrate's House to the sacrifice at the Altar of Zeus.[3]

Certain aspects of Greek religious custom which were transformed by the Macedonians under Alexander are essential to the understanding of later Hellenistic religious festivals and their processions, held under the auspices of his successors.

Alexander's Macedonian army introduced variations of the traditional, civic religious festivals in their isolated, foreign milieu when athletic contests were frequently arranged in connection with a procession and offerings to a god. For example, while sacrificing to Asklepius at Soloi, Alexander staged gymnastic and musical competitions, as well as a procession in which he and the troops marched (Arr. *An.* ii. 5, 8; cf. ibid., ii. 24, 6; iii. 5, 2; Plut. *Alex.* xxix). The presence of the army was an important innovation which became standard practice. The external circumstances behind the army's worship were the direct cause of a second change, namely the removal of the religious celebrations from any ritualized civic context tied

---

[1] H. W. Parke, *Festivals of the Athenians* (London, 1977), 18 ff.; Caspari, 'Studien', 401–2.

[2] L. Deubner, *Attische Feste* (Berlin, 1932), 138 ff.; A. W. Pickard-Cambridge, *The Dramatic Festivals of Athens* (2nd ed., Oxford, 1968), 61 ff.

[3] P. Stengel, *Die Griechischen Kultusaltertümer* (3rd ed., Munich, 1920), 190 ff.; J. Swaddling, *The Ancient Olympic Games* (B. M. Publications, London, 1980), 37–9.

to specific cult practice. As a result, the content of the celebrations varied; for example, some of Alexander's festivals honoured several gods at the same time (Arr. *Ind.* 36, 3) rather than a single god upon the occasion of his annual festival in the Macedonian religious calendar. These two changes affected the future course of Greek religious festivals. Alexander's troops took part in the processions because they may have been the only Greeks available to participate, and also because these festivals were clearly intended as a means of maintaining the morale of men far from home and familiar customs. However, time and again, reference is made in our sources to the arms and formations of the troops. Although the Athenian cavalry and infantry were involved in the Panathenaic procession (Thuc. vi. 56, 2; Arist. *Ath. Pol.* xviii. 4; cf. the Parthenon Frieze), this citizen army joined its fellow citizens in the traditional festival in honour of the city's patron-goddess with the result that the focus of the proceedings was the religious festival and the glorification of city and god. This differs in intent and effect from the Macedonian army arrayed in battle formation (cf. Arr. *An.* i. 18, 2) in a foreign setting removed from any civic tradition; as a result, the religious aspects of their celebration became subservient to its secular nature. The enlargement of the festivals to include several gods is equally significant. Although gods had been frequently worshipped in company with other gods in traditional religion, the broad scope of Alexander's celebrations broke the previously close tie between the procession and specific religious ritual since the former was no longer a prescribed part of the larger ritual in the same way. The procession became a method of worship in its own right, and honorands, participants, and ritual elements changed at the organizer's will since they were no longer regulated by civic cult practice.

The ritual purpose of the procession may have shrunk in these and other ways in direct proportion to its isolation from the traditional religious festival, and this process may be seen in the new festivals founded in the new cities by Alexander's successors. Although based upon the precepts of Greek religion from the homeland, these festivals were grafted on to a foreign setting and celebrated by a disparate population. Moreover, new and different gods, for whom cult ritual had to be created and developed, were worshipped with the introduction of the ruler-associated cults in the empires. Only in time did this 'new' religion become the standardized, traditional religion of the Hellenistic world. The Grand Procession of Ptolemy Philadelphus must be considered against this background as one of the most important pieces of evidence for early Hellenistic religion.

The general organization of Kallixeinos' account of the Grand Procession is fairly clear since the author prefaces his description with a thumbnail sketch of the proceedings (197D). The first individual procession to appear is that of the Morning Star (Eosphoros), followed by one 'named after' οἱ τῶν βασιλέων γονεῖς. (The meaning of this phrase will be discussed below. It has been translated as 'the ancestors' or 'parents of the kings' or 'the parents of the king and queen'.) The various processions of all the gods follow these first two, and precede that of Alexander. The event is concluded by the procession of the Evening Star (Hesperos). After this survey, Kallixeinos states that his account will be selective, and he refers the reader seeking additional information elsewhere. From the processions of all the gods, Kallixeinos selects the one in honour of Dionysus for fuller treatment. The components of this procession are recorded in detail and consecutively until about 201F when the thread of the narrative becomes confused; the end of the Dionysiac procession and random parts of other processions are described in a cursory fashion and in no perceivable order. The account ends in 203B with reference to some kind of coronation ceremony and honours bestowed upon members of the royal family. It is not clear whether this final section belongs to the Grand Procession or to another part of the festival of which the procession forms only one part. In this place, Athenaeus may no longer have followed Kallixeinos' narrative directly but may have joined unconnected passages excerpted from a full text of *About Alexandria*.

A diagram of the Grand Procession shows the sections into which the text has been divided for the purposes of discussion. Some divisions are subjective and may be disputed, but they seem at least to order the proceedings in accordance with a recognizable thematic progression.

I.   The beginning of the Grand Procession.
    A.   The procession of the Morning Star (197D).
    B.   The procession τοῖς τῶν βασιλέων γονεῦσι κατωνομασμένη (197D).
    C.   Processions of some gods? (The order of the divine processions, and the place of the Dionysiac one among them, is not clear).
II. The procession of Dionysus (197E ff.).
    A.   Prelude of marshals, preliminary offerings, heralds, personified figures of Penteteris and Eniautos, and Satyrs bearing vessels (197E–198B).
    B.   Philikos and the Guild of Dionysus, followed by Delphic tripods (198B–C).
    C.   Tableaux from the 'life' of Dionysus.
        1.   Cart carrying a statue of the god, followed by religious officials and worshippers (198C–E).

2. Cart carrying a statue of Nysa (198F).
3. Celebration of wine. Cart carrying a wine-press (in which Satyrs and Silenoi trample grapes) (199A), and another an askos (199A), followed by a long parade of gold and silver vessels (199B–200B). Refreshments for the spectators.
4. The bridal chamber of Semele (200B).
5. Cart carrying a cave with the representation of Dionysus being reared by Hermes and the Nymphs (200B–C).
6. Triumphal return of Dionysus from India (200D–201C).
   (a) Dionysus in triumph on an elephant (200D).
   (b) The symbolic army of Dionysus (200E).
   (c) Parade of exotic animals, spear-captives, and tribute of ivory, ebony, and precious metals, followed by hunting spoils and more wild animals (200F–201C).
7. Dionysus at the Altar of Rhea fleeing the wrath of Hera (201C).
8. Cart carrying statues of Alexander, Ptolemy Soter, Arete, Corinth, and Priapus, followed by women dressed as Greek cities (201D–E).

D. The end of the Dionysiac procession. Parade of the ritual objects of Dionysus (201E). Other animals, and further carts with statues of kings and gods (201F). Choral band with kithara players (201F). Procession of sacrificial animals (202A).

III. The rest of the Grand Procession.
   A. The processions of Zeus, other gods, Alexander [and the Evening Star] (202A).
   B. Miscellaneous items from the other processions, dedications to various gods, and display of treasure (202B ff.).
   C. Parade of infantry and cavalry (202F–203A).

IV. Crowning ceremony and dedications to the royal family (203A–B).

In 196A, Athenaeus confirms that the Grand Procession, whose description was included in a work entitled *About Alexandria*, was held in the capital city of the Ptolemaic Empire and the home of its royal family, which was the obvious location for a civic event on such a scale. Although no detailed information is given about the route of the Grand Procession, Kallixeinos says that it passed through the city stadium (197C; line 2). A Greek stadium with its tiered seating arrangements would have been an optimal vantage point for viewing a procession, and it could also have been used fc other activities associated with the festival, such as athletic contests. Considerations of comfort and visibility suggest that the area inside the stadium was reserved for the official guests and the royal box, and this is supported by the fact that special refreshments are distributed to

those in the stadium during the Grand Procession (see pp. 77-8). This structure is also mentioned elsewhere in the text: marshals dressed as Satyrs
range themselves along each side of the stadium (197E; line 14), and
'stadium', not 'the parade' is probably to be understood in the incomplete
phrase καὶ συνωρίδες καμήλων ἕξ, ἐξ ἑκατέρου μέρους τρεῖς (i.e. three
pairs of camels marched along each side 'of it'; 200F; line 172). Whether
or not Kallixeinos was an observer of the procession, the information
about the event was clearly recorded by someone who took the stadium as
his point of reference. The author or his source may have been accorded a
place there among the official guests, possibly in order to compile an
official record of the proceedings.

The third-century stadium used for the Grand Procession was certainly
not the hippodrome mentioned by Strabo (795, 10) beyond the Canopic
Gate on the road to the later site of Nicopolis. This extra-mural location
would have been an unlikely one for a carefully arranged spectacle held
under royal auspices since it is some distance from the pavilion described
by Kallixeinos within the 'Inner Palaces'; this structure was probably used
in the festivities surrounding the procession (see below). The stadium in
question must have been the one located close to The Palaces, which was
the scene of many of the demonstrations against Agathokles at the end
of the third century (Plb. xv. 30-3).[4] This stadium would have been ideal
for the official guests viewing the Grand Procession, since it was convenient to the centre of the city, the royal residences of the sponsors, and
the pavilion, but its exact location cannot be pinpointed. The Palaces were
a large area contiguous to the harbour which covered as much as one third
of the whole city, and which included the 'Inner Palaces' (containing the
actual royal residences) as well as several other structures.[5] Given the size
of this area, a stadium could have been located nearby without infringing
on royal seclusion. This larger Palace area can be generally located in the
northern central area of the city close to the shoreline; this would have
been the most pleasant area of the ancient city and therefore the one
naturally appropriated for royal residences as well as for other important civic buildings.

Since Greek religious processions moved from one point to another,
or else made a circular route around a city, the Grand Procession would
not have been confined to the stadium alone, but would have progressed
out of the stadium onto the streets of Alexandria. One would expect a

[4] For a discussion of the various Alexandrian stadia, and the identification of the
stadium mentioned in Polybius as the one used for the Grand Procession, see *Ptol.
Alex.* ii. 99 ff., n. 231.

[5] For a discussion of The Palaces and the 'Inner Palaces' see ibid., i. 14 ff.; 22-3;
the general position can be seen on the map after p. 8.

civic spectacle on such a scale to have been made visible in this way to as many spectators as possible, and certain details in the text indicate that the route of this procession extended beyond the stadium. Kallixeinos mentions a 'mystic' crown which was to be placed on the door of the Berenikeion (202D; line 250), a shrine of unknown location but certainly outside the stadium. Also, marshals dressed as Silenoi hold back the crowds at the beginning of the procession of Dionysus (197E; line 11). Such officials would have been required along the city streets, clearing the processional route from spectators jostling for position, rather than within the confines of the stadium since crowds would not be milling about the central area. Finally, the carts carrying the wine-press and askos are said to trickle liquid along the street (199A–B), surely the city streets which formed the processional route. The procession, therefore, had both to enter and leave the stadium. Depending upon the shape of the structure, the participants either made a U-shaped loop around the stadium, entering and leaving the single entrance in the rounded side, or else, if the structure was open on both ends, entered by one gate, marched straight through, and left via the other one. There is no archaeological evidence for the shape of this Alexandrian stadium, but, given that it was used for the Grand Procession, it is reasonable to suggest that it did not have a U-shape, but was oblong and open at both ends, like the Hellenistic stadium at Miletus; in view of the size of some of the objects and carts which had to be manœuvred, it is easier to assume that the procession marched straight through the stadium. A single entrance for those both entering and leaving would have caused a severe traffic jam and constant hitches in the flow of the procession. Once out of the stadium and into the city, the procession would have moved along at least one of the main avenues of Alexandria, which would have provided ample room for the carts, the participants, the troops marching in formation, and the greatest number of spectators. The third-century street-plan of the city is unknown, but in the first century BC, there was a rectangular plan with wide main streets; two of these were more than 100 feet wide and one went from east to west across the city from Necropolis to the Canopic Gate (Strabo 793, 8; 795, 10). A similarly broad east-west street (if the Ptolemaic street was not the same or the predecessor of the one mentioned by Strabo) would have been ideal for the processional route. Given the layout of the city, an east-west street would have been longer than a north-south one, and could have passed fairly near the Palace area where the participants joined it after leaving the stadium.

Indirect evidence for part of the route of the Grand Procession can be adduced from information about the ornamental pavilion, or marquee, which Kallixeinos describes immediately before the procession (196A–197C

= Appendix I F 2), if this can be shown to be related to the procession. There are strong linguistic grounds for assuming a connection between them. The direct quotation of Kallixeinos begins in 196A with the words ὅς φησι, and it is clear that he describes the pavilion as a preface to his account of the procession: 'Before beginning [i.e. the account of the procession], I will describe the pavilion which was constructed within the enclosure of the Akra . . .' He makes a similar connection between his subjects at the end of his description of the pavilion (197C; line 1): 'Since we have considered the subject of the pavilion in detail, we will also describe the Grand Procession.' Since the procession directly follows the description of the pavilion in *About Alexandria*, and since the author explicitly connects them, a relation between the subjects is clearly implied. A link between them is also suggested by the many similarities in decorative detail as well as over-all effect. Both reveal a similar grandeur in scale and conception, coupled with exaggerated luxury and an overwhelming emphasis on extravagance and expense. Comparable artistic details include gold and silver plate, statuary in materials lighter than stone, and clothing embroidered with precious materials. Even as the procession was a great occasion, so too must the pavilion have been intended to complement some great occasion. Furthermore, if Kallixeinos gave disproportionate emphasis to the procession of Dionysus in his account of the Grand Procession because it was especially important and magnificent in relation to the whole, then certain iconographic connections between the decoration of the pavilion and the Dionysiac procession may be significant. The entire pavilion can be interpreted as a Dionysiac bower, a luxuriant arbour which is often associated with the god especially when reclining or feasting. The pavilion was situated in a natural bower in the Palace gardens, and many of its decorative elements are Dionysiac: the middle columns of its main supports have the form of thyrsoi (196C), and Dionysiac symposia scenes appear in the recesses of the epistyle of the pavilion, composed of figures from tragedy, comedy, and satyric drama (196F). These tableaux are separated by niches containing Delphic tripods, the traditional prizes in the performance of the dithyramb in honour of Dionysus. The animal skins on the inside of the curtains surrounding the peristyle (196D) may connote hunting spoils which also figure in the return of Dionysus from India in the procession (201B; line 184). The purpose of the pavilion also suggests a relation to the procession. It was designed as a dining hall (the arrangement and decorations of the couches and tables are described in 196B and 197B), despite the fact that other kinds of entertainment may also have taken place there. Dionysiac feasts were frequently held in bower-like surroundings such as this (see p. 60), but one special, magnificent feast must have been intended for this pavilion. Its architectural daring and perishable materials are alike incomprehensible if it was conceived as a permanent structure, and not as a temporary erection for a specific occasion (although it may of course have remained standing for a short period after the festival). The luxuriant surroundings and atmosphere show in any case that important guests were to be entertained here, and Kallixeinos states that the pavilion was separate from the place where the soldiers, artisans, and tourists were entertained (196A). The festivities associated with the Grand Procession present the obvious special occasion for the use of the pavilion, both in terms of the feast to be served and the guests to be entertained there. The 2,000 oxen which march in the procession (202A; line 222) are the intended victims at the sacrifice which was the climax of this, as of all, Greek festivals. Since a feast was a concomitant part of the sacrifice, these sacrificial oxen may have provided the meal for the guests entertained in the pavilion, who were in this case the theoroi invited to Alexandria for the Grand Procession and its festival, as well as priests and other religious officials.

This combined evidence supports a connection between the pavilion and the procession, and suggests that the former may have been built purposely for the occasion of the latter. The site of the pavilion is therefore relevant to the reconstructed processional route. It probably did not serve as another viewing stand for the procession: its surrounding gardens would have impeded visibility, and the statement that it was removed from the place where the general populace was entertained gives the impression that it was somewhat isolated. Its specific location 'within the enclosure of the Akra' (196A), which was a citadel of the city fortified by a wall and gates,[6] reinforces the suggestion that it was not a viewing stand since many of the objects appearing in the Grand Procession could hardly have been manœuvred inside such an enclosed area. Although the procession probably did not pass in front of the pavilion, its progress may have been visible in the distance since the Akra was elevated. On the other hand, the pavilion was probably in the general vicinity of part of the processional route for the convenience both of the guests coming from the procession and sacrifice to the feast, and of those transporting the sacrificial meal to the pavilion. The precise position of the Akra in Alexandria cannot be determined, but it is at least known that it was in the larger Palace area since those in revolt from Ptolemy IV returned to the Akra from the palace (Plb. v. 39, 3). Its proximity to the royal part of the city is also suggested by the fact that in the tradition regarding the seventy translators of the Septuagint, who were hired expressly on the orders of Ptolemy Philadelphus, these were lodged near the Akra (*Ep. Arist.* 181).

---

[6] For a discussion of the Akra and its location see ibid., i. 30 ff.

The Akra may therefore have been close to, or even within, the 'Inner Palaces', the area of royal residences within the boundaries of the Larger Palaces which seems to have been located around the southern base of the promontory of Lochias (the approximate site of the modern headland Silsileh). This location can also be inferred from Kallixeinos on grounds of convenience, since the royal guests, who were entertained in the pavilion in the Akra and who watched the procession from the stadium contiguous to the larger Palace area, may have been housed in the royal residences within the 'Inner Palaces'. It is likely, therefore, that the grove around the pavilion was part of the extensive royal gardens and parks.

If it is correct that the pavilion and procession are related, that the Akra was near the 'Inner Palaces' and that the stadium was near the larger Palace area, then the procession probably passed through the north-eastern section of ancient Alexandria, and then along the main thorough-fares of the city. The use of this area reflects the procession's royal patronage, and the proximity of stadium, pavilion, and Palaces would have facilitated official participation and hospitality.

The beginning- and end-points of the Grand Procession can only be conjectured. The participants and organizers would have needed a large area in which to muster before the procession began. Although Alexandria may have had a *pompeion*, such as Athens had near the Dipylon Gate to store ritual objects for the annual Panathenaic processions, there is no known trace of one, but any large open space would have sufficed, the park areas of the larger Palaces being obvious candidates. This eastern side of the city would be the logical starting place for the procession if it was to progress westwards through the town after leaving the Palace area. If the procession mustered here, fairly near the stadium, it would have arrived at the stadium in good time and order for the benefit of the dis-tinguished spectators within. This area would have been convenient in terms of the objects and participants too. Since the procession was pre-pared under royal direction, areas within The Palaces may have been made available for constructing and storing some of the elaborate tableaux, and for adding their final touches immediately before the event. The Palaces would also have been the safest place to guard the assembled gold, silver, and other treasure which appeared in the procession, even if it was nor-mally housed elsewhere in temple depositories. The large number of exotic animals in the procession surely either came from, or were destined for, the famous royal zoo of Alexandria founded by Philadelphus (see below, p. 86). If, as seems likely, the zoo was located within the parks and gardens of the royal quarter, the difficulties of collecting, harnessing, and transporting all the animals to the parade route would have been greatly mitigated.

Greek religious processions either headed for the main shrine or temple of the honoured god where sacrifice was made and appropriate worship given, or, in the case of the circular processions where the divine statue was carried around the city, both started and finished at the temple. The final destination of the Grand Procession is not certain, but since several gods are honoured in the smaller processions within the Grand Procession, each sectional procession may have continued on its own after a certain point to the shrine of its own deity. (If the 2,000 bulls in 202A belong to the Dionysiac procession, as suggested below, pp. 110 ff., the other processions may also have had their own victims intended for separate sacrifices at altars before the temples of their respective gods.) The sacrificial animals and divine dedications may have proceeded to the temples even if the parade of carts and participants returned at some point to the Palace area in order to disperse. It is also possible, and perhaps more likely, that the Grand Procession continued as a unified parade to a central point where its climax was a single large public sacrifice for all the honorands (whether each procession contained its own god's animals or whether the large herd in 202A was intended for all the honorands). The gigantic Altar of Hieron II at Syracuse and the Great Altar of Zeus at Pergamon are monumental altars of the type which would have been appropriate for a large, public sacrifice in Alexandria; although there is no known trace of a comparable permanent monumental altar in the city, a temporary structure may have been erected. Since the Grand Procession was obviously calculated to have the maximum effect upon the spectators, its climax in a single public sacrifice would perhaps have been a more fitting finale than a comparatively quiet dispersal of the sectional processions to sacrifices at temples in different parts of the city. After the sacrifice, the individual processions could have gone to the various temples of the gods to deposit offerings and dedications while the populace was preparing for the feast.

Although the year in which the Grand Procession occurred is one of the most difficult problems to be considered, other chronological questions are easier to settle. The season of the year can be fixed if the pavilion was erected for the festivities surrounding the procession and its festival since Kallixeinos states that the entertainment held in the pavilion occurred in the middle of winter—the most natural season in view of the summer heat—which made the floral profusion in the grotto surrounding it appear all the more wondrous to visitors from less moderate climates (196D–E). The time of the beginning and end of the procession is also known: the first sectional procession honoured the Morning Star since the Grand Procession began at that hour (197D; line 4), and the end was marked by the procession of the Evening Star, which was the corresponding hour of the finale. Although the sidereal limits of the procession are thus established, its duration is not. The whole Grand Procession may have lasted from the morning to the evening of one day, or from the morning of one day until the evening of the next. Instead of maintaining that the procession lasted until night only because it took place on a short winter's day,[7] one might rather suggest that one day would barely have sufficed, given all the sectional processions, the inevitable stops and starts, delays, and breaks. A day-long procession would surely have continued well after dark, despite its stated end at the hour of the Evening Star's appearance, since it has been calculated that the march-past of the troops could itself have lasted up to ten hours, depending on their pace and formation.[8] It is questionable, however, whether the detailed tableaux and the elaborate objects of the type appearing in the Dionysiac procession were intended to be seen in less than full daylight for their maximum effect. Since the festival of which the procession was a part lasted more than one day in order to encompass the dramatic, musical, and other activities which are indicated by the text (the Guild of the Artists of Dionysus could not have both marched and performed at the same time, for example), the Grand Procession may have been spread over several days, even though Kallixeinos does not say so. Since the Grand Procession was composed of several smaller processions, it could easily have been broken up over several days, with the end of any one procession providing a convenient stopping place for that day. Likewise, the beginning of any sectional procession could have inaugurated the next day's proceedings. Possibly the parade of troops, the sacrifice, and the crowning ceremony occupied the final day, with the feast as the climax of the celebrations. Roman triumphal processions, which frequently lasted for more than one day (cf. Plut. *Aem.* xxxii), provide a later analogy for this suggestion. A great procession lasting several days in Alexandria would have been a major focus for admiration and acclaim, and such a spectacle may well have been drawn out deliberately for the greatest possible effect. Any time not taken by parts of the Grand Procession could have been filled by performances, competitions, and other activities associated with the festival.

I. THE BEGINNING OF THE GRAND PROCESSION

A. *The Procession of the Morning Star* (197D)

The Grand Procession begins with the individual procession of the Morning Star, which, like the corresponding concluding procession of the Evening Star, is described only in title and not by content. The function of these

---

[7] Cf. Kramer, *Tischgesellschaft*, 35; Caspari, 'Studien', 409–10.
[8] Caspari, 'Studien', 411–12.

two processions as indications of the time of the beginning and end of the Grand Procession explains their inclusion and position in the festivities. The ancients knew that the Morning and Evening Star is a single star which appears at both times, but through poetic convention it was often represented in myth and literature as two different stars, one bringing the dawn, the other the evening.[9] Here too, the necessity of depicting the two limits of the duration of the Grand Procession explains the division of one star into two different stars. The personifications of these stars can be traced as far back as Homer (*Il.* xxii. 317; xxiii. 226), along with similar natural phenomena such as Helios, Selene, Eos, etc. In the fourth century and later, personifications of natural phenomena often had a role in addition to their primary representation of nature; for example, personified stars could serve as recording angels in comedy (Plautus, *Rudens*, based on Diphilos; cf. Platonic School, *Epinomis*).[10] The Eosphoros and Hesperos here are similar 'extended' personifications since, in addition to representing particular stars, they provide information about the duration of the procession. Although it has been claimed that contemporary scientific advances in astronomy (the observation of stars and their movements) gave new life and an added sanction to the long-established personifications of stars,[11] and although significant strides in astronomy were undoubtedly achieved in Alexandria,[12] the extended use of these particular personifications of nature in the procession may equally be due to the increasing popularity and use of personifications in general in the Hellenistic age, which is clearly reflected by the other types of personification which appear in the procession.

Little can be said about these opening and closing processions in the Grand Procession. Since statues of the honorands appear prominently in the presumably analogous divisional processions of Dionysus and Alexander, statues of the personified Eosphoros and Hesperos were probably drawn on carts as the central feature of their respective processions, perhaps as counterparts to each other. The earliest representations of stars were boys, or youths, as riders, but later Eosphoros and Hesperos were commonly shown as winged youths, sometimes holding torches, to symbolize their light.[13] Something along these lines may be imagined for their representations here, with Eosphoros perhaps holding his torch aloft to symbolize the approaching dawn, and with Hesperos holding his torch low to signify the fading day.

    [9] Ibid., 410; *RE* s.v. Hesperos, 1250 ff.

    [10] T. B. L. Webster, *JWCI* xvii (1954), 13.

    [11] Ibid.

    [12] See *Ptol. Alex.* i. 396 ff., for a discussion of some of the famous mathematician-astronomers working in Alexandria.

    [13] *RE* s.v. Hesperos, 1252-3.

B. *The Procession* τοῖς τῶν βασιλέων γονεῦσι κατωνομασμένη (197D)

The second divisional procession is the one called ἡ τοῖς τῶν βασιλέων γονεῦσι κατωνομασμένη, a phrase whose meaning is not clear, and whose interpretation has important ramifications both upon the date of the Grand Procession and the state of the ruler cult at that time. Even the translation of the phrase has been disputed. It seems clear in any case that οἱ γονεῖς means 'parents'. Although the word has the connotation of 'ancestors' in some earlier writers (Hdt. i. 91; Isae. 8, 32; Arist. *GA* 772ᵃ 8), and in at least one Imperial inscription from Teos (*CIG* 3098), in the formulaic language of Ptolemaic inscriptions it always means 'parents'. It seems therefore unlikely that Kallixeinos, who wrote standard Hellenistic Greek, used the term in any other sense. If οἱ γονεῖς must mean 'parents', the uncertainty in the translation is confined to the term οἱ βασιλεῖς. The phrase has usually been translated as 'the procession named after the parents of the king and queen', although in inscriptions from Ptolemaic Alexandria the ruler and his queen were never called οἱ βασιλεῖς before the time of Ptolemy XII and Cleopatra Tryphaena in the first century BC (cf. *SB* 5827, 16 = 6154; 6236, 3, 22, 49). There is no epigraphical evidence that Ptolemy II and either of his two wives were ever called οἱ βασιλεῖς in any official document of his reign from Alexandria, nor does the phrase refer to them in papyri.[14] Furthermore, the translation of the term as 'king and queen' must mean that Philadelphus had a living consort at the time of the Grand Procession. Although the king was

---

[14] Cf. Preisigke–Kiessling, *Wörterbuch d. Gr. Pap.* i. s.v. βασιλεύς iii. Abschnitt 2. The term does occasionally appear in papyri of the 2nd century in references of the reigns of Ptolemies VI, VIII and Cleopatra II (*UPZ* 114, 10: Βασιλεῦσι Ζωἰς Ἡρακλεῖδου; *SB* 7457, 8: ἄγω μὲν τὰς ὑπὲρ τῶν βασιλέων θυσίας; 11: θύομεν ὑπὲρ τῶν βασιλέων). The difference in terminology must reflect the *de iure* co-regency which existed among various of these royal siblings at various times. Cleopatra was the first queen to be a *de iure* co-regent on the throne and to be given regnal years along with the male Ptolemies. *UPZ* 114 is dated to 29 April 150, in which year Ptolemy VI and Cleopatra ruled jointly on the throne (see T. C. Skeat, *The Reigns of the Ptolemies, Münch. Beitr. z. Papyrusforsch u. Ant. Rechtsgesch.* xxxix (1954), 14); by right and by law, therefore, Cleopatra was as much a '*βασιλεύς*' as her husband. An analogous situation occurs in *SB* 7457, year 15 (dated to 167–166 BC; Skeat, 13) when all three siblings ruled jointly. The title βασιλεῖς is used in an informal way in both papyri, in contrast to official documents where the co-regents are each given separate titles, βασιλεὺς Πτολεμαῖος καὶ βασίλισσα Κλεοπάτρα (cf. Preisigke–Kiessling, ibid., iii. Abschnitt 2); although Kallixeinos' text may be considered an example of similar 'informal' usage, the term βασιλεῖς is nevertheless not found referring to Philadelphus and Arsinoe II in informal papyrological contexts. For example, it does not appear in *PEnteux.*, a collection of requests and pleas addressed to the Egyptian king in the 3rd century (although all are later than Philadelphus) in which a less formal titulature may be expected (in *PEnteux.* 27, 18, Ptolemy III and Berenike II are each given their separate titles of 'king' and 'queen'). Since Arsinoe II was not a *de iure* co-regent on the throne like Cleopatra II, there is no reason for her to have been considered more than a queen-consort or for her to have shared the title βασιλεύς.

married twice, neither wife is named or referred to anywhere in the Grand Procession especially where honours or crowns are being given; this would lead to the obvious conclusion that the king was unmarried at the time were it not for the phrase οἱ βασιλεῖς. If this does mean 'king and queen', either all other references to the wife have been omitted from what is admittedly a fragmentary text or else the queen had no part in the Grand Procession; although both these suggestions are possible, neither is particularly probable nor satisfactory, since it is difficult on other grounds to fit either wife into the role of consort during the Grand Procession.

Philadelphus' first queen was Arsinoe I, the daughter of Lysimachus of Thrace and Nicaea, and although the date and duration of their marriage is unknown, Arsinoe bore three children and was repudiated on a charge of conspiracy against her husband (Schol. Theoc. xvii. 128). If, as seems likely, they were married in 289/8 to cement the alliance of Lysimachus and Ptolemy I against Demetrius Poliorcetes,[15] Arsinoe could hardly have been disgraced and sent away (whether justifiably or not) before her father's death in 281. Another suggestion for the date of such a potentially valuable dynastic marriage is 285, when Philadelphus was associated upon the throne with his father.[16] Either date, or one in between, would allow for the birth of three children before 281, the *terminus post quem* for the date of her disgrace. It has often been assumed that the king remained married to Arsinoe I until the arrival in c.276 of Arsinoe II, who ruthlessly instigated the queen's downfall when she realized that marriage to her own brother was her last hope of a throne.[17] This theory arises largely from Arsinoe II's formidable reputation and should be tempered by the reflection that Philadelphus, who needed his sister's brains in that difficult decade, had as many advantages to be gained from the incestuous marriage as his sister had.[18] (Moreover, evidence from the Pithom Stele may suggest that the entrance of Arsinoe II was unrelated to the departure of Arsinoe I; if the statement that Philadelphus journeyed alone to Pithom in the sixth year of his reign means that he had no consort in 279,[19] Arsinoe I must have already been sent away by then.) If Arsinoe I is queen consort during the Grand Procession, the festival must have occurred between c.285 and c.281. A procession in honour of the parents of Philadelphus and Arsinoe I, οἱ βασιλεῖς in this case, would only need to celebrate the parents of the king, Ptolemy I and Berenike, since, on the analogy of Ptolemaic inscriptions proclaiming the lineage of a particular royal couple, a wife who is not the consanguineous sister of her husband is

---

[15] W. W. Tarn, *JHS* liii (1933), 60.

[16] K. J. Beloch, *Griechische Geschichte* (Berlin and Leipzig, 1927), iv (2), 130.

[17] Ibid., iv (1), 582 ff.   [18] W. W. Tarn, *JHS* xlvi (1926), 161.

[19] E. Naville, *The Store-City of Pithom* (4th ed., London, 1903), 19, line 7.

without exception assumed to be part of her husband's family and is given the same ancestors (e.g. *OGIS* 56, 21–2, referring to Ptolemy III and Berenike, the daughter of Magas of Cyrene). It is consequently not necessary to assume that a procession would have been held in honour of Arsinoe I's parents, since the queen would be officially considered, and styled, the child of Ptolemy I. The omission of the consort Arsinoe I elsewhere from the text is perhaps easier to accept than that of her more powerful successor Arsinoe II, who was in effect a co-regent, and may perhaps even be explained as the result of a later, otherwise unattested 'damnatio memoriae'. Even if Arsinoe I did originally figure in the festival as consort, she could have been expunged from Kallixeinos' official sources for the event by royal order after she was disgraced and replaced in fact and memory by Arsinoe II. In this case she would naturally be missing from his description.

Two factors, however, argue against the acceptance of Arsinoe I as queen consort during the Grand Procession, as signified by the use of the title οἱ βασιλεῖς. The first is the improbability that Arsinoe I, a consort, would have been included in this title of official recognition when her successor, a *de facto* co-regent who shared in the national policy of her brother's kingdom, was never included in such a plurality of title with her brother in inscriptions or papyri. The second is that the Grand Procession would then have had to take place before *c.*280, and although this date has the one advantage of excluding any connection of the Grand Procession with the Ptolemaieia festival (which is argued below; see pp. 182 ff.), it nevertheless must be rejected on one issue. A Grand Procession in these years could indeed have celebrated an earlier occasion altogether, namely Philadelphus' association on the throne with his father in 285, or his own coronation after 283 (although nothing in the text argues in favour of any of these events over any other). The procession, however, could not have taken place so early because in it Ptolemy I and Berenike are given posthumous divine honours, both separately and in the procession 'named after' οἱ τῶν βασιλέων γονεῖς (Philadelphus is certainly one of the βασιλεῖς, regardless of his counterpart, so his parents are among the honorands here). Soter's deification is marked by the establishment of the Ptolemaieia *c.*280/79 (see p. 182), when his queen may still have been alive since she is not mentioned in the decree of establishment (*SIG*[3] 390; for the date of the death of Berenike, see p. 122). The Grand Procession must postdate their mutual deaths and respective deifications, which makes a date in the 280s unacceptable.

Philadelphus' second wife, Arsinoe II (called Philadelphus) was his consanguineous elder sister and an outstandingly able woman of great power, which she exercised while queen to the extent that she may be regarded as a *de facto*, although not a *de iure*, co-regent on the throne with her brother (see p. 38 and n. 14). After the first Syrian War she was granted extraordinary honours by the king, and was deified while still alive (*PHib.* 199, 11-17; cf. *Ptol. Alex.* i. 215). She was worshipped as a goddess after death, and her ideas on foreign policy continued to affect Philadelphus at least publicly as late as the eve of the Chremonidean War (*SIG*³ 434-5, 16-17). If Philadelphus and Arsinoe are understood to be married at the time of the Grand Procession, certain restrictions are put upon the possible dates for its celebration. Their marriage occurred at an uncertain time after the spring of 279, when Arsinoe II was widowed by the death of her second husband Ptolemy Keraunos (Justin xxiv. 3, 9-10), but before 29 June 273, the date given by the Pithom Stele for a joint trip by king and queen.[20] Arsinoe probably did not return to her native Egypt before *c.*276, since until that date (when Antigonus Gonatas finally established himself as king of Macedon) she had been in Samothrace directing the claims of her son by Lysimachus to the Macedonian throne.[21] If the words οἱ βασιλεῖς mean that Arsinoe was married to her brother at the time of the Grand Procession, it must then have taken place between 274/3 (at the latest) and July 270, when Arsinoe died.[22] (The acceptability of a year within this period for the Grand Procession is discussed in Chapter 5). Although one may argue that this queen may have been *entitled* to be called one of οἱ βασιλεῖς because of her influence over the throne (despite the fact that the lack of evidence for the title at this date suggests strongly that she never actually *used* it), it then becomes incredible that, although alive during the Grand Procession, she is neither honoured nor even mentioned by name anywhere else in the text, especially in the crowning ceremony at the end. Her absence would be all the more curious in view of the fact that her parents, by that time lesser royal figures than the current rulers, are celebrated with a procession partly in their honour, receive divine honours elsewhere in the Grand Procession, and do appear in the concluding crowning ceremony. The difficulty increases with the suggestion that Arsinoe II died before the Grand Procession but was commemorated here as βασιλεύς along with her husband, since her posthumous importance and worship actually increased in various ways and was publicly recorded in Athens before the Chremonidean War (*c.*266/5). If Philadelphus is considered to have been a widower at the time of the Grand Procession, its date would have had to be long enough after Arsinoe II's death for her influence to have waned (perhaps well into the 250s), or else her omission from the rest of the text

---

[20] Ibid., 20, line 15; cf. P. M. Fraser, *BCH* lxxviii (1954), 57 n. 3.

[21] W. W. Tarn, *JHS* xlvi (1926), 161.

[22] Cf. the Mendes Stele, Sethe, *Hierogl. Urk.* ii. 40; *Ptol. Alex.* ii. 937 n. 415.

is incomprehensible; but so late a date is unlikely on other grounds to be right (see pp. 164-5). The *dikeras* illustrates this difficulty: this double cornucopia was the special symbol of the queen, but was probably only associated with her after her death. Although it does appear in the Grand Procession (202C, line 246; ? 202B, line 231; see textual note), and has been interpreted as referring to the queen, the object seems to be only a minor ritual object or divine attribute without that particular significance which might be expected if it did symbolize Arsinoe. Its lack of special prominence as her symbol here cannot be reconciled with Arsinoe's posthumous prestige (see Appendix II for a discussion of the *dikeras*).

The obscure phrase οἱ βασιλεῖς apart, the balance of evidence from the text weighs against Philadelphus being married at the time of the Grand Procession. If, however, this phrase does not refer to a consort, the king may well have been 'between wives' from *c*.280 to 275 (he could hardly have been on the throne long before he married Arsinoe I, and, as above, he was probably not a widower when the procession took place). To be consistent with both linguistic usage and historical restrictions, οἱ τῶν βασιλέων γονεῖς can be interpreted in either of two ways. Kallixeinos could have used it in a proleptic sense of Arsinoe II: if Philadelphus was not yet married to her at the time of the Grand Procession (which explains why she is not mentioned within the text), Kallixeinos, writing in later years when Arsinoe II was a goddess and a major deity in the ruler cult, may have found it natural to refer to her with that status. Soter and Berenike would naturally, in this case, be called 'the parents of the king and queen' even though Arsinoe was not queen at the time. This suggestion may explain the omission of Arsinoe from the text, but it still does not obviate the difficulty of οἱ βασιλεῖς as a title for king and queen when it is otherwise unattested before the first century BC.

The more likely solution is that οἱ βασιλεῖς is translated as 'kings' (i.e. male rulers).[23] The phrase is used in this general sense in many Ptolemaic inscriptions when several ruling monarchs from various countries or generations are referred to, especially when none is mentioned by name (*OGIS* 90, 31; *SEG* 8, 529, 8, 11-12, 27). Since οἱ γονεῖς means 'parents', the parents in question would be those both of Ptolemy I and II. Ptolemy I obviously appears as one of the honorands as the father of Philadelphus, but there is reason to think that his own parents may have been similarly honoured. His mother Arsinoe had a vital place in the dynastic stemma of the Ptolemies as the vehicle of their officially claimed divine and royal

---

[23] Tarn, *Ant. Gon.* 261 n. 10; *Hermes* lxv (1930), 447 n. 2, argued for this interpretation, although his final view of the problem was that the phrase meant 'ancestors of the kings', *JHS* liii (1933), 60. This is impossible because of the translation of οἱ γονεῖς as 'ancestors' rather than 'parents' (see above, p. 38).

descent, since she was purported to be a descendant of King Amyntas I of Macedonia through whom a blood tie with Dionysus and Alexander the Great was contrived by the Ptolemies.[24] The line originates with Zeus through his sons Herakles and Dionysus, and is traced down through Amyntas and Arsinoe (the mother of Soter) to Soter (cf. the official version of this genealogy in Satyrus, *FGrH* 631). Other descendants of Amyntas were the forefathers of Philip II and Alexander. Soter's father Lagus also claimed a divine descent. The Adulis inscription calls Soter a descendant of Herakles through his father and of Dionysus through his mother (*OGIS* 54, 4–5), and Theocritus states that Alexander and Soter, the son of Lagus, numbered Herakles as their furthest ancestor (xvii. 27). The importance of the Ptolemaic relationship to Alexander and Dionysus is clearly shown in the 'Indian Triumph' pageant in the Dionysiac procession (see pp. 82 ff.), and a divisional procession partly in honour of Lagus and his wife Arsinoe would also emphasize the Dionysus-Alexander link and Ptolemaic claims of legitimacy as Alexander's rightful heirs in Egypt. This interpretation of οἱ βασιλεῖς accords well with the dynastic propaganda so evident elsewhere in the Grand Procession, and it has the considerable advantage of removing both wives as candidates for βασιλεύς.

However its honorands may be understood, this divisional procession remains the most difficult to interpret because of the terminology used to describe it. Unlike the names of the other processions, which consist of the word πομπή plus the genitive of the name of the honoured god (e.g. ἡ ⟨πομπὴ⟩ Ἑωσφόρου; αἱ τῶν θεῶν ἀπάντων) or the noun with a ktetic adjective (τῆς Διονυσιακῆς πομπῆς), this procession is described obliquely as the one *named after* (κατωνομασμένη) the parents τῶν βασιλέων. The explanation for the difference in terminology may be that these honorands, whoever they are, are not gods in the same sense as the other deities worshipped with processions, but are rather deified or glorified mortals. If this procession partly honours Soter's parents, Arsinoe and Lagus, they were not divine themselves (despite their purported divine ancestry) nor were they worshipped in Alexandria. On the other hand, Soter and Berenike were both deified singly in Alexandria by the date of the Grand Procession, and the unique name of the procession which is partly in their honour may reflect the stage of their deification at that time and its relation to the official dynastic cult. A joint cult of the Theoi Soteres was established in their honour probably by about 270 (possibly referred to in Theocritus xvii. 121 ff.; see below, p. 122), but this cult presumably began after the Grand Procession because here Soter and Berenike are not called the Theoi Soteres, an official cult title which would have been used had it

[24] Cf. Tarn, *JHS* liii (1933), 58–9.

existed; for example, this procession could have been called ἡ τῶν θεῶν Σωτήρων πομπή plus the names of the other honorands. The Grand Procession, therefore, probably only indicates their deification as individual gods. Despite the single and joint deification (regardless of the exact date of the latter), Soter was not included in the dynastic cult until the reign of Ptolemy IV, a curious phenomenon the explanation of which is unknown but which may have been in accordance with Soter's own wishes.[25] The peculiar omission of Soter from the state dynastic cult and his resulting slightly ambiguous position among the gods may further help to explain the equally ambiguous position of Berenike, and the still more ambiguous position of Arsinoe and Lagus, in divine company, and may be why their procession was only 'named after' them; it did not honour them in the same way that Dionysus' procession worshipped his divine, Olympian godhead. A similar contrast is seen between the procession 'named after' οἱ τῶν βασιλέων γονεῖς and the only other one in honour of a deified mortal, namely Alexander. The positions of these two processions are exactly comparable (the former following the procession of the Morning Star, the latter preceding that of the Evening Star, and both framing the various processions of the Olympian gods), but Alexander's procession is described in the same way as those of the Olympian gods (202A; line 226): καὶ μετὰ ταῦτα Διὸς ἤγετο πομπὴ καὶ ἄλλων παμπόλλων θεῶν, καὶ ἐπὶ πᾶσιν Ἀλεξάνδρου. Like Soter and Berenike, Alexander was a deified mortal, but his personal cult (established by Soter and different from the original Founder Cult) was the origin of the dynastic cult.[26] This god, who had a public, 'national' cult, differs from the other deified mortals and his procession is therefore described directly in terms akin to those used for the Olympian gods.

At the end of his thumbnail sketch of the constituent parts of the Grand Procession, Kallixeinos includes a comment to his readers about the sources which they should consult for more information about the occasion (197D; line 8: τὰ δὲ κατὰ μέρος αὐτῶν εἴ τις εἰδέναι βούλεται, τὰς τῶν Πεντετηρίδων γραφὰς λαμβάνων ἐπισκοπείτω). Certain suggestions are offered in Chapter 4 about the identity of these sources and the possible forms they may have taken, but apart from recording the existence and accessibility of some type of public record, this sentence is important for the interpretation of the text, the author, and the occasion. The explicit reference to sources containing information shows that the transmitted account is not a complete description of all the contents of the Grand Procession, but an abbreviation by the author and therefore perhaps not a true reflection of either the substance or the effect of the original event. Secondly, the reference to the sources has been taken as evidence by many scholars that Kallixeinos need not have been an eye-witness observer of the Grand Procession in order to describe it, but could have been totally dependent upon secondary sources. This suggestion, if true, affects the possible dates proposed for Kallixeinos (see Chapter 4 D). Finally, this statement sheds some light upon the occasion of the Grand Procession, since, if an account of it was contained in αἱ τῶν Πεντε-τηρίδων γραφαί (whatever these may have been), it follows that this procession must have been part of a penteteric festival, that is, one held every four years. The knowledge that the festival was a regularly recurring event, and not a special extravaganza staged once for a particular occasion, affects any decisions reached about its historical interpretation (see Chapter 5).

II. THE PROCESSION OF DIONYSUS

A. *The Prelude to the Dionysiac Procession* (197E–198B)

The description of the magnificent Dionysiac procession begins with a long introductory section (197E ff.) which prefaces the central part celebrating the life and *aristeia* of the god. The first participants establish the general atmosphere and thematic congruity of the procession. At the head march Silenoi who restrain the crowds and whose appearance announces the beginning of the new procession which came at least third in the order of the Grand Procession. The parade route is thereby cleared of the crowds milling about in the hiatus between the end of one procession and the beginning of the next. The Satyrs who follow (line 13) officially begin the Dionysiac procession, carrying torches which may have a religious, purifi-catory purpose in addition to lending an air of dignity and solemnity to the proceedings. The ivy decoration thereon immediately introduces a Dionysiac theme. The Satyrs range themselves on both sides of the stadium, which suggests that their function was primarily ceremonial; they may in this case have remained in place throughout the Dionysiac proces-sion (instead of marching out of the stadium along the processional route) as a type of guard of honour for the other participants passing between them. Satyrs and Silenoi naturally appear in various capacities throughout the Dionysiac procession as the traditional companions of the god. Some visual distinction is probably indicated between them since they are always differentiated by Kallixeinos, and the most likely difference is that of age: although the two types of creatures once had an identical iconography and interchangeable names,[27] by the fourth century Satyrs came to be represented as youthful creatures and Silenoi as their older counterparts,[28] perhaps under the influence of Praxiteles who sculpted youthful Satyrs and Satyriskoi. No other intrinsic difference between them in the procession would seem evident from their costumes or attributes. The fact that these characters are men dressed as mythological creatures gives some information about their basic costume aside from the special features which are described in detail. Loin-cloths would have been a necessary article of apparel as the mode of attachment for the artificial tails and gigantic phalloi which were part of legendary Satyrs. Men representing Satyrs in Greek vase-paintings without exception wear such loin-cloths.[29]

The next part of this introductory section consists of the presentation of incense; there appear Nikai with censers, a double altar, and boys bearing frankincense, myrrh, and saffron (197E; lines 15 ff). The appearance of the incense in the opening stages of the Dionysiac procession perhaps indicates its purificatory function (possibly anticipated by the torches carried by the Satyrs) as preparation for the epiphany of the divine statues and ritual objects. Although incense was often used as an accompaniment to sacrifices, no sacrificial animals appear until the end of the Dionysiac procession in 202A, and its presence is better understood here as a preliminary offering to Dionysus. Incense was ubiquitous in religious contexts in Ptolemaic Egypt as it was in other parts of the Greek world, and frankincense, myrrh, and saffron are frequently mentioned in papyri. The first two gums were burned to produce a pleasant smell, and the Ptolemies went to great lengths to maintain trade routes to ensure a supply of these indigenous Arabian products to Egypt, and also encouraged their production in Egypt.[30] These spices may have actually been burning in the censers and on the altar during the course of the procession, being replenished as necessary from the supply carried by the boys. In Roman times, saffron was mixed with water and sprinkled about to give a pleasant odour (Lucr. ii. 416; Seneca *Lucil.* 90, 15; Lucan ix. 808-9; Prop. iv. 1, 1), and although similar olfactory considerations may have been relevant in this public spectacle, saffron was a common symbol of divine purity and majesty, and, as such, was an appropriate offering to the gods who are in literature frequently described as wearing saffron-coloured garments.[31] The statue of Dionysus which appears later is dressed in a saffron-coloured cloak (198C; line 49) and has a saucer full of saffron at its feet (line 52).

---

[27] F. Brommer, *Satyroi* (Würzburg, 1937), 2 ff.

[28] Ibid.; *RE* s.v. Silenoi und Satyroi, 36-7.

[29] Cf. J. Boardman, *JHS* lxxviii (1958), 6, Fig. 2; 7 and n. 8; F. Brommer, *Satyrspiele* (Berlin, 1944), Pls. 2-6.

[30] *Ptol. Alex.* i. 175 ff.; G. W. van Beek, *JAOS* lxxviii (1958), 141 ff.

[31] *RE* s.v. Safran, 1729-30.

An unusual item appears between the Nikai and the boys carrying incense, a βωμὸς ἐξάπηχυς διπλοῦς (line 18), a double altar with elaborate ivy and vine decoration again symbolic of Dionysus. Paired altars are well attested in antiquity: two chthonic altars may exist side by side,[32] a chthonic *eschara* may be placed beside a regular 'Olympian' altar,[33] and, e.g. at Olympia, two 'Olympian' altars may be placed side by side, or one altar dedicated to two gods (Paus. v. 14, 4 ff.). Although the last two categories have been called 'double' altars,[34] neither is an adequate description of an altar specifically called διπλοῦς, which is in any case a portable, free-standing structure, not a permanent or ground altar. The physical appearance of this altar may be similar to that of a double Rhodian funerary altar,[35] which consists of two cylindrical altars carved from one piece of stone and encircled by a single garland, or to the unusual tripartite ceremonial altar before the Doric Temple in the Foro Triangolare at Pompeii.[36] On the other hand, it may conceivably have consisted of two discrete altars appearing side by side and linked by garlands. In view of its size, the double altar was probably wheeled on a cart rather than carried, and made not of stone but of hollowed terracotta or wood (which could both have been gilded and highly decorated). Full-size terracotta altars which were light enough to be carried did exist elsewhere in the ancient world,[37] and questions of weight must have determined the material to be used here. This altar must have been intended for the burning of incense rather than any animal sacrifices, and was in essence an enlarged version of a miniature altar, or arula, which was normally used in religious ritual for burning incense. A double altar of this size is of course hardly 'miniature' by any standards other than the colossal scale of the Dionysiac procession, but the large amount of incense carried by the boys would require a proportionately large 'arula'. The double altar is nevertheless an enigma, since the paired altars mentioned above served two divinities combined in worship at the same shrine, be they both chthonic, both Olympian, or a combination. The worship of two aspects or cults of one god may also explain a double altar. Even the Rhodian funerary altar, whose anomalous form is probably due to economy of time and money in the mass-production of such common monuments, preserves the same underlying concept of doubleness since it commemorates two people. The obvious conclusion to be drawn from the presence of this double altar is that it honours two gods, or two aspects of one god. Many other Olympian gods do feature in

[32] C. G. Yavis, *Greek Altars* (Saint Louis, 1949), 134, Nos. 6–7.
[33] Ibid., 92–4.
[34] E. N. Gardiner, *Olympia: Its History and Remains* (Oxford, 1925), 198–9.
[35] P. M. Fraser, *Rhodian Funerary Monuments* (Oxford, 1977), 33 and n. 176; Pl. 91 (*a*).
[36] Yavis, 183, No. 18.   [37] Ibid., 170–1 sub No. 64.

the mythological scenes of the life of Dionysus which appear later in the procession, but Dionysus is not specifically paired with any of them, and nothing argues convincingly that one or another was honoured with him on this altar. Perhaps the closest implicit link which is made in the procession is that between Dionysus and Alexander, since the elaborate pageant of Dionysus' Indian Triumph can only be interpreted in the light of Alexander's recent successes in the East (see p. 83). It is therefore conceivable that the double altar honours Dionysus in combination with his 'human counterpart' (at least in the context of this procession), but if this or any other divine combination of cult was made explicit to the spectators of the procession, Kallixeinos does not make it clear to his readers. Another possibility is that two aspects, or cults, of Dionysus are being worshipped on the double altar. Numerous aspects of Dionysus were recognized and worshipped in antiquity, and indeed in Ptolemaic Egypt the god had important cults for his chthonic associations in addition to those for more traditional worship.[38] The Dionysus of the procession is honoured primarily as the god of wine, secondly as the Indian Triumphator, and less emphatically, as the patron of drama. The double altar may celebrate this multiple divine role presented in the procession, but if it was meant to honour his chthonic cult in addition to his 'traditional' worship, it is particularly odd that these connotations are totally excluded elsewhere in the procession in favour of his connection with wine and the East.

Forty crowned Satyrs carrying a large gold crown of vine and ivy are the final participants in this introductory section (line 23). The prodigious ceremonial crown must be a dedication intended for Dionysus, and appears with the altar and incense as a preliminary offering to the god. This section forms a suitable prelude to the central part of the Dionysiac procession. An appropriate tone of official ceremony has been established by the Satyrs and Silenoi, and an atmosphere of dignified religious ritual is created by the incense and initial offerings. The way is paved for the epiphany of Dionysus and the celebration of his life, and his sovereignty as the god of wine (an aspect of his godhead which is emphasized throughout the rest of the procession) is established immediately by the decorative preponderance of vines.

The next two figures, dressed as a herald and a trumpeter,[39] signal the

---

[38] *Ptol. Alex.*, i. 202 ff.

[39] Athenaeus refers to a lost epigram of Poseidippos which describes the obese Aglais, who 'blew the trumpet for the procession in the first great parade at Alexandria' (415A-B): καὶ γυνὴ δὲ ἐσάλπισεν ᾿Αγλαὶς ἡ Μεγακλέους ἐν τῇ πρώτῃ ἀχθείσῃ μεγάλῃ πομπῇ ἐν ᾿Αλεξανδρείᾳ τὸ πομπικόν . . . (cf. Ael. *VH* i. 26). If Fraser, *Ptol. Alex.* ii. 381 n. 335, is right that this anecdote refers to the Grand Procession, Aglais is probably not the trumpeter with the herald since it is doubtful that a woman

beginning of the main section of the Dionysiac procession (198A; line 27), the approach of the divine epiphany in the form of his statue. A herald and a trumpeter are frequently seen at the head of Greek religious processions, including Dionysiac processions in classical Athens where they lead the participants,[40] and these officials perform exactly the same role. They are followed by the personified figures of Eniautos (the 'Cyclic Year'), Penteteris (a 'Five-Year Span'), and the four Horai (198A–B; lines 29 ff.). The respective attributes of these figures (the horn of plenty, a persea crown, and seasonal fruits) and their position after the herald suggest that they replace and represent kanephoroi,[41] the bearers of baskets of offerings, notably first-fruits. Kanephoroi were long-established, regular participants in Greek religious processions including Athenian Dionysiac festivals, and they often occupied a prominent position at the head of the proceedings.[42] Kanephoroi played an important role in Ptolemaic as well as Attic religion: the term 'kanephoros' was used later for the eponymous priesthood in the official cult of Arsinoe Philadelphus.[43] Consequently, kanephoroi may reasonably be expected to participate in this procession, and these personified figures are the obvious candidates because of their position. Although their attributes are pertinent to each particular personification (see below), they may also be intended as the actual or symbolic first-fruits offered to Dionysus. In this procession, the kanephoroi are represented by figures which are in fact personifications of something else, but this convoluted notion is paralleled by scenes on two Attic vases,[44] where female personifications of Πομπή (identified by inscriptions) are depicted beside processional baskets. 'Pompe', a personification of the procession who also represents the kanephoros in it by metonymy,[45] furnishes an analogy for this unusual type of 'double personification' in the Dionysiac procession.

Even if these figures represent processional kanephoroi in general, they

would have had this role in a public procession, and, in any case, Kallixeinos specifically states that these heralds are Silenoi, and therefore presumably male. Furthermore, this section of the Grand Procession seems to have been too dignified for a participant who would be considered risible, especially if all these figures are associated with the Guild of the Artists of Dionysus (see below). Perhaps Aglais blew her trumpet in a comedy or Satyr play attached to the festival.

[40] *SIG*³ 728 A; A. Frickenhaus, *JDAI* xxvii (1912), 66, 71; S. Eitrem, *Beiträge zur Griechischen Religionsgeschichte* (Kristiania, 1920), iii. 83.

[41] Frickenhaus, 75; Eitrem, 90.

[42] J. Schelp, *Das Kanoun der Griechische Opferkorb, Beitr. zur. Arch.* vii (Würzburg, 1975), 15 ff.

[43] *Ptol. Alex.* i. 217.

[44] G. M. A. Richter and L. Hall, *Red-Figured Athenian Vases in the Metropolitan Museum of Art* (New Haven, 1936), i. Nos. 160, 169.

[45] Deubner, 103.

have a primary, specific role in terms of what they personify directly. Eniautos, Penteteris, and the Horai must have a temporal, chronological significance as far as the procession and its attendant festival are concerned, although it is perhaps surprising that these figures appear in the context of the Dionysiac procession and not in a less specific part of the Grand Procession. The figure of Penteteris must surely signify that the festival of which the procession was a part was a penteteric one, occurring every four years like the Olympic Games, a detail which is also known from Kallixeinos' statement that his sources were contained in the 'penteteric records'. There is no other reason why a representation of such an artificial span of time should be included. The notion of the penteteris as a recurring cycle of time, which is implicit here because the festival is celebrated again at the end of each successive four-year period, holds the key to the interpretation of the other figures. The figure representing the 'Year' is significantly called ἐνιαυτός and not ἔτος. Much has been written about these two terms, and the generally accepted distinction between them is that ἔτος is a year, a specific chronological period be it civic, regnal or calendaric, but that ἐνιαυτός is a year-long span of time, a 'twelve-month' as we may call it. This span does not necessarily coincide with any calendar 'year' and may be reckoned from any point, and always contains the idea of a recurring cycle of time.[46] Eniautos is therefore a twelve-month period, a cycle recurring four times to make up a penteteris. The Horai may also be seen in this light as the recurring seasons which make up an *eniautos*. (They were in fact associated with Eniautos as far back as the fifth century; cf. Pindar, *Paean* i. 5 ff.) The notion of the Eniautos-Daimon has often been connected to cycles of nature as a symbol of the recurring fruitfulness of a new year, the harvest, the death and rebirth of nature, etc.;[47] although this connotation is often overstated, and is absent altogether when the word is used in inscriptions to describe periods of time,[48] all of these personified figures do carry symbols of nature. Eniautos has the horn of Plenty (indicative of the year's fruitfulness), Penteteris, a crown from the traditionally ever-fruitful Egyptian persea tree, and the Seasons, fruit appropriate to each of them. The very presence of the Horai in this group may connect these cycles to natural cycles even if this is not their primary connotation in the procession.

The periphrasis ὃς προσηγορεύετο Ἐνιαυτός suggests that his name was announced as the figure passed by or that he was preceded by a labelled banner, in which case his costume and attributes alone may not have

---

[46] A. Wilhelm, *SB Wien Akad.* cxlii (1900); G. Murray, *JHS* lxxi (1951), 120 ff.; C. J. Emlyn-Jones, *Glotta* xliv–xlv (1966–7), 156 ff.

[47] Murray, op. cit., 120 ff.; J. E. Harrison, *Themis* (Cambridge, 1912), 184–6.

[48] Wilhelm, op. cit.

yielded an immediate identification. His horn of Amaltheia is an attested attribute to signify the year's fulfilment,[49] but the reason for the tragic costume is not clear. It may simply be a tribute to the fact that Dionysus, in whose procession Eniautos appears, is portrayed, *inter alia*, as the patron of drama: the pavilion contains scenes of figures from tragedy, comedy, and Satyr plays, dramatic masks hang from the canopy shading the statue of Dionysus (see below), and the Guild of the Artists of Dionysus follows this group of personified figures in the procession. If Eniautos, Penteteris, and the Horai are actually members of the Guild (see below), Eniautos would naturally be dressed in a dramatic costume. Penteteris is not described, but the specific mention of her extreme height suggests that she, like Eniautos, has a tragic costume including high cothurni, and wears it for the same reason. The palm branch and the crown of persea are symbols of victory (even if the persea itself connotes fruitfulness), and the victory she alludes to may be those in competitions associated with the festival; dramatic contests are specifically indicated by the presence later of Delphic tripods intended as prizes for the victorious choregoi of dithyrambic contests. Such attributes are particularly appropriate to Penteteris if she is a member of the Guild. This personified figure is paralleled by a Trieteris portrayed on a Greek mirror dating from the first half of the third century BC, who, along with the personifications of Oinē and Phallodia, acts as a nursemaid to the infant Dionysus.[50] Trieteris is depicted as a typical Hellenistic draped female, which is no help in determining the iconography of Penteteris, but her existence shows that the idea of visually personifying artificial spans of time was not unique to the Dionysiac procession. Personifications of the Horai are common in art and literature from the time of archaic vases and Hesiod. Although they were originally shown as three women in identical dress who probably represented various recurring natural and agricultural cycles, their number increased to four by the end of the fifth century, and as they came to be identified with the Seasons, their attributes were accordingly differentiated.[51] The Horai here may be pictured as elaborately dressed, beautiful young women, who perhaps carried their appropriate fruits in kana, processional baskets.

[49] The description of a cup elsewhere in Athenaeus shows that the horn of Amaltheia must have been a common attribute of Eniautos (783C: ὅτι ἐστὶ ποτήριον 'Αμαλθείας κέρας καὶ 'Ενιαυτὸς καλούμενον).

[50] W. Züchner, *Griechische Klappspiegel* (Berlin, 1942), 43, KS 54; see F. Bechtel, *Die attischen Frauennamen* (Göttingen, 1902), 51 ff., 125 ff., for personal names derived from calendaric or festival names (e.g. Theoria, Penteteris, Panegyris, etc.).

[51] Harrison, *Themis*, 186 ff.; R. Hinks, *Myth and Allegory in Ancient Art* (London, 1939), 43 ff.; F. W. Hamdorf, *Griechische Kultpersonificationen der vorhellenistischen Zeit* (Mainz, 1964), 39-40, 100-1.

B. *Philikos and the Guild of Dionysus* (198B-C)

Immediately before the tableaux representing scenes from the 'life' of Dionysus, the Guild of the Artists of Dionysus and their priest march together along the processional route (198B-C; line 40). Their appearance provides important evidence both for the place of drama in Ptolemaic Egypt and for the date of the establishment of the Egyptian Guild. Drama occupied no less prominent a position in Hellenistic festivals than it had in classical ones. In the kingdoms of the Diadochi, dramatic performances played a major role in both traditional and newly established civic religious festivals with the result that this most popular and influential form of culture was preserved and spread throughout the Greek world for several hundred years.[52] The Ptolemaic kingdom shared this common interest in drama. The very existence of the Guild of Artists of Dionysus in Egypt, which is well attested quite apart from the reference to it in the Grand Procession, proves that dramatic performances were popular enough for the artists to form themselves into a formal group, perhaps because of the professional and financial privileges which developed from a centralized organization (see below). Drama continued to be written in Ptolemaic Egypt. An inscription from Ptolemais-Hermiou of the Guild of Dionysiac Artists names as members the tragic poets Phainippos and Diognetos, and the comic poets Stratagos and Mousaios (*OGIS* 51, 31-6).[53] Other dramatic creations may have come from the famous group of Hellenistic tragic poets known as the Pleiad (some of whom lived during the reign of Ptolemy II), who may have had a link with Alexandria although neither the kind of link nor its extent can be determined.[54] Yet dramatic performances did not only depend upon an active body of dramatic writers producing new plays on new themes; revivals of classical tragedies, comedies, and Satyr plays were common,[55] and in addition, many 'new' plays may have been simple adaptations of old subjects.[56]

Dramatic performances grew from the confines of an isolated civic occasion in classical Greece to new international levels with the establishment of the panhellenic festivals in the Hellenistic kingdoms. Authorities were eager to secure for their festivals the best international performers, who had to travel throughout the Mediterranean in order to appear at the various prestigious festivals. Recognized organizations of artists were doubtless to the convenience of both the local organizers, who could be assured of the appearance of the best possible artists, and of the artists, who could be guaranteed employment at a particular festival. The Guilds

---

[52] Cf. G. M. Sifakis, *Studies in the History of Hellenistic Drama* (London, 1967).

[53] For references to many other obscure poets and dramatists in Ptolemaic Egypt see P. M. Fraser, *JEA* xlv (1959), 80 n. 4.

[54] *Ptol. Alex.* i. 619 ff.   [55] Sifakis, *Drama*, 1-2.   [56] *Ptol. Alex.* i. 619.

which developed provided the regular, accepted connection among the artists and the cities and courts at which they appeared,[57] and were in a position to demand international protection for their members as sacred servants of Dionysus, guarantees of inviolability which were important to actors travelling across national boundaries in an age of frequent warfare and changing balances of power. These Guilds are known from all over the Greek world. The earliest Guilds in mainland Greece, the Isthmian-Nemean and the Athenian, both seem to have been founded *c.*279 BC, a date which can be pinpointed from three inscriptions providing the *termini post* and *ante quem* for their establishments.[58] An inscription of the cities of Euboea, dated within the years 294 to 288, shows no recognition of organized Guilds of Artists since the professional arrangements are made with individual artists only (*IG* XII (9) 207), but two slightly later decrees from Delphi attest their existence. The first, which gives certain honours to the *koinon τῶν τεχνιτᾶν τοῖς ἐν Ἰσθμὸν καὶ Νεμέαν συμπορευομένοις* (*SIG*³ 460 = *FD* III (1) p. 85 n. 1) is dated to an unspecified time before the Gallic invasion of 279 BC.[59] The second records the immunity granted by the Amphictyony to *οἱ ἐν Ἀθήναις τεχνῖται* (*IG* II² 1132 A; another copy in *SIG*³ 399 = *FD* III (2) 68), and this decree can be dated precisely to 278/7 BC.[60]

The Guilds of the Artists of Dionysus in Egypt were thought to have come into existence only a few decades later than *c.*280 BC, which still put them among the earliest to be established, but Kallixeinos' reference to the Guild, be it the local Alexandrian branch or the national body, combines with other considerations to argue for an earlier date of establishment. Two decrees of the Guild from Ptolemais-Hermiou are the most detailed pieces of evidence for the Egyptian body. Both record the honours granted by the Guild to various individuals (*OGIS* 50-1), although it is not clear if this is the national Guild or a local branch at Ptolemais-Hermiou. The date of these inscriptions has been debated, but their titulature makes it clear that both are earlier than 243/2, the date of the establishment of the cult of the Theoi Euergetai.[61] The terminology used for the Guild of Artists in both decrees is *οἱ περὶ τὸν Διόνυσον καὶ θεοὺς Ἀδελφούς*; since the names of sovereigns associated with the Guilds changed as the reigns of

---

[57] For an account of the Guilds see Sifakis, *Drama*, 136 ff.; Pickard-Cambridge, *Dram. Fests.*², 279 ff.; G. Nachtergael, *Les Galates en Grèce et les Sôtéria de Delphes* (Brussels, 1977), 301 ff. (with bibliography).

[58] P-C, *Dram. Fests.*², 281 ff.

[59] For a discussion of the date of this decree see Nachtergael, 297 n. 10.

[60] Ibid., 297. Nachtergael, 301, says that the foundation of the Guild of the Athenian *περὶ τὸν Διόνυσον τεχνῖται* can be dated to '*c.*290', but cf. pp. 195-6 and n. 298, p. 297 for the date of Hieron, the archon in question.

[61] *Ptol. Alex.* i. 219.

the sovereigns changed, and were not accumulated and retained in successive reigns (cf. dedications of οἱ περὶ τὸν Διόνυσον καὶ θεοὺς Εὐεργέτας in *OGIS* 164; 166),[62] the decrees from Ptolemais-Hermiou should belong either to the reign of Philadelphus (after the establishment of the cult of the Theoi Adelphoi in 272/1) or to the early years of the reign of Euergetes before 243/2. The Theoi Adelphoi would normally have been mentioned on their own only within this period. A date in the reign of Philadelphus has been advocated for the decrees on palaeographical grounds (*c.*275 to 250),[63] and since the Guild seen in the second decree is clearly not a new foundation, but one whose complex internal organization is shown by the list of members arranged by categories according to a hierarchy of membership, it must have existed for some years before the date of the decree. This is confirmed by the Guild's appearance in the Grand Procession.

The other references to the Egyptian Guild of Artists of Dionysus support this suggestion of its early establishment. A passage of the *Dikaiomata* states that the king released from the salt tax τ[οὺς νέμοντας] τὰ περὶ τὸν Διόνυσον in Egypt (*PHal.* 1, xii. 260 ff.). This document is dated by its editors to either the end of the reign of Philadelphus, or to the beginning of the reign of Euergetes, with a slight preference for the former date.[64] However, the only sure *terminus post quem* is *c.*276 BC, since in the text (line 179) Edfu (Apollonopolis) is called 'Arsinoe near Apollonopolis', and this renaming in honour of Arsinoe II would probably not have occurred before her marriage to Philadelphus, although a date after her deification and death some six years later may be even more likely. Unless the surviving papyrus document is a later copy of an original with the new name inserted in place of Apollonopolis, the *Dikaiomata* could date from any time after *c.*276. Regardless of the date of the written document (which, on palaeographical grounds, could date as late as *c.*245; cf. ed. p. 11), the privileges granted to the Guild show that it had been established for some time. Since the salt tax was an important one in Ptolemaic Egypt (it may have been the only per capita tax of its time),[65] the Guild members must have occupied an honoured position indeed to have been exempted from it, αὐτοί τε καὶ ἔκγονοι. Furthermore, it seems likely that the Guild may have been in existence long before the *Dikaiomata* was actually written to have been a well-established and honoured institution entitled to such a profitable tax exemption. Even if the *Dikaiomata* dates from the end of the reign of Philadelphus, the Guild could well have existed for some

---

[62] G. Klaffenbach, *Symbolae ad Historiam Collegiorum Artificum Bacchiorum* (Diss. Inaug. Berlin, 1914), 22.

[63] *Ptol. Alex.* ii. 870 n. 1.

[64] *Dikaiomata* (*PHal.* 1), ed. Graeca Halensis (Berlin, 1913), 11–12.

[65] F. Übel, 'Die frühptolemäische Salzsteuer', *Atti XI Congr. Pap.* (Milan, 1966), 325–68.

decades. Philadelphus' generosity to Dionysiac performers as early as the time of his marriage to Arsinoe II is attested by Theocritus, who states that the king rewarded the performers with special gifts (xvii. 112 ff.). Although this passage does not mention an organized Guild of Dionysiac artists, it does show the prevalence and prominence of the performers by the third decade of the third century in Alexandria.

The passage in Kallixeinos appears to be the earliest datable mention of the Guild in Egypt. The evidence from Ptolemais-Hermiou and the *Dikaiomata* shows that the Guild must have existed for some time before the end of Philadelphus' reign to have developed its complex internal organization and recognized prestige, but if the Grand Procession took place before *c.*276 BC (see Chapter 5), the appearance of the Guild in the first decade of Philadelphus' reign shows that it was even then a defined unit under an official leader. This in turn implies that the Guild must have existed for some years before the date of the Grand Procession. Its prominent inclusion in a festival staged as a royal *tour de force* indicates that the Guild was moving into the royal favour shown to dramatic performers, which is first attested by Theocritus and which culminated in the Guild's exemption from the salt tax. If the appearance of the Guild of the Artists of Dionysus in the Grand Procession can be dated as early as *c.*276, and by inference some years before, the date of the establishment of the Egyptian Guild seems to have been at least contemporary with that of the Athenian and Isthmian-Nemean Guilds in mainland Greece, and it may well have been earlier. If that is so, then the Egyptian Guild is the first recorded Guild of Dionysiac Artists, and the impetus for the organizations of the artists spread not from the mainland to Egypt but from Egypt to the mainland. If this hypothesis can be upheld, possible reasons for the creation of the Guild in Egypt may include the considerations that greater financial and professional benefits were to be gained in a kingdom with an economy and culture under direct royal control, and that this was matched on the other side by the wish of the new rulers to attact prominent artists to their courts.

The procession of the Guild in the Grand Procession was led by a certain Philikos, the poet-priest, who, on the analogy of other Dionysiac Guilds where priests were the chief officials (e.g. Nachtergael, Nos. 3-5, 7-10), was probably the president of the organization. Two priests of other Guilds, Philonides of Zakynthos and Pythokles of Hermione (*IG* XI (2) 113, 25; Nachtergael, 15 *bis*) are known to have been actors as well, which suggests that the leaders of the Guilds for any one year were elected from the ranks of the Guild members; the poet Philikos appears to be in the same category since several poets are mentioned among the members of the Guild at Ptolemais-Hermiou (cf. *OGIS* 51). Given the similarity in date and occupation, this Philikos may be the tragedian active in Alexandria who was a member of the Pleiad, Philikos of Corcyra, whose Suda *Life* says that he was a priest of Dionysus and lived during the reign of Ptolemy Philadelphus.[66] If the identification is correct, the Grand Procession and a branch of the Egyptian Guild of the Artists of Dionysus can be connected with a known tragedian who was a prominent member of the Alexandrian literary circle. His very presence reinforces the view that the occasion was an especially prestigious one, and it may strengthen the suggestion that this Guild was the national body, not a local branch.

The presence of Philikos and the Guild in the Grand Procession provides some information about the rest of the great festival. The obvious implication is that dramatic performances or competitions were included, and that the Artists of Dionysus participated in those events, which must then have been scheduled at a time other than that allotted for the procession. (The question of the Guild's participation aside, it is hardly likely that any part of the festival would have been allowed to conflict with the procession itself, which was surely conceived as the main focus of public attention. This supports the view that the festival must have lasted more than one day.) The performance of the dithyramb is the only kind of dramatic performance in the festival which can be inferred from the appearance of the Guild here (see below), but one might suppose that the usual tragedies, comedies, and Satyr plays were also included. Some of the preceding participants in the introductory section of the Dionysiac procession may have been members of the Guild in their role as actors. The initial entry of the Guild may have been signalled by the appearance of the ceremonial heralds (198A). Each event in dramatic contests was regularly announced by such a trumpeter and herald, and these functionaries were members of the Guilds of Dionysus as well.[67] The trumpeter Thrasymachus appears as a signatory of one of the two Ptolemais–Hermiou inscriptions (*OGIS* 51, 65), which must indicate that he was a bona fide member of that local Guild. The victor-list of the Sarapieia festival at Tanagra, in which a trumpeter and a herald appear among the victors and are presented with crowns of medium value (*AE* 1956, 34 ff. lines 3–4, 23–4) may suggest their elevated status in the hierarchy of dramatic participants. The trumpeter and herald in the Grand Procession may well have been members of the Guild who would later perform their usual function of announcing the dramatic events at the festival, but who here proclaim the first appearance of the Guild in the proceedings (which culminates in the formal procession of Philikos and the other members). The

[66] *Ptol. Alex.* ii. 859 n. 407, which also discusses the correct form of his name; *RE* s.v. Philiskos (4), 2379–81.

[67] P-C, *Dram. Fests.*[2], 304.

figures of Penteteris, Eniautos, and the Horai who immediately follow the heralds may also be connected with the Guild. If Eniautos was a Guild member, his tragic costume would be appropriate to an actor who may have participated in the later dramatic performances. (Similarly, Penteteris and the Horai may have been male members of the Guild dressed in female costume.) The suggestion that Eniautos represents the revolving 'year' which composes the penteteric cycle of this particular celebration is supported by the fact that the concept of the revolving year, ἐνιαυτός, is attested by an inscription of the Isthmian-Nemean Guild (*SIG*³ 457, 21 ff.: καὶ ὅπως ἂν ὁ ἐνιαυτὸς μετατεθῆι, ἐν ᾧ ὁ ἀγὼν γίνεται . . .). Penteteris may have a similar interpretation. Her palm branch and crown may be symbolic of victory in the later dramatic competitions, and her personification of a four-yearly festival may also connect her to an idea which seems to have been important to the Guilds, since individual festivals are often referred to in Guild inscriptions by names derived from their chronological periodicity, e.g. the Trieteris (*OGIS* 51, 27-8; *FD* III (1) 351, 18). The censers and the altar which follow the Horai and precede Philikos may represent the private offerings of the Guild to their patron deity (198B; line 36), and it is possible that the large oinochoe and karchesion borne next by the Satyrs (198B; line 39) were other votive offerings from the Guild to Dionysus as the god of wine. These Satyrs may not have been connected to the Guild also; their importance here lies in the ritual vessels which they carry.

The identification of the particular dramatic competitions in which the Guild is to perform depends upon a textual question concerning the Delphic tripods which are carried immediately behind the members (198C; line 42): τούτων δ' ἐφεξῆς ἐφέροντο Δελφικοὶ τρίποδες, ἆθλα τοῖς τῶν ἀθλητῶν (in the manuscript reading) χορηγοῖς, ὁ μὲν παιδικὸς ἐννέα πηχῶν τὸ ὕψος, ὁ δὲ πηχῶν δώδεκα ὁ τῶν ἀνδρῶν. These Delphic tripods ˙ are stated to be prizes, the smaller for the choregos of the boys' class and the larger for the choregos of the men's class, but the phrase ἆθλα τοῖς τῶν ἀθλητῶν χορηγοῖς is foreign to a context which concerns dramatic, not athletic, events. This is clear from the proximity of the Guild of the Artists of Dionysus and the fact that choregoi were leaders of dramatic choruses. L. Robert's correction of ἀθλητῶν to αὐλητῶν is palaeographically minimal, and necessary to the sense.[68] Fluteplayers, who occur in the list of members of the Guild of Ptolemais-Hermiou, played important roles in ancient drama, and their prominence here represents a significant contemporary change in music and drama.

Robert's emendation shows that this passage refers to the performance

---

[68] *Études Épigraphiques et Philologiques* (Paris, 1938), 31 ff.

of the dithyramb by the artists of Dionysus, since all the elements of a dithyrambic performance are present here according to the analogy of the traditional Athenian dithyramb as it was performed at the City Dionysia:[69] choregoi for a boys' and a men's chorus, a flautist to accompany them, and tripods which were presented to the victorious choregos. A dithyrambic performance by the Guild in the festival associated with the Grand Procession is appropriate since from its creation the dithyramb was primarily, although not exclusively, Dionysiac.[70] Moreover, the dithyramb would not have been out of place in an Alexandrian festival, since its performance is widely attested epigraphically at many Hellenistic festivals.[71] However, there was a change from the style of the Attic performance in the Hellenistic age which is reflected in this passage from Kallixeinos. In the fifth century BC, the most important elements of the dithyrambic performance were the poet, the choregos, and the choruses, while the flute was regarded solely as accompaniment. Gradually, 'virtuoso' musical performances gained in popularity until the flute came to be considered the principal element in the performance: in effect, the chorus accompanied the flute, not vice versa.[72] This change is illustrated by the regular inscriptions on choregic monuments which record the name of the choregos, the poet, and the flautist. In the first half of the fourth century, the name of the flautist follows that of the then more prominent poet (*IG* II^2 3065), but in the second half of the century, the flautist's name precedes that of the poet (*IG* II^2 3042), an indication of the increasing importance of the music. The specific reference to flautists in this passage of the text of the Grand Procession also shows the change to a greater emphasis on music in dithyrambic performances of the Hellenistic age, even to the extent that here the choregoi are called 'choregoi of the flautists', although their more usual role was the training of the choruses. Despite the emphasis on the flutes, the dithyramb was to be performed in the festival associated with the Grand Procession in the traditional manner, with choruses of boys and men whose choregoi were rewarded with victory tripods. The members of the Guild of the Artists of Dionysus were probably concerned with this performance, either as choregoi, performers, or flautists. Although the passage bears witness to a contemporary change in musical style, it shows that the festival of which the procession was a part continued traditional competitions as a means of worshipping the Olympian gods.

---

[69] P-C, *Dram. Fests.*^{2}, 74 ff.; id., *Dithyramb, Tragedy, and Comedy* (2nd ed., Oxford, 1962), 35 ff.

[70] P-C, *DTC*^{2}, 6.

[71] P-C, *DTC*^{1}, 75–9.

[72] P-C, *DTC*^{2}, 55–6; id., *Dram Fests.*^{2}, 78–9; L. Robert, *Ét. Ép. et Phil.*, 34–5.

C. *Tableaux from the 'Life' of Dionysus*

1. *Divine statue and retinue* (198C-E)   The main part of the Dionysiac procession consists of large carts carrying various statues and tableaux relating to the mythology of the god. All of these are pulled by men, most probably slaves, whose number is determined by the size and weight of the individual carts. Manpower may have been considered more aesthetic than groups of draught animals controlled by shouting drivers with whips, or perhaps it was thought that draught animals would detract from the effect of the other animals who were bona fide participants in the procession. Hundreds of animals, for example, appear in the triumphal train of Dionysus.

The first cart holds the statue of Dionysus, whose divine epiphany has been prepared in the introductory section by the symbolic followers, purificatory rituals, and preliminary offerings (198C-D; lines 45 ff.). The elaborately garbed statue appears to pour a libation from a golden karchesion, but since Kallixeinos does not say that the statue actually pours a libation (like the following statue), it was probably just positioned to suggest the action, a pose which is common for statues of gods.[73] This statue may have been an actual cult statue of the god taken from one of his urban temples for the procession, if it was not a special statue constructed for this occasion. The material of this statue and of the other over-life-size statues being drawn along cannot have been marble, whose weight would have been too great for the carts, but must have been a lighter substance analogous to that of the statues in the symposiac scenes on the epistyle of the ornamental pavilion (196F-197A). These were over-life-size in order to be seen from the ground, yet light enough not to affect the balance of a tent with wooden supports. All these statues are comparable to the movable statues placed in the bower of Aphrodite and Adonis (Theoc. xv). Since the statue of Adonis was to be carried to the shore the next day by the female worshippers (lines 132 ff.), it must have been constructed of a light material such as wax, plaster, or hollowed wood or terracotta, with a surface coloured realistically.[74] Alexandrian artists were evidently highly skilled in this kind of work, to judge from the complexity and popularity of these statues. The over-life-size male Greek wooden statue in Alexandria (which has traces of paint and plaster) may indicate the types of statues created for the procession.[75]

This first appearance of Dionysus gives added emphasis to the statue's

---

[73] Cf. Erika Simon, *Opfernde Götter* (Berlin, 1953); see pp. 48 ff. for representations of Dionysus in this pose.

[74] A. S. F. Gow, *JHS* lviii (1938), 198.

[75] Graeco-Roman Museum, Alexandria. In March, 1979, the statue was in the centre of Room XVIII (inv. No. 23351-2).

iconography, which introduces the aspects of the god which will recur throughout the rest of his procession. He is represented as the patron of wine by the krater at his feet and by the karchesion from which the libation appears to be poured. The latter vessel has already appeared as an offering to the god in the introductory section of his procession, and a fragment from Old Comedy shows that it was characteristic of the god and his circle, (Kratinos, *CAF* (Kock) i. fr. 38). Before the statue lie cassia and saffron, and a *thymiaterion* on which to burn them, in order to purify the atmosphere surrounding the divine presence. The canopy which shades the statue also emphasizes aspects of his divinity. Its decorative ivy, vine, thyrsoi, crowns, fillets, drums, etc., connote the god's orgiastic associations as the patron of wine and its ensuing revels, and the dramatic masks which also hang from the canopy reflect the importance of his role as the patron of drama. Ornamental canopies appear elsewhere as coverings for divine statues (one covers the tableau of Aphrodite and Adonis, for example; cf. Theoc. xv. 119 ff.), but in its Dionysiac context it can be interpreted as a bower, a typical feature of representations of Dionysus because of its luxuriance and the opportunity it affords for displaying some of the vegetation sacred to the god. The bower–grotto was a frequent setting for Dionysiac symposia, and the ornamental pavilion whose description precedes that of the procession is in fact an elaboration of a Dionysiac bower. Similar coverings appear elsewhere in the Dionysiac procession. The statue of Nysa which follows Dionysus also has a canopy (198F), and the Cave of the Nymphs where the infant Dionysus is reared is shaded with ivy and yew (200C). Such bowers and caves later became important features of the rituals in the Mysteries of Dionysus as the site of meetings, feasts, etc.[76]

Dionysus' statue is followed by a long parade of his religious officials and symbolic followers (198E). Since several priests and priestesses are mentioned in this train, this procession is probably not a celebration staged by one particular Dionysiac cult with its few officials. The numbers of priests and priestesses may be the combined religious officials of all the cults of Dionysus in Alexandria who march in concert on the occasion of his procession, but some at least may be the priests and priestesses of the Dionysiac thiasoi, the organizations of local celebrants of Dionysiac orgiastic rites.

The reading περσειστελεταί (line 57) is meaningless as it stands, but, given the context, must hide a reference to a functionary in a cult of Dionysus, although no emendation has provided the necessary clarification.

---

[76] For some examples of the uses of grottoes and bowers in Dionysiac legend see M. P. Nilsson, *The Dionysiac Mysteries of the Hellenistic and Roman Age* (Lund, 1957), 61 ff.

Many aspects of this procession are either elements of, or contain elements of, features which were common in the Dionysiac Mysteries which became increasingly popular in later Hellenistic and Roman times. (These are discussed in the commentary as they appear in the text.) There is no evidence that formal Dionysiac Mysteries existed as early as the third decade of the third century BC, but the combination of the 'mystic' features in the procession may suggest that certain mystic cults did exist at that period, either on their own, or as part of an older series of Mysteries out of which the later, formal Mysteries of Dionysus developed (see Chapter 5 for further discussion). The procession itself is not a mystic ritual, but if Dionysiac mystic cults were celebrated in Alexandria, then a procession like this, which was not part of an annual religious festival in honour of a single divine cult, may well have comprised various mystic elements in addition to features from the more traditional cults of Dionysus. Like the bower of Dionysus, which was a feature of the traditional Dionysiac cults just as it was part of the mystic cults, the thiasoi which appear in the god's train had traditional orgiastic, as well as 'mystic', connotations. These comments serve as an introduction to a consideration of the proposed solutions of περσειστελεταί, which sounds as though it may incorporate a reference to τελεταί, the initiation rites at various sets of Mysteries.[77] Such a reference would be important evidence for the development of Dionysiac mystic cults, if not actual Mysteries, in third-century Alexandria, and the relation of either to this festival. For example, Schweighäuser's emendation πέρυσι τελεσταί ('Last Year's Initiates') is perhaps the most attractive palaeographically, but it would reflect a well-established system of Dionysiac Mysteries which accepted initiates on a yearly basis, like the Eleusinian Mysteries. Such a level of sophistication, organization, and differentiation seems unlikely at this date even if individual 'mystic' cults may have existed in honour of Dionysus. Attempts to elucidate the attested reading consequently make assumptions for which there is no real warrant (cf. also Preller), but the garbled manuscript reference to some kind of initiation may combine with other hints in the text to indicate the procession's adoption of certain mystic features.

Various maenads complete the train of followers in this section (198E; line 58), and their presence clearly indicates the importance of contemporary orgiastic cults of Dionysus. The women are all called Maketai, a name for Macedonian women,[78] but it is impossible to know if they are

---

[77] Rohde's conjecture ἱεροστολισταί (printed by Gulick, Loeb) is clever, since there were officials in native Egyptian religion concerned with the ritual robing of divine statues, but it is unlikely that these officials would have taken part in a Greek procession.

[78] *RE* s.v. Maketai, 773–4.

true Macedonians or if this is a name used for female worshippers of
Dionysus because the inhabitants of northern Greece had well-known
associations with the god. Beyond this general classification, they are
described by various names: 'Mimallones' (said by Plutarch (*Alex.* ii.
5) to be among the women in Macedonia engaged in orgiastic cults of
Dionysus),[79] 'Bassarai' (a well-known name for a Bacchant, used inter-
changeably with 'Maenad'),[80] and 'Lydai'. This last name must derive
from the Maenads in legend which Dionysus brought with him from the
East (N.B. the chorus in the *Bacchae* of Euripides are Lydian Women).[81]
The transference of the term explains why 'Macedonian' women can also
be called 'Lydian' women. (The word Λῆναι, a proposed change by Wilamowitz (ad loc.), appears first in the title of Theocritus xxvi, but the word
is rare,[82] and emendation here unnecessary.)

2. *Statue of Nysa* (198F)   Immediately behind the followers of
Dionysus appears another statue on a cart, a representation of 'Nysa'
(whoever she may be; see below, p. 65), lavishly dressed and bedecked
with typical Dionysiac attributes (198F; line 63). This statue is noteworthy not only in iconography but in structure; it had a self-activating
mechanical device which enabled it to stand up and sit down, and belonged
to the class of so-called automata. Nysa apparently actually poured a
libation from her phiale (or else Kallixeinos could hardly have known that
the substance was milk), and thus also differs from those statues which are
portrayed as if pouring a libation (the preceding Dionysus statue is probably
in this category). A real libation may have been an added feature to
increase the verisimilitude which was already emphasized by her automatic
movement. Since a fixed stance is common in statues of gods making
offerings, Nysa's sitting-to-standing movement was probably not ritually
significant since it was not required in order to indicate a libation; as an
attraction added for its effect on the spectators, however, the display of
mechanical facility is comprehensible in a procession so full of ostentation
in other respects. The automatic mechanism of this statue must be considered against the background of the advances in applied sciences and
mechanics made in the Hellenistic age, especially in Alexandria. In common with the rest of the Greek world, the Alexandrian Greeks seem to
have felt that although theoretical sciences and mathematics were admir-
able and worthy of study, applied mechanics were not.[83] This latter field
thus lagged behind the others because the advances made by the pure

[79] *RE* s.v. Mimallones, 1713. The relevant texts are quoted in L. R. Farnell, *The Cults of the Greek States* (Oxford, 1909), v. 293.

[80] *RE* s.v. Bassarai, 104; A. Vogliano, *AJA* xxxvii (1933), 249.

[81] *RE* s.v. Lydai, 2119–20.

[82] Gow, *Comm. Theoc.* ad loc., p. 475.

[83] *Ptol. Alex.* i. 425 ff.

sciences were rarely given any practical application. It seems that most of
the practical application, little though it was, happened in Alexandria, to
judge from the evidence of several ingenious mechanical objects of Roman
Alexandria described by Heron, which are probably traceable to Ptolemaic
originals.[84] Vitruvius (x. 7, 5) classes all of these as toys, and although
Nysa may belong to the same category, she could not have been produced
without the kind of mechanical knowledge which could have been applied
to more practical machines.

It has been suggested that Nysa was the work of the famous third-
century inventor Ktesibios, who lived and worked in Alexandria during
and after the reign of Philadelphus.[85] The coincidences of date and location make this suggestion attractive, and the statue is also the sort of ingenious toy for which Vitruvius says Ktesibios was famous (his remark
that these inventions were toys refers specifically to Ktesibios). Other
considerations support this identification. At a slightly later date than that
proposed for the Grand Procession, Ktesibios and his inventions are known
to have been popular with the royal family. He was the inventor of the
famous rhyton in the form of the Egyptian god Bes which automatically
produced a musical tone when the wine flowed out. This rhyton was dedicated, probably by the inventor, in the temple of Arsinoe-Zephyritis,
perhaps placed upon a plinth or pedestal upon which was inscribed the
associated epigram by Hedylos commemorating the dedication (Gow-Page,
HE 1843 ff.).[86] The fact that the rhyton was dedicated in the temple of
Arsinoe-Zephyritis, which was itself consecrated by the admiral Kalli-
krates during the lifetime of Arsinoe II when the queen became associated
with the marine Aphrodite,[87] indicates some connection between the
inventor and the royal family, even if it was only a gesture of thanks for
past patronage or a compliment in hope of future patronage. Furthermore,
if the commemorative epigram links Hedylos closely to Poseidippos and
the court circle, this link perhaps encompasses Ktesibios also, who, along
with his invention, is the real subject of the poem.[88] If the epigram of
Hedylos commemorates an offering made at the time of, or shortly after,
the dedication of the temple before Arsinoe's death in 270, then it seems
that Ktesibios was associated with the royal family during the second half
of the 270s, only a few years after the Grand Procession.

The other consideration which may connect Ktesibios with Nysa is the
specific type of mechanical device which was used to operate her. Since
the statue appears on a moving cart, many devices which could otherwise

---

[84] Ibid., 426.
[85] Ibid.; for a discussion of the man and his date (some have argued that there
were two homonymous inventors) see vol. ii. 622 n. 445; *RE* s.v. Ktesibios, 2074–6.
[86] *Ptol. Alex.* i. 413, 571.   [87] Ibid., 239.   [88] Ibid., 413, 571.

explain her mechanism satisfactorily, such as those based on hydraulics and pneumatics, must be ruled out. Since all automata require an initial source of energy, the obvious source for Nysa is to be found in the revolving wheels of the cart. A simple 'camshaft' arrangement could have harnessed, and changed the direction of, this energy to transfer the forward, circular motion of the cartwheels into the up-and-down linear movement which caused the statue to stand and sit.[89] Nysa's generous drapery suggests that all of the mechanisms which moved her could have been concealed from view underneath. If the motion of the wheels was harnessed underneath the cart by a type of camshaft, the lever which would be moved up and down by the shaft had to be connected to the statue somewhere, and the seat of the throne would be the logical place. If the statue was placed upon a throne with a solid base and high back and sides, the bottom of the statue could have been attached invisibly to a shaft which pushed it up from the throne and pulled it back down as the shaft itself moved up and down from the movement of the wheels. As an extra cover, Nysa's chiton and shawl would be alternately folded around her back and sides as she sat down, and hanging loose around her as she stood up. Nysa must have been constructed with hinged joints for this motion to be possible, but articulated limbs had been a familiar feature of terracotta and ivory figurines in Greece for some time.[90] If her hands were attached to the sides of the throne and her arms hinged at the elbow so that they could straighten, this would keep her from bending forward at the hip as she stood up, and could also explain how the libation of milk was poured. If a container of the liquid (perhaps an askos with a controlled opening) was concealed in her sleeve, the arm would straighten as the statue stood up, and the container would point downwards and release a small quantity of milk into the phiale. As the figure sat down, the concealed container would be horizontal and the flow would cease. Since the cart would not have been moving quickly in any case, both because of the slow pace of the forward movement of the procession and because it was pulled by hand, the wheels would have been turning fairly slowly (very slowly if they were large), and the statue would not have bobbed up and down at a dizzy pace.

Ktesibios is known to have experimented with changing the direction of forces created by an energy-source and harnessing them in order to move objects. Vitruvius' description of Ktesibios' famous water clock (ix. 8,

---

[89] See H. Hodges, *Technology in the Ancient World* (London, 1970), 183, for the suggestion that the cam was one of the simple devices behind many of the inventions of this period.

[90] A. Chapuis and É. Gélis, *Le Monde des automates* (Paris, 1928), i. Ch. I; A. Chapuis and E. Droz, *Automata: A Historical and Technological Study* (Neuchâtel and London, 1958), Ch. I.

4 ff.) shows that he employed a rack-and-pinion mechanism which moved several figures attached to the clock. (A rack and pinion is one version of the system of cog-wheels, consisting of a toothed wheel (the pinion) paired to a shaft (the rack) with teeth along one edge. As the wheel revolves, its teeth engage with those of the shaft, and the circular motion is thereby converted into rectilinear motion.[91]) It has been suggested that Ktesibios himself invented the rack and pinion and used it for the first time in the clock on the grounds that Vitruvius, in quoting the writings of Ktesibios, describes the instrument completely.[92] This invention (even if premature in that it was not used in other clocks) has been dated to about 280 BC, and it may have been the first stage of the use of the principle of cog-wheels, out of which the other types developed.[93] If Ktesibios was at this time experimenting with changing the directions of energy, he may at least have supervised the design of Nysa, which, on this hypothesis, incorporated the transference of circular to linear motion. In view of his links with the royal family, and, in any case, because he was certainly the most famous inventor of his day in Alexandria, it is easy to believe that his help was sought for a festival in which no expense was spared. Even if he was not himself involved, Nysa may have been designed by other Alexandrian inventors who were influenced by his experiments.

Nysa is one of many historically attested automata. Others include a self-revolving hearth (*ID* 104–10, 10 (= *IG* II^2 1639): ἐσχάρα . . . αὐτό-στροφος), flying birds, walking statues, and a stag with moving feet,[94] but perhaps the most interesting parallel to Nysa in terms of context is the snail of Demetrius of Phalerum (Plb. xii. 13, 11), which appeared at the Dionysia in the procession which he staged during his archonship in Athens in 309/8. The snail moved along the processional route under its own energy, leaving a trail of mucus, and may have been operated by a tread-mill hidden inside its shell. While, however, Demochares (who appears as an opponent of Demetrius of Phalerum) sees the snail in the procession as an abomination indicative of the decline of Athens under Demetrius, Nysa may be considered in perfect accord with the rest of the lavish, unusual features of the Grand Procession.

The difficulty of interpreting the mechanism of the statue is matched by that of the actual subject of Nysa, who can be only one of the several possible 'Nysas' connected to the corpus of Dionysiac myth. Some sign or

---

[91] For a discussion of the ancient use of cog-wheels see F. M. Feldhaus, *Die Technik der Vorzeit, der geschichtlichen Zeit und der Naturvölker* (Leipzig and Berlin, 1914), s.v. Zahnrad; A. G. Drachmann, *The Mechanical Technology of Greek and Roman Antiquity* (Copenhagen and Madison, 1963), 200 ff.

[92] Drachmann, 192.   [93] Ibid., 202–3.

[94] For these automata see R. G. Austin, *JRS* xlix (1959), 17–18; for the snail of Demetrius (mentioned below) see A. Rehm, *Philologus* xcii (1937), 317 ff.

banner must have told the spectators that this statue was Nysa, but if it was obvious to them which Nysa it was meant to be, it is not obvious to the reader of Kallixeinos' text, who is not told of any distinctive iconographic feature which determines the identification. Nysa most probably represents either the legendary female Nysa, the mortal nurse to whom the baby Dionysus was entrusted, or the location Nysa, where Dionysus was raised, usually in the Cave of the Nymphs, or a combination of both ideas. (Other mythological Nysas derive from ancient conflations of these ideas: sometimes the Nymphs at Nysa are also named Nysa themselves, or, when Dionysus was reared elsewhere by the Nymphs, they too may also be named Nysa'.[95]) Although there has been disagreement about the identification of Nysa, her interpretation as the personification of the geographical Nysa fits best into the context of the rest of the Grand Procession and into the contemporary view of Dionysus which began with Alexander the Great's march to India. The appearance elsewhere in the Grand Procession of women personifying the various cities of Greece, the Islands, and Ionia (201 D-E; line 205) shows that the idea of Nysa as a personified location would not have been out of place, and, moreover, the recognizable order and theme of the whole Dionysiac procession tends to suggest that the nurse Nysa, the mortal daughter of Aristaeus, would not appear at all, much less in this section of the procession. The scenes of the birth and youth of the god only begin with the appearance of the Thalamos of Semele (200B; line 134), and a statue of the nurse would be out of place away from the context of the scenes of his birth and upbringing. Also, the position of this statue immediately behind the statue of Dionysus and the parade of his followers, the focus of the Dionysiac procession, gives it a prominence which is arguably inappropriate if applied to the nurse, who was not, after all, a major character of Dionysiac myth. Finally, a statue of the mortal Nysa would conflict with the later tableau of the Cave of the Nymphs, with Dionysus and Hermes present (200B-C; line 136). This scene represents the version of the Dionysus legend whereby the infant god was entrusted to Hermes by Zeus to be taken to the Cave of the Nymphs and brought up in safety. Several Nymphs are included in this tableau, but, although the description of the scene seems complete, there is no mortal Nysa, nor any one Nymph called Nysa who is singled out as the chief nurse. A statue of the mortal Nysa elsewhere in the Grand Procession would provide contrary, and confusing, information about the youth of Dionysus. Although these conflicting legends existed in mythology, they are unacceptable in a context as compact and self-contained as that of the sectional procession of Dionysus. These difficulties are removed if Nysa

[95] See *RE* s.v. Nysa (1), 1628 ff., for an analysis of the different 'Nysas' known in mythology.

personifies the place where the god was reared. Although the appearance of the personification of Nysa, as the location of the god's childhood, might more logically appear later amid the scenes of the life of Dionysus, it is comprehensible at the beginning of his procession as a celebration of the place whence Dionysus had come to attain his present position among the gods. Thus, the god's childhood home, and the glorification due to it from his presence there, are presented right after the appearance of the god's statue: the god, the origins of the god, and the main aspect of the god (the long celebration of wine which directly follows Nysa) form the first three elements of the procession.

The prominence given to the statue of Nysa by its position in the procession reflects the contemporary significance which the origins of Dionysus had. One of the largest sections of the Dionysiac procession is the 'Triumphal Return of Dionysus from India', and it is maintained that this aspect of Dionysus was only emphasized after the time of Alexander the Great (see below, p. 83). Whether or not Alexander had seen himself as a new Dionysus repeating the journey which the god had made previously, it is clear that during the expedition to India much attention was given to identifying signs that the god had passed that way before the Macedonians (the fact that the various identifications of landmarks were dubious is less important than the fact the Macedonian army believed in them). The association of Alexander and Dionysus was emphasized later by the Diadochi and especially by the Ptolemies. This is clear in the triumphal section of the Dionysiac procession, where, it has been maintained, Alexander rather than the god is the true hero.[96] A personification of the locality where Dionysus was reared is therefore appropriate because the place played a large part in the Indian campaign of Alexander, which is itself a central theme of the procession. The Macedonian expedition discovered the supposed birthplace of Dionysus in the Swat Hills when a mountain which was covered in vines and called Μηρός was interpreted to be the thigh of Zeus from which Dionysus was born, and it was named Nysa. Although Arrian (*An.* v. 1, 6) says that the mountain was named after the nurse of Dionysus, the important point is that it was the *locality* where Dionysus was born which they had found so far from home. The nurse was a thing of the past, but the place survived and represented a continuing link with the past and with Dionysus. It is the locality of Dionysus' birth and nurture which is important as far as both Alexander and the procession are concerned.

The iconography of the statue does not argue against its identification as the location; Nysa pours a libation of milk and is crowned by ivy leaves

---

[96] *Ptol. Alex.* i. 202.

and grape clusters. Grapes, like the thyrsos which she holds in her left hand, are of course a common Dionysiac attribute, but here they could refer specifically to the fact that Dionysus is said to have invented wine as a child at Nysa (D.S. iii. 70, 8). Milk is the essential characteristic of nurses, to be sure, but here it could signify the fruitfulness of the region, the general fertility and productivity as in the biblical 'Land flowing with Milk and Honey'. Even if the milk should be thought to refer more narrowly to the suckling of Dionysus, it could be an attribute of the place where the nurture occurred as well as of the nurse.

3. *Celebration of wine* (199A-200B)   The next section of the Dionysiac procession is a long celebration of wine (199A-200B; lines 73-131), consisting of a cart holding a *lenos* (wine-press), another holding an askos, and a long parade of gold and silver vessels of all types used in the various stages of wine preparation, storage, and consumption. Although the display of plate appears in a practical guise to accommodate the vast quantity of wine which precedes it, the costly vessels are surely dedications to Dionysus, whether previous votive offerings in his various temples around Alexandria now brought out on display in the Grand Procession, or new offerings from the worshippers on the occasion of this festival. The disproportionate length and prominent position of this section devoted exclusively to wine, apart from providing the pretext for the presentation of an ostentatious display of treasure which suits the extravagance of the occasion, underline the importance placed upon this aspect of Dionysus, namely, Dionysus first and foremost as the god of wine. The iconography of the statue of the god which had already passed in procession introduced this side of his worship (along with his dramatic role), but that initial view of Dionysus is elaborated and emphasized in the rest of his procession to the extent that his patronage of wine almost supplants all his other attributes.[97] The connection between Dionysus and wine is familiar from pre-classical times: the Athenian Anthesteria festival in honour of Dionysus was the time for sampling the year's new wine, and countless vases show Dionysus crowned with vine leaves in the company of drunken satyrs and maenads. This was a large part of the traditional Greek Dionysus, but hardly his exclusive role; he had other important cult associations, notably chthonic ones. If the Dionysus of the Grand Procession appears primarily as the patron of wine, this aspect must have been prominent in Alexandria; even though it does not reflect the only focus of his civic worship, it must have been deliberately chosen for emphasis. It is unfortunately impossible to determine from independent sources how faithful a view this was of civic worship of Dionysus in Alexandria since the Dionysiac procession

[97] Ibid.

provides the only detailed picture of his cult at that period. Given the royal sponsorship of the Grand Procession and its festival, this portrayal of Dionysus must reflect royal favour, and may consequently have influenced popular feeling to some extent.[98] The attraction of this aspect of Dionysus to the Ptolemies may result at least partly from the importance which viticulture, and wine-production, had in the economy, which is seen in the royal support and encouragement given to this industry. Large quantities of wine were imported from Greece into the Ptolemaic kingdom, and substantial areas of Egypt were put under cultivation for the growth of vines from whose grapes native wine was produced. Papyri attest direct government interest in the industry and the tightly controlled scale of taxes to which it was subject.[99] The emphasis on wine in the procession may be partly a reflection of the increasing importance and success of new viticulture in Ptolemaic Egypt, quite apart from the joyful atmosphere which a plenitude of wine would lend to any festival.

The vintage begins with trampling the grapes, and a cart holding a wine-press is the appropriate introduction to the celebration of wine (199A; line 73) besides providing a pleasing spectacle for the onlookers: figures moving to musical accompaniment, with the results of their labours flowing down on to the processional route as a physical reminder of wine throughout the rest of the Grand Procession. Satyrs trampling grapes in a *lenos* is a scene familiar from Attic vases,[100] which may be used as evidence for the general appearance of the wine-press in the procession: a large, rectangular 'box' on four legs with a spout on one side. This *lenos* would be mounted on the cart, with the spout at the bottom of the basin extending over the street. The cart measures 20 cubits in length by 16 in width (about 30 by 24 feet), although the size of the *lenos* is 24 by 15 cubits (about 36 by 22½ feet). This discrepancy in length led Kaibel (ad loc.) to suspect the text, but it is not known how the *lenos* was positioned on the cart. If the four legs of the *lenos* were fixed near the four corners of the cart, the body of the basin may well have been larger than the perimeter of its base, and could have overhung the cart at the front and back, which would ensure that the grape-juice flowed into the street at the back instead of on to the cart. The difference in length between cart and *lenos* would only be some three feet in front and back, which does not seem impossible or dangerously out of balance. The grape-trampling scene raises certain

[98] Ibid.

[99] For Ptolemaic viticulture see ibid., 166 ff.; M. I. Rostovtzeff, *A Large Estate in Egypt in the Third Century BC* (Madison, 1922), 93 ff.; id., *SEHHW*, 353-5; M. Schnebel, *Die Landwirtschaft im hellenistischen Ägypten, Münchener Beitr. z. Papyrusforschung u. antiken Rechtsgeschichte* vii (1925), 239 ff.; Cl. Préaux, *Les Grecs en Egypte d'après les archives de Zénon* (Brussels, 1947), 22-6.

[100] B. A. Sparkes, *BABesch* li (1976), 47 ff.

questions about the time of year when the Grand Procession occurred. If it is correct to connect the Grand Procession and its festival with the ornamental pavilion, the statement that the entertainment in the pavilion took place in the middle of winter (196D-E) must also be applied to the festival (see above, p. 35). Attempts to connect a mid-winter festival in Alexandria with known vintage times (when so many ripe grapes would have been available) are luckily unnecessary; although climatic conditions could have caused the time of the main grape vintage to vary from its normal mid- to late-summer schedule,[101] it seems unlikely that a seasonal variation would have caused a grape harvest in the middle of winter, and there are only a few tenuous references in later papyri to a small, secondary grape harvest in some years in winter.[102] Ripe fruit may have been imported from somewhere with a harvest cycle independent of the Nile flood, although such a procedure would require greater care in transport and refrigeration than seems likely at this date. It is perhaps more likely that the grape-trampling scene was staged. Some grapes, if picked underripe and kept out of light and heat, could have been reserved for this occasion from the harvest of the previous summer since the festival must have been planned months in advance. Even if the grapes had rotted by mid-winter, it would hardly have mattered for the purpose of the *lenos* scene, since the juice was only to be expelled on to the street, not used for making wine. On the other hand, the Satyrs may not actually have been trampling grapes at all, but only simulating the activity for the tableau. In this case, there may have been a large container of grape-juice (or a substance which resembled it) with a controlled opening hidden in the body of the *lenos*, the contents of which duly flowed out of the spout and into the street.

An immense askos made of leopard skins follows the *lenos*, also wheeled on a cart and trickling its contents over the parade route (199A-B; lines 79 ff.). Kallixeinos is careful to mention that the wine flowed out κατὰ μικρόν; the stream, like that from the container full of grape-juice (if used on the previous cart), was no doubt deliberately restricted in order to last for the whole processional journey and to prevent an unattractive, empty askos at the end. Skin askoi were the traditional means of transporting wine locally, since clay amphorae were restricted to imports and exports.[103] The normal askos was, and is, where still encountered, a goatskin stitched up to form a bag, and larger containers could be made from several skins stitched together with their seams covered in pitch to prevent leakage. This

---

[101] Schnebel, 275-7.

[102] Cf. *PFlor.* 236; *SB* 5810; cf. R. Clothilde, 'La Coltura della vite e la fabbricazione del vino nell'Egitto Graeco-Romano', *Studi della scuola papirologica, R. Academia scientifico-letteraria* iv (1) (Milan, 1924), 48 ff.

[103] V. R. Grace, *Amphoras and the Ancient Wine Trade* (Excavations of the Athenian Agora, Picture Book No. 6) (Princeton, 1961), unnumbered, p. 9.

leopard-skin askos is of the size, material, and ostentation suited to the Grand Procession. The size of its cart, 25 by 14 cubits (about $37\frac{1}{2}$ by 21 feet), is comparable to that carrying the *lenos*, but it is drawn by twice as many men, surely because of the formidable weight of the liquid.[104] To judge from the shape of the cart, the askos was probably a flat rectangle similar to a modern water mattress, although it may have been supported by some kind of frame (see below). Bizarre as this cart may sound, it has parallels in Roman art which depict a multi-skinned askos on a cart. This method must therefore have been one standard way of transporting large quantities of wine locally by road. The cover of a Roman sarcophagus shows two oxen pulling a large askos on a cart, which has wooden slats enclosing the askos to hold it in place.[105] Three other representations of cart-drawn askoi appear in wall-paintings from rooms attached to a tavern in Pompeii.[106] Two of the scenes are similar, and show pottery amphoras being filled with wine from a large askos on a cart which is drawn by mules or horses. The askoi must consist of several skins because of their size, but they have the shape of a single goatskin, drawn tight at the neck. The amphoras are filled from a spout formed from one leg of the animal. In one painting, the askos is held in shape and place by curved slats which encircle it and are attached to the cart. In the second painting, slats are joined into an over-all framework which supports the askos around its diameter. These scenes suggest that the tavern bought wine from a local producer who transported it to them in this way, or that the tavern sold wine in bulk to private customers, transporting it in a cart-drawn askos. The askos in the procession of Dionysus probably reflects a typical way of transporting large quantities of native wine by land around Egypt (although river transport was probably used wherever possible). This rather mundane method of transport is enhanced for the occasion of the Grand Procession by increasing the size of the container dramatically and by making it from leopard, not goat, skins.

The length of the following parade of gold and silver vessels, and its position in the middle of the Dionysiac procession, emphasize all three of the reasons for its inclusion: as prominent former or future offerings to Dionysus, as symbolic vessels for the wine which has gone before in the procession, and as an exhibition of treasure to proclaim

[104] Franzmeyer, 37, calculates that the askos held nearly twice as much liquid as the celebrated Wine Cask in the Heidelberg Schloss.

[105] R. Garrucci, *Monumenti del Museo Lateranense* (Rome, 1861), 54 and Pl. xxxii, 2 (he discusses neither the date nor the provenance of the piece); for a drawing see Daremberg-Saglio, s.v. Vinum, p. 920, Fig. 7514.

[106] W. Helbig, *Wandegemälde der vom Vesuv verschütteten Städte Campaniens* (Leipzig, 1868), Nos. 1486–8. Drawings of 1487–8 are found in the *Tavole* of the Real Museo Borbonico (Naples, 1824–57), iv. Pl. A; v. Pl. xlviii.

the wealth of the Ptolemaic kingdom and to satisfy the general love of ostentation so prevalent in that period. Since no contextual nor thematic anomalies appear in this section, only points of particular interest need be discussed here, notably the difficult textual problems. The archaeological and historical importance of this section lies in its witness of the flourishing metal-working industry in Alexandria from the time of the city's foundation.[107] Alexandria always had the reputation of being a centre, if not the greatest centre, of toreutic art in the Hellenistic age, but these claims are supported mostly by indirect evidence since there are relatively few extant examples of metal-work from Ptolemaic Egypt. The pieces which do exist, even though they may not come from Alexandria itself, reinforce the city's claimed reputation in this field because of their uniformly high quality, and the plentiful production of varied objects in precious metal can be traced back to the earliest Ptolemaic period. Indirect evidence for Greek metal-work in Egypt can be adduced from the numerous examples of pottery which are clearly based on metal prototypes in both shape and decoration,[108] but the most vivid picture of the industry is provided in written sources. The description of the Grand Procession unmistakably reflects a long-established familiarity with the techniques of metal-working and the artistic skill necessary for their successful application. The Zenon papyri present some evidence for the existence and use of gold and silver plate outside Alexandria itself in the third century (*PCZ* 59021, 59038, 59044, 59071, 59074, etc.), and there is a reference to a goldsmith's shop in the Square Stoa in Alexandria at the end of the first century BC (*BGU* 1127, 8-10). The display of gold and silver vessels in the procession reads not unlike the account of the objects in the gift of Philadelphus to the Temple at Jerusalem, preserved in the *Letter of Aristeas*. Although this 'letter' may have been composed in the middle of the second century,[109] its Alexandrian origin is certain and may be invoked as another reflection of Alexandria's fame in metal-working. Even if the gift to the Temple is fantasy and if the letter reflects the situation of the second century rather than the third, the attested wealth in precious metals, the reputation of Philadelphus' Alexandria as a toreutic centre, and the description of the objects themselves, could hardly have been invented, or preposterously exaggerated, if they furnished an entirely false picture of Alexandria a century earlier. Kallixeinos reflects the contemporary level of toreutic art in the Alexandria of Philadelphus, while Aristeas reflects it indirectly in his later view of the same period, although his description is ecphrastic rather than realistic.[110] The question of the

---

[107] See *Ptol. Alex.* i. 136 ff., for a brief discussion of the metal-working industry in Alexandria.   [108] Ibid., ii. 241 n. 32.   [109] Ibid., ii. 970 n. 121.
[110] For suggestions that the author of the *Letter of Aristeas* may have drawn

origin of this vast quantity of gold and silver cannot be considered in detail here, but an abundant, convenient source of precious metal must have been a prerequisite for an industry developed on such a scale. Gold had been, and would continue to be, obtainable from the mines of the eastern desert in Egypt, but silver is not found in the country. It is difficult to suppose that the Ptolemies had obtained this much silver from Spain through the Carthaginians at that early period,[111] or had by then reopened the desert gold mines which had lain dormant since the late dynastic period.[112] This treasure may have resulted at least in part from Ptolemy I's share of Alexander's eastern booty. The ancient sources attest that this was vast, but do not specify how it was divided up among the Diadochi after Alexander's death.[113] Some could have been taken to Egypt by Ptolemy. The large quantity of gold and silver vessels from the Macedonian tombs at Vergina and elsewhere shows that precious metals were sought, obtained, and worked to a high degree of skill also in other parts of the early Hellenistic world.

The vessels in this parade are grouped loosely by material. Gold vessels precede the silver plate, and the display is concluded by more gold plate. Beyond this over-all order, the great variety of shapes, the variable quantities and sizes, and the lack of a discernible pattern in the presentation reinforce the notion that this is a random selection of treasure brought together and not a special matching collection made specifically for this occasion. Among the first group of vases appear vessels called 'therikleioi', named after the classical Corinthian potter Therikles. The exact type of vase to which this name refers is still disputed, but their appearance here shows that they were still known, if not actually made, in Alexandria, and that they were sometimes of precious metal. The name of this vessel may refer more to its technique than to its shape. Since the fine ribbing or fluting which was characteristic of earlier Achaemenid vases was applied to many types of Greek metal vases as well as to their clay imitations, it has been argued that the special shine developed by Therikles on black glazed pottery may have been connected with this style of reeding or fluting.[114]

heavily on the text of Kallixeinos see *Aristeas to Philocrates*, ed. M. Hadas (New York, 1951), 48. Against this view, see *Ptol. Alex.* ii. 975 n. 133.

[111] *Ptol. Alex.* i. 152 ff.

[112] Philadelphus may have acquired these mines by the 270s at the earliest, cf. ibid., ii. 297 n. 342, but it is unlikely that they had gone into full production before the date of the Grand Procession.

[113] Cf. Arrian, *Hist. Alex.*, ed. P. A. Brunt (Loeb, Cambridge, Mass., 1976), i. 517.

[114] B. Shefton, *Ann. Arch. Arabes Syriennes* xxi (1 and 2) (1971), 110; Daremberg-Saglio, s.v. Thericlea Vasa. For other therikleioi in third-century Ptolemaic contexts, cf. a gilded therikleios referred to by Istrus, the follower of Callimachus (*FGrH* 334 F 47); *IG* XI (2) 161 B, 27, where a Θηρίκλειος κύλιξ is dedicated at Delos by Soter or Philadelphus. See now T. B. Mitford, *The Nymphaeum of Kafizin, Kadmos* Suppl. ii (Berlin and New York, 1980), Nos. 40–2, 46, where three ceramic

The 'therikleioi' here may have been various types of vases classified together because they had been made with the same technique, or else several vases of one particular shape to which the technique was so frequently applied that it had, by this date, attracted the name to itself.

An extraordinarily large krater appears next by itself on a cart (199 B-C; lines 86 ff.). The description of this vase, with its many figures in relief in various friezes,[115] is reminiscent of the Derveni krater, which suggests that there was a certain uniformity in style and sophistication in the metal-work produced throughout the late classical and early Hellenistic world. The small zone on the neck of this krater is designated by the words ὑπὸ τὰ χείλη, and the main frieze on the belly by ⟨ὑπὸ⟩ τὰ ὦτα. The emendation ἐπὶ τὴν βάσιν for the manuscript reading ὑπὸ τὴν βάσιν shows that there was a third frieze of decoration around the foot of the vase, where there is embossed decoration on both the Derveni and Vix kraters; figures carved 'ὑπὸ' τὴν βάσιν (*under* the foot) is a curious notion unless the krater stood upon a separate pedestal which was itself covered with relief work.

Two kylikeia, stands for kylikes, appear next in this parade (199 C; line 90). The specification of their length and height shows that they were types of 'sideboards' upon which cups and other vessels were normally placed, although it is not stated whether or not vessels were displayed upon these stands in the procession. Kylikeia appear frequently as items of furniture in *Totenmahl* scenes in East-Greek grave reliefs, where they are comparable in size to the three-legged tables placed before the couches of the deceased (cf. Studniczka, 166 ff. and Abb. 51; E. Pfuhl and H. Möbius, *Die Ostgriechischen Grabreliefs* (Mainz, 1977-9), ii. 366 and n. 161). The main interest in the kylikeia in the procession lies in their decoration, consisting of finial ornaments on the top, and of figures presumably attached to the body of the stands in various places. Ἐπὶ τῶν ποδῶν must refer to the legs of the stands (where tall tripods often had decorative figures), but the meaning of ἐν ταῖς γάστραις κύκλῳ is not clear. Ἡ γάστρα properly means a 'swelling' or a paunch-like shape, and it is frequently applied to vases with a bulging, convex body. The sides of the kylikeia may have been curved to a similar convex shape, with the 'circle' referring either to a frieze of figures encircling the bodies of the stands as decoration, or to circular arrangements of figures on each of the swelling sides of the stands.

The phrase εἶτα λέβητες ἐξ βανωτοὶ εἴκοσι τέσσαρες . . . (199 C; line

kantharoi and (probably) a lagynos are inscribed Θυρεικλεῖον, and dedicated to the Nymph by a flax company in Ptolemaic Cyprus between the years 225–218 BC.

[115] The emendation τετορευμένα in place of the ms reading τετορνευμένα is clearly right here and in line 110 since it shows that the figures are embossed upon the surface of the vase, a type of repoussé work common in Hellenistic gold and silver plate; cf. M. J. Milne, *AJA* xlv (1941), 390 ff.

95) has been emended by many editors in order to elucidate the unusual word βανωτοί, but the transmitted text is acceptable. A βανωτός or βανώτιον is a well-attested word in papyri for a container of various substances including wine (see, for example, *PSI* 428, *passim*; *PCZ* 59194). Although no conjunction separates the *banotoi* from the preceding lebetes (which has also led to attempts to emend the phrase), the syntax can stand since similar examples of asyndeton are common throughout this catalogue-type list of gold and silver plate. *Banotoi* were prosaic clay vessels, perhaps made in various sizes, but apparently in a distinctive shape which differentiated them from generalized clay containers called κεράμια, since both names appear side by side in papyri. These humble containers were reproduced in precious metal for the occasion of the Grand Procession along with other vases in this section which were usually made in clay: Panathenaic amphorae (199D; line 104), *bikoi* (199D; line 97, which are common clay containers in papyri, cf. *PSI* 428, 25, 82–3, 102, etc.), and *kōthōnes* (199F; line 114, canteen mugs originally used by Laconian soldiers and surely of clay).

A series of tables precedes the appearance of Delphic tripods (199D; lines 97). These are called both τράπεζα and τρίπους; the former is a rectangular table since it is measured by length, and although the latter word can also mean 'tripod', it here signifies three-legged tables whose circular shapes are indicated by the fact that the measurement of the largest is given in terms of its circumference. These τρίποδες are distinguished in terminology, and therefore in form, from the Δελφικοί τρίποδες which follow. The latter are the tall, three-legged stands for vessels, and without exception Kallixeinos uses the adjective Δελφικός in conjunction with τρίπους when he means 'tripods' instead of 'three-legged tables' (cf. 197A; 197B; 198C (line 42); 198D (line 51); 199D (line 99); 202C (line 240)). Also, the 'Delphic' tripods are always measured by their height in cubits (except in 199D where the text is lacunose), not by their circumference like the tables. The eighty Delphic tripods are said to be ἐλάττους τῶν προειρημένων, that is, smaller than the two intended as prizes for the victorious choregoi in 198C; these are the only Delphic tripods to have been mentioned before in the text of the Grand Procession, and they measured $13\frac{1}{2}$ and 18 feet in height. The description of this second group of Delphic tripods is marked by textual confusion. The manuscript reading is meaningless even with the obvious emendation τετραμέτρητοι for τετράμετροι; the former adjective means 'holding four measures' and makes no sense modifying either αἱ γωνίαι (the joints of the legs of the tripods) or indeed τρίποδες, which are elsewhere measured by height, not by the volume of the vessels they support. A lacuna must therefore be placed after γωνίαι in which there was probably a description of figures or other decorative elements attached to the legs of the tripods, and perhaps a more specific measurement of the height of the tripods. Τετραμέτρητοι may modify the twenty-six hydriai which appear next in the parade, or another type of vessel whose name has fallen out in the lacuna.

Large, ornate kraters appear at the beginning of the final parade of gold plate (199E; line 107), and textual adjustment is also required here. The sentence clearly begins with the intention of listing several gold objects, all in the accusative case in apposition to τὰ χρυσώματα, but κρατῆρας Λακωνικούς are the only vessels mentioned before the construction switches to the nominative with the word τετραμέτρητοι (the emendation from τετράμετροι is again obvious). A lacuna has therefore been conjectured after ἀμπελίνους in which the descriptions of other vessels (no doubt kraters; see below) were given in the accusative in continuing apposition to τὰ χρυσώματα. Τετραμέτρητοι in this case modifies vessels, now lost in the lacuna, which were originally described after the construction had switched to the nominative; the adjective cannot modify the following Corinthian vessels because they are each said to hold eight measures (line 112). (If the text of this section has no lacuna but is only severely truncated, which seems on balance unlikely, τετραμέτρητοι must be emended to τετραμετρήτους, in order to modify κρατῆρας Λακωνικούς, with a full stop placed after it. Such an error could easily have arisen by attraction from the following ἕτεροι.) The names of the types of Corinthian vases are not given in the text, but they are surely kraters since their decoration as described is common to ornate kraters (cf. the one with relief decoration described in 199B): ⟨κρατῆρες⟩ can be supplied from the surrounding context, either from κρατῆρες Λακωνικοί (which is the preceding type of vessel if the text is complete), or from a third type of krater whose description is lost in the lacuna, but which immediately preceded the Corinthian vessels. Two types of figures are described on these vases, both called τετορευμένα, but distinguished by the adjectives περιφανῆ and πρόστυπα. This must mean that the figures on the neck were in the round while those on the body were in low relief.[116] Although τετορευμένα properly refers to embossed work on metal, it can also be applied to figures in the round which were made with a similar technique (either hammered over a mould or made with the repoussé method). These kraters seem very similar to the Derveni krater with its four figures in the round seated on the shoulder of the vase. Kallixeinos describes the figures on the shoulder as ἐπιμελῶς πεποιημένα (likewise figurines on the shelves of the gold chest which follows later in 199F). These critical comments suggest that Kallixeinos, or a source he was using for this information, had actually seen the vessels (either in the procession or at any time

[116] Ibid., 397.

afterwards), or else a visual representation of them. These considerations are germane to later discussions of the author's date and sources (see Chapter 4D-E).

The final group of gold plate contains two glass vessels described by the adjective διάχρυσα (199F; line 119). There are several preserved fragments of Hellenistic gold-glass made in the so-called 'sandwich style'[117] (gold leaf between two layers of glass); διάχρυσα probably indicates that these vessels were made in this technique. Alexandria was formerly considered the obvious place of manufacture for gold-glass since the city had an important glass industry,[118] but although the discovery of gold-glass fragments in the excavation of an ancient Rhodian glass factory may point rather to Rhodes as the major centre of production in the Hellenistic period,[119] the vessels in the procession attest the existence of gold-glass (whether imported or local) in early third-century Alexandria.

At the end of this parade of gold and silver plate, a number of youths appear who carry refreshments for the guests in the stadium (200A-B; line 127): μεθ᾽ οὓς ἄλλοι παῖδες ἔφερον κεράμια πρὸς τὴν τοῦ γλυκισμοῦ χρείαν . . . καὶ κερασθέντων ἐν ταῖς ὑδρίαις καὶ πίθοις πάντες κοσμίως ἐγλυκίσθησαν οἱ ἐν τῷ σταδίῳ. It is clear that portions of wine are being distributed to the privileged spectators; γλυκισμός is the usual word used for such a distribution, and the information that the substance had been mixed must refer to the normal dilution of wine with water among the Greeks. The appearance of these refreshments serves a double purpose: the opportunity of drinking real wine is the obvious culmination of the preceding lengthy celebration of wine in its various aspects, and this activity would have afforded a welcome interval between parts of the Grand Procession, since it presumably took some time for the wine to be distributed and consumed. The procession probably halted at least during the distribution. The consumption of refreshments by audiences at spectacles is well attested from classical times.[120] It was a standard feature of the City Dionysia at Athens, and an understandable one in a festival consisting of continuous dramatic performances throughout the day. The wine and food in that case may have been either brought by the spectators or sold in the theatre,[121] but in the Grand Procession the refreshments are provided by the authorities since the distributors appear in the line of the procession. It was also a well-known practice for civic officials to provide γλυκισμός for the populace; inscriptions attest it as the public

---

[117] For a list of these see A. Oliver, Jr., *JGS* xi (1969), 9 ff.; for discussions of various pieces see A. von Saldern, *JGS* i (1959), 45 ff.; D. B. Harden, *JGS* x (1968), 38 ff.; for gold-band glass vessels see Oliver, *JGS* ix (1967), 20 ff.

[118] *Ptol. Alex.* i. 136-7.   [119] G. Weinberg, ΑΔ xxiv (1969), Mel. 147.

[120] Philochorus, *FGrH* 328 F 171; Arist. *Eth. Nic.* x. 1175ᵇ 12.

[121] Parke, *Festivals*, 131.

acknowledgement and celebration of the attainment of an office or honour, and it was clearly intended as a gesture of good will (*I Priene* 108, 257 ff., 272-4; 109, 192 ff.; 111, 238-9; *IG* VII 2712, 68). The distribution of γλυκισμός during the Grand Procession can be understood as a combination of both ancient practices. On the one hand it was a gesture of beneficence and generosity on the part of the authorities towards the honoured guests, and, on the other, the guests needed some refreshments in the middle of the day-long proceedings. (Similar refreshments may also have been provided during other sectional processions.)

The sweet wine and water seem to have been mixed in the right quantities in hydriai and pithoi during this interval in the procession, and then distributed by the youths carrying the diversified keramia. The hydriai and pithoi must have been in the stadium where the mixture was decanted into more manageable vessels to be carried around and distributed in portions to the guests; if the large containers did not appear in view, Kallixeinos or his source could hardly have known that the mixture was prepared in those types of containers. If these refreshments were intended only for those in the stadium, which seems likely as the only practicable proposition, the boys carrying the keramia probably fell out from the procession when it restarted, since their task was finished.

The emendation ἐγλυκίσθησαν provides the correct meaning in this context. It is the passive form of γλυκίζω, to which γλυκισμός is cognate, and is used in inscriptions to describe the distribution of γλυκισμός (*IG* VII, 190, 17; 2712, 75-7). The phrase used in this passage merely means 'all those in the stadium received their due portion of γλυκισμός'. The form ἐγλυκίσθησαν involves a change of only one letter from A's attested reading ἐγλυκάσθησαν, which, like Cobet's emendation ἐγλυκάνθησαν, gives the wrong meaning. These passive forms of, respectively, γλυκάζω and γλυκαίνω mean 'to be sweetened up' in the literal sense and imply that the spectators, having consumed a sweet substance, 'became much sweeter' because there was a greater amount of sweet material inside them. These verbs do not adequately describe spectators who have simply received a portion of γλυκισμός.

4. *The bridal chamber of Semele* (200B)   After the interval and refreshments, the second major part of the Dionysiac procession starts in 200B with a series of scenes representing 'events' in the life of the god, beginning chronologically with the birth and rearing of Dionysus, and continuing through his adult exploits. The description of the Chamber of Semele appears first, and is related in the third person as part of Athenaeus' abbreviation of this part of the text of Kallixeinos (line 132). The exact contents of this scene are not specified, but it may have portrayed Semele and Zeus in the *thalamos* before his revelation to her of his true form. The

later birth of Dionysus in the charred remains of the chamber would hardly be fitting visually, nor do these figures, dressed in golden, jewel-encrusted clothing, seem to be portrayed at a moment of death and tragedy. Literary sources depict Semele's chamber as a luxuriant 'Dionysiac' bower wreathed in ivy and vines (Eur. *Phoen.* 649-56 and schol. ad loc.), and, to judge from the lavish clothing of these figures and the fact that the scene is included among those which are described as θέας ἄξια πολυτελῶς κατεσκευασμένα, a similar iconography, combined with a certain ostentation in the portrayal, may be imagined in this scene. Since it is implied that there are several figures in this scene, some of the attendants of the couple may have been included.[122]

Other references to Semele in Alexandrian literature show that she was a well-known mythological figure there. Callimachus wrote a poem about her, according to the list of titles given in his Suda *Life* (Suda K 227), and in Theocritus' *Idyll* xxvi (the story of Pentheus' dismemberment by Ino, Agave, and Autonoe), the three women set up three altars for Semele and nine for Dionysus (lines 5-6), which may indicate that Semele and Dionysus had a joint cult in Alexandria[123] as they are known to have had elsewhere.[124] Although the prominence of her Thalamos in the procession is therefore not surprising, and its general subject is comprehensible, the textual context of this part of the Dionysiac procession is confused, per-haps because it is summarized by Athenaeus. As the text stands, six-foot-long tables, on which various tableaux (including the Thalamos) are arranged, appear to be carried along. (These could be analogous to the legged platforms carried in various Holy Week processions in modern Spain, which contain elaborate scenes from the Passion of Christ, often with several figures.) If the text is sound, it is difficult to suggest what the other θεάματα on tables may have been in the story of the life of Dionysus; his conception in the Chamber of Semele must have come first, and the next named scene is the cart carrying the rearing of the infant god in the Cave of the Nymphs which should follow the Thalamos scene thematically. Nothing is said about the method of locomotion of these tables, which may be due to Athenaeus' summary rather than to Kallixeinos since this is the only place in the Dionysiac procession where such information is

---

[122] For references to various artistic representations of Semele see *RE* s.v. Semele, 1345.

[123] Gow, *Comm. Theoc.* ii. 475, thinks that the poem could be connected with, or suggested by, religious ritual.

[124] Hesiod, *Theog.* 942; Pindar, *Dith.* fr. 75, 19 (S-M); Eur. *Phoen.* 1755; *Bacch.* 998; Eur., *TGF* (Nauck) fr. 586. A joint altar was dedicated to Dionysus and Semele at Magnesia (*IMag.* 214), and at Thebes the Thalamos was worshipped as a shrine, *RE* s.v. Semele, 1342. For an account of various divine manifestations of Semele see H. Jeanmaire, *Dionysos* (Paris, 1951), 343 ff.; *RE* s.v. Semele, 1342 ff.

omitted. The tables would hardly be drawn on the carts used elsewhere, as this would form an unnecessary double platform for the scenes, but in view of their smallness they could have been carried if the statues were of some relatively light material. This sudden change from carts with scenes to tables with scenes cannot be explained, nor can the fact that these scenes alone were created 'in miniature' when everything else in the Grand Procession was conceived on a massive scale.

Kaibel found this interpretation unacceptable, and suggested a lacuna after the reference to the tables in which the description of carts containing the Chamber of Semele and the other scenes originally appeared: ἐξῆς τούτοις καταλέγει τετραπήχεις τραπέζας . . . ἐφ' ὧν πολλά . . . κτλ. This emendation makes carts the standard vehicles for all the scenes in the procession of Dionysus (removing the awkward change of locomotion introduced by the tables), and the separation of the relatively small tables from the scenes of the god's life allows the Chamber of Semele to be presented on a larger scale comparable to the other scenes in the Dionysiac procession. Kaibel's suggestion has further merit in the context of this section. The mention of tables, as tables, is more appropriate to the preceding description of the refreshments than to scenes from the life of Dionysus. After the account of the distribution of sweet wine, Kallixeinos may have proceeded to describe tables with food which were brought for the guests in the stadium (cf. the inscriptions recording γλυκισμός as a civic benefaction which show that food was also distributed with it; *IG* VII, 2712, 68). A lacuna in the text may explain the absence of the description of the number of tables and their contents, as well as of the mention of the cart for the following scene of the god's birth. The tables may equally have signalled a resumption of the parade of gold and silver plate after the break for refreshments, since various vessels may have been displayed on them.

There is, however, one factor which may support the appearance of tables in a representation of the Chamber of Semele. Although the over-all meaning of *Idyll* xxvi of Theocritus is far from clear, even a conservative interpretation may allow that it connotes some kind of mystic or orgiastic cult of Dionysus,[125] one which may have included his mother Semele in some way, especially in view of the fact that she seems to have been worshipped herself in Orphic Mysteries. One curious reference to Semele in Hesychius (s.v. σεμέλη) may shed some light on the part played by Semele in these mystic cults: σεμέλη. τράπεζα. παρὰ δὲ Φρυνίχῳ ἑορτή (Phrynichus, *TGF* i (Snell) 3, F 23). Keune[126] has suggested that the τράπεζα was a special mystic object for Semele because of its appearance

---

[125] Gow, *Comm. Theoc.* ii. 475, 482 (cf. lines 27-32).
[126] *RE* s.v. Semele, 1343.

in the Orphic *Hymn* to her which apparently refers to some kind of Orphic rites in her honour (xliv. 8-9): ἡνίκα σοῦ Βάκχου γονίμην ὠδῖνα τελῶσιν/ εὐίερόν τε τράπεζαν ἰδὲ μυστήριά θ' ἀγνά. He tentatively identifies the εὐίερος τράπεζα (which seems to be linked with the celebration of Semele's birth-pains) as a table holding natural produce, and suggests that this association may be a partial explanation of the entry in Hesychius. Since a table holding natural produce is an appropriate attribute for Semele (who is sometimes considered an earth-goddess[127]), the possible mention of tables in connection with her in the Dionysiac procession may be of some importance. If the text is sound, although truncated through Athenaeus' abbreviation, the tables may be related to various Orphic aspects of Semele. The scene of the Chamber may have appeared upon one of the tables in miniature since tables are associated with birth-pains in the context of the Orphic text. Since the Orphic *Hymn*, though written many centuries later, implies that Semele appears in some sort of mystic celebration, probably within the larger framework of the Dionysiac-Orphic Mysteries, the appearance of these tables and the Chamber of Semele in the procession may be connected with such mystic cults. This corroborates the evidence seen throughout the procession that mystic cults existed in the early third century in Alexandria, even if it is impossible to unravel their threads (see Chapter 5). That this scene had vague mystic associations is perhaps supported by the fact that the following scene, the Cave of the Nymphs, is also known to have had mystic importance.

5. *The infant Dionysus in the Cave of the Nymphs* (200B-C)   The next episode in the life of Dionysus is centred on the cave where Hermes brought the infant god to the Nymphs who would rear him. The cave is described as a delightfully idyllic Hellenistic grotto in which all the appropriate characters are placed (200B-C; lines 136 ff.). The scene of the Chamber of Semele is related in the text as part of the summary of Athenaeus, and at some unspecified point his direct quotation of Kallixeinos' text begins again. Kaibel indicated the beginning of the direct quotation in the cave scene with τήνδε 'τὴν τετράκυκλον ...', and Jacoby at an equally arbitrary place, κισσῷ καὶ μίλῳ. 'ἐκ τούτου περιστεραί ...'. The phrase πᾶσαι δ' αἱ περὶ αὐτὸν Νύμφαι, which appears a line or two below, is central to this question since αὐτόν has no antecedent.[128]

---

[127] Ibid.; J. E. Harrison, *Prolegomena to the Study of Greek Religion*[2] (Cambridge, 1908), 404 ff.; W. F. Otto, *Dionysos: Mythos und Kultus* (Frankfurt, 1933), 66 ff.

[128] Although περὶ αὐτόν was emended by Cobet to περὶ αὐτό, which refers to the ἄντρον and removes the masculine pronoun for which there is no antecedent, it is even less acceptable that *any* reference, however incomplete, to the god, should be missing from the scene of which he is the main subject. Περὶ αὐτόν should therefore be retained.

Although Dionysus must be understood as the focus of attention, it is most surprising that the god's name appears nowhere in the description of this cart. This confusion is unlikely to have arisen if the text of Kallixeinos is quoted verbatim here, but it is comprehensible if Athenaeus is still the abbreviator. He may have paraphrased the original description of the scene by Kallixeinos rather carelessly, omitting the name of Dionysus whose appearance he took for granted, and failing to notice that his summary did not actually name the main character of the scene. By far the easiest suggestion is that his paraphrase continued through the cave scene and that his direct quotation began again at the beginning of the following scene, the Triumphal Return of Dionysus from India (200D).

The representation of the rearing of Dionysus by the Nymphs is the logical sequel to his birth-scene. Artistic representations of the god being entrusted to his divine nurses are common,[129] especially as the cult of the Nymphs increased in popularity in the Hellenistic Age. These Nymphs may reasonably be interpreted as those inhabiting Nysa, if the statue of Nysa represents the god's supposed birthplace. The more popular version of the legend of the rearing of Dionysus, where Hermes and not Zeus brought the infant to the Nymphs,[130] is the one depicted in the procession. The cave contains typical Dionysiac elements as part of its idyllic decoration: fountains of milk and wine bubble forth, which were apparently simulated on the cart since Kallixeinos says what the liquids are. Askoi with controlled openings may have been concealed on top of stepped rocks in the cave so that the milk and wine could be seen to 'bubble' down over the rocks and collect in pools on the 'ground'. These two liquids have already appeared in connection with the statue of Nysa, whose head was crowned with vines and who poured a libation of milk. The cave of the Nymphs who inhabit Nysa naturally reflects the same features, and here too the milk probably symbolizes the nursing aspect of the region (as well as of the Nymphs) in addition to its general fertility. Since wine appears in the cave, this scene perhaps commemorates the invention of the substance by the divine baby soon after his arrival at Nysa. The inclusion of this scene in the procession of Dionysus may also reflect certain mystic elements in the cult of Dionysus: when children were later admitted to the fully developed Mysteries of Dionysus, the representations of the childhood of Dionysus, especially the legend of his rearing by the Nysaean Nymphs, assumed a greater symbolic significance within the ritual of the Mysteries.[131]

6. *Triumphal Return of Dionysus from India* (200D–201C)   The central part of the procession of Dionysus is a pageant celebrating his triumphal return from India, which is depicted as the most important

---

[129] Cf. H. Heydemann, *Dionysos' Geburt und Kindheit* (Halle, 1885), 18 ff.
[130] *RE* s.v. Dionysos, 1036.   [131] Nilsson, *Dionysiac Mysteries*, 111 ff.

episode in the life of the god (200D ff.). The next cart contains the god reclining on a statue of a richly caparisoned elephant, directed by a Satyr-iskos sitting upon its neck (note the similar picture of Dionysus' Triumph in D. S. iv. 3, 1), and followed by a lengthy parade of his victorious army (200E ff.): 500 girls and 120 Satyrs in assorted panoply lead a long cavalry procession composed of asses ridden by Satyrs and Silenoi and chariots drawn by various exotic animals. These chariots were driven by boys dressed as charioteers and ridden by girls dressed as warriors (200F; line 167), representing the ἡνίοχοι and παραβάται of real Greek combat. This 'army' is followed by the fruits of victory: captive women, vast amounts of tribute, hunting spoils, and a long parade of animals, both wild and domesticated. This pageant is undoubtedly elaborated in detail by Kallixeinos because it contains much of the most fascinating exotica in the Grand Procession, and the theme of Dionysus' triumphal return from India was a convenient peg on which these elements could be hung. Although this may have been one reason for its prominence and length in the Dionysiac procession, the scene has much greater significance in terms of contemporary political propaganda.

Dionysus was a god who from early times was at home in military con-texts. He and Silenos had participated in the primeval battle against the Giants (Eur. *Cyclops* 5 ff.), and in some cults at Thrace and Sparta Dionysus was endowed with warlike attributes.[132] These associations were especially connected with Dionysus' exploits in the East. The Dionysus in the *Bacchae* of Euripides was portrayed as a god who had come from the East to conquer Greece (cf. lines 13-20) even as he had already conquered the eastern peoples. His route to Greece, the next 'unconquered land', could be seen as a triumphal procession from India. However, this triumphal aspect was not emphasized until the Hellenistic age, when the eastern successes of Alexander the Great provided a parallel to the Indian triumph of Dionysus. It has been disputed whether or not Alexander himself was the first to recognize, and emphasize, the comparison between his own victories and those mythical ones of the god.[133] Alexander may have been conscious of himself as the 'Neos Dionysos' since he was familiar with the worship of the god from his childhood in Macedonia, where the frenzied, orgiastic aspects of Dionysiac cult were especially popular. (Alexander's mother Olympias is said to have been one of the most un-inhibited leaders of the women's rites in the yearly festival of Dionysus.) The historians of Alexander frequently made the analogy between Alexander and Dionysus explicit, tracing how the notion of Dionysus as an

---

[132] Farnell, *Cults*, v. 292; cf. 60.
[133] For the view that Alexander was conscious of himself in this role see V. Ehrenberg, *Ost und West* (Brunn, 1935), 164-8.

earlier conqueror of the East assumed a special significance for the Macedonian. Gradually, Alexander's expedition to India took on the appearance of following the footsteps of the god, and the troops interpreted landmarks along the way as signs that Dionysus had passed that way before them, and they believed the Indian traditions of the god's presence (Arr. *An.* v. 1, 1 ff.; vi. 28, 1 ff.; vii. 20, 1 ff.; *Ind.* 1, 1 ff.; 5, 8 ff.; see above, p. 67). The similarity in route and role between Dionysus and Alexander may perhaps be seen in the latter's religious celebrations. Marked comastic elements are present in the week-long, drunken festivities held after the near-fatal march through Gedrosia, in which Alexander and his Companions led a procession on a wagon pulled by eight horses and were followed by the officers and friends on canopied carts through streets strewn with flowers and crowns (Plut. *Alex.* lxvii; Curt. Ruf. ix. 10, 24-7). Although Arrian doubts the whole episode, he says that the revel was meant to be in imitation of Dionysus' own progress (*An.* vi. 28, 1). On the other hand, this comparison between Alexander and Dionysus may not have been current during the former's lifetime and may have resulted wholly from the interpretation given to his expedition by the historians.[134] Even if stories like the finding of Nysa at Mount Meros were historically true, the tales concerning the Dionysiac reaction of the army may have been exaggerated later (Arrian suggests this himself; *An.* v. 2, 7), and a historical visit of Alexander to those places may not in itself have involved a conscious assimilation of Alexander to Dionysus.

In any case, there can be no doubt from the procession itself that such an assimilation *was* made between Alexander and Dionysus in Ptolemaic Alexandria. Although the other Diadochi also claimed a relationship with Alexander in order to ensure their own political legitimacy in those parts of his empire which they ruled after his death,[135] and although their adoption of elements of his Indian campaign (such as the elephant-scalp headdress, which derived from the fact that the elephant was first introduced into Greek warfare in Alexander's Indian campaigns) made explicit their tie with Alexander as the Conqueror of the East, this tie was with Alexander alone, and not with Dionysus. The Ptolemies took a further step and connected themselves with Alexander through Dionysus. The Ptolemaic kings appear as blood descendants of Dionysus through Soter's mother in the official Ptolemaic genealogy preserved in Satyrus (see above, p. 42), and there was one unofficial, and certainly false, story in circulation that Soter was an illegitimate son of Philip II of Macedon, and was

---

[134] A. D. Nock, *JHS* xlviii (1928), 21 ff. = id., *Essays on Religion and the Ancient World*, ed. Zeph Stewart (Oxford, 1972), i. 134 ff.; for the origin of this picture of Alexander, see now P. Goukowsky, *Essai sur les origines du mythe d'Alexandre* (Nancy, 1978-81), ii (*Alexandre et Dionysos*); cf. Addendum *supra*, vi.

[135] Goukowsky, i. 145 ff.

thus not only a half-brother of Alexander, but a closer relation of Dionysus since he could also claim the god as an ancestor through his supposed father's Argead blood. (In this story, Soter's mother Arsinoe, who was Philip's mistress and pregnant by him, was given in marriage to Lagus before the birth of her child, who was then accepted as Lagus' own; Paus. i. 6, 2; Curt. Ruf. ix. 8, 22.) These official and unofficial stories show beyond doubt that the Ptolemies were eager to associate themselves by blood as closely as possible with Dionysus and Alexander, himself a descendant of the god through the Argead house. Finally, it is possible that the stories in which Alexander's Indian campaign is approximated to that of Dionysus had an Alexandrian origin; Cleitarchus, himself perhaps an Alexandrian, may have been the originator of many of these stories. They were known to Eratosthenes in Alexandria (who criticized them), and passed into the *Vulgate* tradition of Alexander-history.[136]

The 'Return of Dionysus from India' in the Grand Procession is perhaps the most emphatic statement of the parallel between Dionysus and Alexander, and the best illustration of the indirect celebration of the latter through the glorification of the former. A Dionysiac procession in Alexandria would emphasize the Ptolemaic claims in a public way in any case, but the triumphal aspects of Dionysus which are particularly celebrated in this procession serve as propaganda for the Ptolemies, legitimised as Alexander's heirs in Egypt. The long section devoted to the Indian Triumph of Dionysus cannot but have been associated with Alexander's successes in the East, and the implicit comparison is made explicit by the similar picture of Dionysus and Alexander as eastern conquerors in the context of the procession: Dionysus appears on an elephant followed by a retinue which includes elephant quadrigae (200D-F), and a statue of Alexander, flanked by the war-goddesses Athena and Nike, later appears in his own procession in a chariot drawn by elephants (202A; line 227). The Ptolemies as the sponsors of the Grand Procession are reflected in the glory derived from this comparison, and share the glory of the eastern triumphs themselves as the heirs of Alexander and Dionysus. In this part of the procession, their personal connection with the East is seen in the plethora of spices, luxury goods, and exotic animals, all of which had been obtained through extensive trading connections developed and maintained under royal control. The extravagant wealth exhibited here recalls the fabulous booty traditionally associated with Alexander's victories, and although

---

[136] See ibid., 136 ff., 149 ff., for a discussion of Cleitarchus; for the origin of Cleitarchus see *Ptol. Alex.* i. 496; ii. 717 n. 3; for Eratosthenes' criticisms see P. M. Fraser, *PBA* lvi (1970), 197 ff.; for all references to the tie between Alexander and Dionysus see E. Mederer, *Die Alexanderlegenden bei den ältesten Alexanderhistorikern* (Stuttgart, 1936), 94 ff.; Goukowsky, ii.

many of the items in the procession come from 'Ethiopia' as well as from the East (on this, see below, p. 98), the precise geographical origin of the goods is less important than their general exotic associations and the fact that the Ptolemies could claim credit for their appearance in Alexandria.

From these beginnings in third-century Alexandria, the picture of Dionysus as the conqueror of India grew in popularity. The theme of the Indian Triumph became popular in art and literature throughout the Graeco-Roman world. Many Roman sarcophagi depict various elements of this triumph,[137] and the Indian campaign with its resulting triumph degenerated into a series of mindless, bloody battles by the time it occupied several books of the *Dionysiaca* of Nonnus. Still, this triumphal theme in art and literature continues to take its iconographic stock from Alexander's eastern expedition.[138]

The appearance of animals in Dionysus' train is thematically comprehensible since many served as mounts for the god's symbolic cavalry, while others may have had some ritual significance. The god was traditionally associated with wild animals: he often rode in a chariot drawn by wild beasts (as depicted on vases as early as the sixth century BC[139]), the leopard was actually sacred to Dionysus (note that several varieties of wild cats appear in 201C), and animals were important features of the orgiastic maenadic rites. Since Dionysus is pictured on his return from India, he had to be accompanied by retinue of oriental followers who were unfamiliar and awe-inspiring to the spectators of the procession. However, the great multitude of animals which appears here outweighs any practical or ritual purpose, and the triumphal procession is partly an excuse for the exhaustive parade of beasts. Their appearance can, however, be readily explained as the result of contemporary royal interest in animals, and of the desire of Philadelphus to display his personal collection. The king's interest in breeding domestic animals is well attested in the Zenon papyri, and his collection of wild animals is known from Diodorus (iii. 36, 3). The exotic animals came to Alexandria not only from hunters who received a substantial reward from Philadelphus, but as political gifts to the king from rulers of lesser domains which were the natural habitats of the beasts (cf. *PCZ* 59075). The animals collected by Philadelphus must have been housed in a zoo, which may have been located in the Palaces area of Alexandria where there were spacious gardens in a location convenient for the king. The animals appearing in this section of the procession were

---

[137] F. Matz, *Die Dionysischen Sarcophage* (Berlin, 1968–75), iv. Index, s.v. Indischer Triumph.

[138] *RE* s.v. Dionysos, 1039–40.

[139] See, e.g., the Phineus Cup; A. Rumpf, *Chalkidische Vasen* (Berlin and Leipzig, 1927), Pls. XL–XLI.

probably inhabitants of the zoo, if they were not new beasts obtained for this special occasion and destined for the zoo later. A royal zoo may be mentioned in the second-century *Memoirs* of Ptolemy VIII (*FGrH* 234 F 2), but since pheasants and guinea fowl (if νομάδες ὄρνιθες = Numidian birds = guinea fowl; see below, p. 94), are alone specified among the animals raised there, it is possible that the king is referring to some breeding ground for the palace kitchens. This establishment, whatever it was, was housed in the Palaces area, and, if it *was* a zoo, it is tempting to suggest that it is a remnant of the earlier one from the time of Philadelphus.[140]

The use of wild animals in Greek religious ceremonies is not unparalleled. Pausanias describes a procession of Artemis Laphria at Patrai, where, in striking similarity to the Dionysiac procession, the priestess rode in a chariot drawn by stags (vii. 18, 12). Polybius attests that the temple of Artemis at Lusi in Arcadia possessed a private collection of animals at the time when the Aetolians threatened to plunder the sanctuary (iv. 18, 9–10). In *Idyll* ii of Theocritus, Simaitha says that Anaxo went to the grove of Artemis on the day when many wild beasts were on show (lines 66–8). Although this *Idyll* may not have an Alexandrian setting and may not refer to a real precinct of Artemis where wild beasts were used in various rituals, it still suggests that comparable customs were known to Theocritus, who lived in third-century Alexandria at the time of the Grand Procession.

The animals in Dionysus' triumphal train are divided into three groups: domesticated and tamed animals are either ridden by, or pull chariots ridden by, members of the god's army; next, dogs and birds appear in the section devoted to hunting spoils; and, finally, a parade of birds in cages and of both domestic and wild animals.[141] (The description of this third group of animals has been abbreviated by Athenaeus, 201B; line 188: εἰπὼν δὲ καὶ ἄλλα πλεῖστα καὶ καταλέξας ζῴων ἀγέλας ἐπιφέρει . . . κτλ. Although the exact subject of Kallixeinos' original text cannot be known, it seems likely that his longer list of more and more types of animals was simply cut by Athenaeus who resumed his direct quotation with the account of the most unfamiliar, and hence the most interesting, group of wild animals).

---

[140] Fraser, *Ptol. Alex.* i. 15; ii. 466 n. 39, accepts that the establishment described by Euergetes II is the actual zoo of Philadelphus. So also Jacoby, *FGrH* II D, p. 659, s.v. 234 F (2).

[141] For other discussions of these animals see G. Jennison, *Animals for Show and Pleasure in Ancient Rome* (Manchester, 1937), 30 ff.; D. B. Hull, *Hounds and Hunting in Ancient Greece* (Chicago, 1964); J. M. C. Toynbee, *Animals in Roman Life and Art* (London, 1973). The standard work on ancient animals remains O. Keller, *Die Antike Tierwelt* (Leipzig, 1909–13), 2 vols.

In the first group, several familiar domesticated animals are ridden by the Satyrs and Silenoi in 200E and pull the chariots in 200F: asses, wild asses or onagers, horses, and goats. Later, mules pull carts full of female spear-captives (200F; line 173). The Zenon papyri furnish ample proof that all these animals were raised and bred in third-century Egypt,[142] and one letter, which records a gift of animals sent to Philadelphus by the Ammonite king, is of particular interest because it mentions horses, asses, and assorted cross-breeds from asses, horses, and wild asses (*PCZ* 59075, 3-5). All these common animals would have been obvious choices as beasts of burden in the procession, either to be ridden or harnessed to chariots. In addition, wild animals appear in the chariot section which are much less familiar and whose identity is in some cases uncertain (200F; line 164): κόλων δεκαδύο, ὀρύγων ἑπτά, βουβάλων δεκαπέντε . . . ὀνελάφων ἑπτά. The fact that these animals all pull chariots, be they ἅρματα (the standard war-chariot with two wheels, two passengers, and three or four draught-animals) or συνωρίδες (a lower, lighter vehicle used for war and racing and pulled by two animals), which are mounted by pairs of boys and girls, has two important corollaries: all the wilder animals in this section must have been able to be tamed sufficiently to walk through the streets of Alexandria and be entrusted with the lives of the children, and many of the chariots could have been less than full size because of their light load, and so could have been drawn by some rather small animals.

From information provided by Hesychius (s.v. κόλον) and Strabo (312), the 'kolos' has been identified as a saiga antelope,[143] a type of antelope found today across the Urals and known there also in antiquity, as shown by a wooden bridle-decoration made in the distinctive shape of the head of this antelope,[144] from the fifth barrow at Pazyryk in southern Siberia (which dates from the fifth or fourth centuries BC). The identification of the 'kolos' with this saiga antelope is likely, but cannot be proved. What can be said is that since oryxes (the familiar African antelope) are mentioned separately later, a 'kolos' should be an animal visually distinct from an oryx, as a saiga antelope with its humped nose certainly is. Such an animal would have been very unfamiliar in Egypt since it came from so far away and was unlike any native quadruped, and on these grounds it may have been in demand for the royal zoo. Saigas would have been available to the Ptolemies through trade with the Greek colonies on the north side of the Black Sea.

Oryxes are common animals in Africa today, and there is no climatic reason to think that they were not common in antiquity. Of the types of

---

[142] See, e.g., Rostovtzeff, *Large Estate*, 107 ff.   [143] Jennison, 31.
[144] *Frozen Tombs: The Culture and Art of the Ancient Tribes of Siberia* (British Museum Exhibition Catalogue, London, 1978), 71 No. 86.

oryx which live in north and east Africa,[145] (the Beisa (common in East Africa), the White or Scimitar oryx (common in North Africa), and the Arabian or Beatrix oryx (native only to Arabia)), the last is perhaps the least likely to have been used as a draught animal since it is the smallest of the oryxes, standing about 3 feet 6 inches at the shoulder. All these oryxes could have been obtained easily by the Ptolemies, and some may at that time have been native to Egypt. Aelian (*HA* xiii. 25; xv. 14) says that there was also an Indian variety of oryx, which the Indians displayed along with deer, gazelles, and other quadrupeds. It is not impossible that the Ptolemies also owned some of these antelopes, which had been shipped west with luxury goods by land and sea. Indian antelopes would have been particularly suitable in the triumph scene, but the African varieties would have been much easier to obtain. Pausanias' story about the stag-drawn chariot at Patrai suggests that deer and antelope-like animals could be tamed for draught purposes.

The identification of the βούβαλος is uncertain, but it has been suggested that it is one of the several varieties of hartebeest.[146] Since Tora hartebeest have long, cow-like faces, this variety may have been the origin of Pliny's remark that the bubalus was similar to a calf and a stag and was sometimes mistaken for a wild ox (*HN* viii. 38). Hartebeest were common along the North African coast until the end of the fourth century AD,[147] and the Ptolemies could have obtained them easily. If these 'boubaloi' were not hartebeest, they may have been one of the types of gnu, which have a generally bovine appearance and are common in Africa. Βουβαλίδες are mentioned by Aelian as animals displayed by the Indians (*HA* xiii. 25); these are differentiated from deer, gazelles, oryxes, and asses, and cannot have been hartebeest or gnus which are indigenous to Africa. If the bovine appearance of Pliny's African bubalus was in Aelian's mind, he may be referring to the nilghai, a cow-like animal found only in India.[148] As with the Indian variety of oryx, the 'boubalos' may have been an Indian animal, or alternatively, an African 'cousin' of an animal known to have come from India in order to fit the theme of Dionysus' Indian triumph.

'Ονέλαφος is a word not otherwise attested. Comparable words are τραγέλαφος or 'goat-deer' (apparently some kind of wild goat or antelope known in Arabia (D. S. ii. 51, 2) and the Phasis (Pliny *HN* viii. 120), and ἱππέλαφος or 'horse-deer' (an Indian animal according to Aristotle *HA* 498[b] 32), but Kallixeinos presumably means something different. This 'ass-deer' may be a type of wild ass distinguishable from the ὄνοι ἄγριοι

---

[145] Hull, 83–4; I. T. Sanderson, *Living Mammals of the World* (London, 1955), 262.
[146] Hull, 205, s.v. βούβαλις; Jennison, 32; Toynbee, *Animals*, 146.
[147] Jennison, 32.   [148] Sanderson, 259.

mentioned before,[149] and the varieties of wild ass catalogued in *PCZ* 59075 attest that many different types were known and bred in the third century.

Ostriches are also yoked to chariots in this section, and their rather surprising use as draught animals is not unparalleled in antiquity or modern times.[150] The chariot of Eros is pulled by two ostriches on a late Imperial gem in Munich,[151] and ostriches are ridden by members of a comic chorus on a black-figure skyphos in Boston.[152] (Although these must have been men dressed as ostriches and not real birds on the stage, the scene still shows that the idea of riding ostriches was not unknown.) Oppian says that ostriches were large enough to carry a youth on their backs (*Cyn.* iii. 482 ff.), and the birds are alleged to have been ridden by Firmus, the rich Pretender in Egypt (*SHA*, Firmus, vi. 2). Some corroboration that ostriches were known as 'beasts of burden' in third-century Alexandria may be provided by Pausanias, who says that on Helicon there was a bronze statue of Arsinoe II mounted on an ostrich (ix. 31, 1).[153] In the last century, two Californian ostrich farms provided cart-drawn rides for visitors,[154] and ostrich-cart races have recently been held in a festival in Nevada, USA, which shows that it would have been practicable for eight pairs of ostriches to be harnessed to the chariots in the procession. The birds were available to the Ptolemies in North Africa and the Syrian desert, although they also lived further afield in Africa.[155]

The inclusion of elephant-ἅρματα in this section is significant because the presence of the animals must be seen against their strategic military role in the third century.[156] The fact that the elephants draw ἅρματα, or quadrigae, clearly implies that four beasts are yoked to each vehicle, which makes a total of ninety-six elephants from twenty-four quadrigae,[157] plus a further four elephants pulling the ἅρμα which carries the statue of Alexander later in his own procession (202A; line 228). From calculations

---

[149] Jennison, 32.

[150] For all ancient references to the ostrich see D'Arcy Wentworth Thompson, *A Glossary of Greek Birds* (2nd ed.; London, 1936), 270 ff.; for ostriches in Roman art see Toynbee, *Animals*, 237 ff.

[151] *AGDS* München I-3 No. 2543.

[152] G. M. Sifakis, *Parabasis and Animal Choruses* (London, 1971), Pls. III-IV.

[153] See F. T. Griffiths, *Theocritus at Court, Mnemosyne* Suppl. lv (1979), 59 and n. 21, who thinks that this bird was a phoenix which was mistaken for an ostrich by Pausanias.

[154] Information received from the Librarian of the Reference Department, The City of Pasadena Public Library.

[155] Jennison, 32; Hdt. iv. 175; 192; Pliny *HN* x. 1.

[156] I plan to deal with this question at greater length elsewhere.

[157] H. H. Scullard, *The Elephant in the Greek and Roman World* (London, 1974), 125, however, maintains that a single elephant pulls each chariot on the grounds that Philadelphus could not have had 96 elephants.

of the number of Indian elephants inherited by Ptolemy I from Alexander's original herd, and those won by him from the other Diadochi in
various battles,[158] it seems highly unlikely that Philadelphus could have
owned as many as 100 Indian elephants by the beginning of the third
decade of the third century. Many must have been killed in battle or else
have died of old age (the survival rate of captive elephants used in war
probably did not greatly exceed forty years); moreover, his original Indian
animals had probably not replaced their numbers through reproduction.[159]
Unless he had obtained more Indian elephants by unknown means, some
of the beasts in the procession may have come from Africa,[160] having been
obtained by the king as a result of his efforts to build up a herd which was
a crucial part of his military strength, and which was supplied from a non-
Indian source, since the passage of Indian elephants to Egypt through
hostile Seleucid territory would hardly have been sanctioned.[161] Ptolemaic
explorations along the Red Sea coast are well known, along with the
resulting trading settlements founded there through which African elephants
were shipped to Alexandria in later years, but no regular commercial
traffic is known to have occurred along this route before the last years of
the 270s.[162] The development of the standard supply route of elephants
from the Horn of Africa via the Red Sea ports should be dated later than
that. The elephants which march in the Grand Procession may have been
African animals procured via a Nilotic route into Nubia and the Sudan,
which was explored and exploited before the Red Sea route became the
standard passage for goods obtained from the interior of Africa. Elephants
are known to have lived along the Nile[163] as well as in the Horn of Africa
in antiquity, and the Meroitic civilization which grew up along the river
used elephants in war and ceremonial. Their trained elephants are depicted
in various functions in relief carvings at the site of Musawwarat-es-Sufra

---

[158] Ibid., 124–5.

[159] William Gowers and H. H. Scullard, *Num. Chron.* (6th ser.) x (1950), 275
n. 16; G. M. Allen, *Proc. Acad. Nat. Sci. Philadelphia* lxxxviii (1936), 25–6 (on age in
captivity); Gowers and Scullard, 273, nn. 8–9; 'Elephant', *Encyclopaedia Britannica*
(1970), 273 (on breeding in captivity).

[160] The African elephant used by the Ptolemies and the Carthaginians was the
now extinct Forest elephant, not the huge Bush elephant; cf. Gowers, *African Affairs*
xlvii No. 188 (July, 1948), 173 ff.; Allen, 19–25; Scullard, 23–4, 60 ff.; F. E. Zeuner,
A History of Domesticated Animals (London, 1963), 279 ff.

[161] Jennison, 30–1, believes that the Seleucids may have allowed elephants to pass
through their territory to the Ptolemies, but this is hard to believe since the Seleucids
had a difficult time themselves getting Indian elephants; cf. Strabo 724, for the
extensive lands ceded by Seleucus I to Chandragupta in return for 500 elephants.

[162] *Ptol. Alex.* i. 178 ff.

[163] Pliny, *HN* vi. 180, quoting Bion for a list of towns found along the Nile; one is
mentioned as the place where elephants began to be found. See *Ptol. Alex.* ii. 297
n. 340 for the view that Bion belongs to the 3rd century. For elephants at Meroe,
cf. Pliny, *HN* vi. 185.

about 100 miles north of Khartoum.[164] It has yet to be determined whether the Ptolemies passed knowledge of trained elephants to the Meroitic peoples (in which case Nilotic elephants could probably not have been trained and shipped north to Alexandria before the procession), or whether a supply of already domesticated African beasts was available there to be traded to the Ptolemies in the early third century.[165] The latter possibility cannot be excluded at the present time because of the uncertain dating of the Meroitic sites and the tentative chronology of the Meroitic king-list, upon which the dates of many of the relevant sites depend.[166] It is tempting to suggest that the elephants in the Grand Procession are African animals which came to Alexandria via the riverain route, and that, as such, were among the first African elephants to be obtained by the Ptolemies. Their appearance in the Grand Procession, which included an emphatic display of Ptolemaic military might, would have been a great *coup* and an unmistakable piece of propaganda for the Ptolemies in view of their smouldering hostilities with the Seleucids, who had hitherto monopolized the supply of Indian elephants.

Camels appear twice in the Dionysiac procession. The first group consists of six pairs, three on each side of the stadium preceding the mule-drawn carts which carry the Indian spear-captives (200F; line 172). A second group carries the loads of spices which form part of Dionysus' Indian booty (201A; line 175). The one-humped Arabian camel, or dromedary, was domesticated in the second millennium BC, but although the animal is ideally suited to Egypt's climate, there is no evidence that it was ever used there until Ptolemaic times (except for Curt. Ruf. iv. 7, 12; see below), when references to camels as beasts of burden and transport appear in papyri from the reign of Philadelphus (*PCZ* 59008, 59143, 59207, 59802; *BGU* 1351, 1353). Strabo (815) states that camels were used on routes across the eastern desert linking Alexandria via Coptos with the ports along the Red Sea. Ptolemy II clearly recognized the importance of this animal to the commerce of his kingdom. Since it had been used extensively in the Arabian trading caravans for centuries (mostly for the transport of incense from Arabia and India), the camel was probably introduced into

---

[164] F. Hintze, *Die Inschriften des Löwentempels von Musawwarat es Sufra*, Berl. Abh. 1962 (1); P. L. Shinnie, *Meroe: A Civilization of the Sudan* (London, 1967), 92 ff.

[165] Hintze, *Kush* x (1962), 183–4; Scullard, 130; Shinnie, 101 (for the view that the knowledge spread from south to north); J. Desanges, 'Les Chasseurs d'éléphants d'Abou Simbel', *Actes du 92ième Congrès National des Sociétés Savantes* (Strassburg and Colmar, 1967), 34 ff. (for the view that the knowledge spread from north to south).

[166] For the difficulties in dating some sites and kings see Hintze, *Kush* x (1962), 177 ff.; id., *Kush* xv (1967–8), 285 ff.; id., *Die Inschriften*, 13–19; Shinnie, 35; B. G. Haycock, *Kush* xiii (1965), 264 ff.

Egypt through the steady trading contact with Arabia. The group of camels which carry the spices in the procession therefore perform one of their very common functions in the Ptolemaic world.[167] Both spices and camels also had connections with India and the East which makes their appearance in this section of the Dionysiac procession particularly appropriate. Herodotus records that camels were used in India as early as the fifth century BC (iii. 102), and Alexander, *en route* to India, is said to have used them to carry water on his march to the Siwah Oasis in Egypt (Curt. Ruf. iv. 7, 12). Of the spices appearing in the procession, frankincense and myrrh were Arabian in origin,[168] but cinnamon and cassia were Indian[169] (although most ancient authors (e.g. Hdt. iii. 107) attributed them to Arabia since they were always funnelled westwards through Arabia as a result of the Nabataean monopoly on Indian goods). Arrian, however, notes the delight of Alexander's army when it came upon spices and incense in their natural habitat (*An.* vi. 22, 4 ff.; vii. 20, 2 ff.; *Ind.* 32, 7; 41, 7). The presence of the camels and spices in the procession thus combines connotations of Alexander, India, and the whole eastern, exotic world even as it bears witness to the contemporary spice trade which was so important to the Ptolemies, and to the introduction of a new animal into the national commerce and transport system.

The second major group of animals in the triumphal return from India accompany the hunters and hunting spoil (201B; line 181). *Kynegoi*, who are apparently some kind of official hunters or keepers,[170] lead dogs, of which the three named types, the Indian, the Hyrcanian, and the Molossian, are all famous breeds of hunting dogs known from the ancient world.[171] Their presence here reinforces the papyrological evidence for the breeding of dogs in Ptolemaic Egypt (*PCZ* 59262, 59710, 59712, 59824; in the famous epitaph of the dog Tauron, who died while defending Zenon against a wild boar, the dog is specifically called Indian, ibid., 59532 = *GVI*

[167] For the use of the camel before, during, and after Ptolemaic times see Zeuner, 338 ff.; A. E. Robinson, *SNR* xix (1936), 17 ff.; J. E. Atkinson, *A Commentary on Q. Curtius Rufus' Historiae Alexandri Magni Books 3 and 4* (Amsterdam, 1980), iv. 7, 12 ad loc.

[168] G. N. van Beek, *JAOS* lxxviii (1958), 141 ff.

[169] Ibid., 147; W. H. Schoff, *The Periplus of the Erythraean Sea* (London, 1912), 82 ff.; J. I. Miller, *The Spice Trade of the Roman Empire* (Oxford, 1969), 153 ff. and Index I, s.v. cassia, cinnamon.

[170] For kynegoi, who may have been members of the army who collected animals when on military expeditions, see *RE* s.v. Kynegoi; P. Roussel, *REG* xliii (1930), 361 ff.; C. F. Edson, Jr., *HSCP* xlv (1934), 226 ff.; *Pros. Ptol.* viii, pp. 225–6 (lists of kynegoi); G. T. Griffith, *The Mercenaries of the Hellenistic World* (Cambridge, 1935), 126 and n. 2.

[171] Jennison, 33; Hull, 27, 29 ff.; Toynbee, *Animals*, 102 ff.; Keller, i. 91 ff.; J. Aymard, *Essai sur les chasses romaines* (Paris, 1951), 244–5, 251–4.

1968). The dead animals and birds which are carried along on trees can be understood to be the catch from the hunting.

At the beginning of the third group of animals, four varieties of birds are carried along in cages (201B; line 186), all of them well known in antiquity, and some with Indian connotations to make them especially appropriate to Dionysus' return from India. Parrots were assumed to have an Indian origin by ancient sources,[172] and they first appeared in the Greek world when Nearchus brought some back after Alexander's Indian campaign (*FGrH* 133 F 9). Peacocks had also been Indian birds originally, although known from early times in Greece from the Heraion at Samos where they were sacred.[173] Aelian states that the largest and best peacocks still came from India (*HA* xvi. 2), so the birds acquired by the Ptolemies may consequently have been Indian ones. A story elsewhere in Aelian (*HA* xi. 33) that a sacred Indian peacock was presented to an unidentified Ptolemy (who dedicated the bird to Zeus Polieus) shows that these birds were revered in Egypt. Like the parrot, the peacock had a special tie with Alexander, who was so stunned by the beauty of the Indian birds that he protected them under a heavy penalty (*HA* v. 21). Peacocks seem to have had a special tie with Dionysus in Ptolemaic Egypt since they are represented in the Dionysiac reliefs along the dromos of the Serapeum at Memphis, which were carved during the early Ptolemaic period.[174] Guinea-fowl originated in Africa but were familiar in Greece since classical times.[175] There was an alternative, and probably incorrect, tradition that they had originated in India (Sophocles, *TGF* (Radt) iv. fr. 830a), which may account for their appearance in the Indian triumph. Despite the familiarity of the birds in Greece, and the fact that they were bred in the Palaces in the time of Euergetes II, these birds were evidently considered sufficiently rare or special to be carried in cages in this part of the procession.

The description of the other birds in this section is confused textually. The manuscripts preserve the following reading (line 187 adnot.): καὶ φασιανοὶ ὄρνιθες καὶ ἄλλοι Αἰθιοπικοί, πλήθει πολλοί, but Athenaeus, in a later discussion of pheasants, quotes Kallixeinos in slightly different words (387C-D): καὶ φασιανοὶ καὶ ὄρνιθες Αἰθιοπικοί, πλήθει πολλοί. In the manuscript version of the text, the substantive noun φασιανός is used as an adjective instead of the common adjectival form φασιανικός (cf. Ath. 386

---

[172] For ancient references to the parrot see Thompson, 335 ff.

[173] Ibid., 277; cf. Menodotos *ap.* Athenaeus 655A.

[174] J.-Ph. Lauer and Ch. Picard, *Les Statues ptolémaïques du Sarapieion de Memphis* (Paris, 1955), Pls. 19-20; for the date of these sculptures see *Ptol. Alex.* i. 255.

[175] Thompson, 198 ff.; J. Pollard, *Birds in Greek Life and Myth* (London, 1977), 94.

D ff. *passim*) and ἄλλοι Αἰθιοπικοί is a strange ellipse even if ὄρνιθες is supplied from φασιανοὶ ὄρνιθες. Moreover, ἄλλοι may imply that many of the preceding birds came also from 'Ethiopia' (which does not have the modern geographical designation, but is a general adjective meaning African), but guinea-fowl are the only native Africans among otherwise Indian birds. Pheasants may also be included in the latter category: as its name implies, the bird came originally from the Phasis River in Colchis and was known in Greece in classical times,[176] but Aelian says that they were raised as treasured pets in the royal parks of India (*HA* xiii. 18). This Indian association, which shows the birds' value in the East, may explain their inclusion in the Dionysiac triumph. Pheasants were, in any case, specially bred in Alexandria in the second century (see above, p. 87). If the alternative, and preferable, text is accepted from Athenaeus 387D, which involves only slight palaeographical changes, φασιανοί appears more comfortably as the substantive noun, Αἰθιοπικοί modifies ὄρνιθες (which removes the awkward ellipse), and the ambiguous ἄλλοι disappears. If, then, 'Ethiopian' birds are mentioned as a separate category, the types are not specified, although possible African birds would have been ibis, egrets, flamingoes, etc.[177]

The list of other animals on parade continues after the abbreviation of Kallixeinos' full list. First march herds of Ethiopian, Arabian, and Euboean sheep (201B-C; line 189). The Zenon Papyri attest that sheep were raised extensively in Ptolemaic Egypt,[178] and the Arabian breed is specifically mentioned (*PCZ* 59287, 59405, 59430; see also Strabo 783-4). Strabo also mentions an Ethiopian breed of sheep (822), and Euboea did have several kinds of sheep which were especially noted for fine, soft wool.[179] Twenty-six Indian cattle appear next, which must be one species of the humped, white oxen well known in India, perhaps the zebu.[180] These animals need not have come directly from India, since that type of white Indian cattle have been bred on the shores of the Mediterranean since the time of the Assyrians and would have been available to the Ptolemies from there.[181] Arrian emphasizes that the Indians were great raisers of oxen (*Ind.* 11, 11), and that Alexander was made a special present of Indian cattle at Taxila (*An.* v. 3, 5), which suggests that these beasts may have a particular significance in the Indian triumph. Ethiopian cattle, which follow the Indian variety in the procession, existed in several varieties and were known in Egypt for centuries, since they are represented in dynastic Egyptian art.[182]

[176] Pollard, 93-4; Thompson, 298 ff.; Toynbee, *Animals*, 254 ff.
[177] Jennison, 34.   [178] Rostovtzeff, *Large Estate*, 113 ff.
[179] Keller, i. 314.   [180] Jennison, 34; Toynbee, *Animals*, 149.
[181] Jennison, 34.   [182] Keller, i. 332.

The single large, white bear has provoked a great deal of discussion. It has been suggested that this is a polar bear, whose presence would have been dramatic evidence of indirect Ptolemaic trade with the furthest points of the known world,[183] but, although it is not impossible that polar bears had been traded from some remote Scythian tribe to a Greek colony on the Black Sea and thence to Egypt (the saiga antelopes may have come via this route), a polar bear would probably not have survived the Egyptian climate for long. Other types of white bears seem more likely. Pausanias says that white bears were indigenous to Thrace (viii. 17, 3), and these may have crossed the Mediterranean through trade arising from the close marriage ties which the Ptolemies once had with Lysimachus, King of Thrace, even before Thrace became a Ptolemaic province in the middle of the 3rd century BC. The bear may also have been an albino specimen—an unusual albino would surely have been much sought after because of its rarity, and this may have been the reason why it marched alone—perhaps of the light-brown Syrian bears,[184] or of a Cyrenaican bear, if the ἄρκος mentioned in a sacral law at Cyrene as the recipient of substantial portions of sacrifices (including the skin and the head) is a real bear and not the title of the priestess (*SEG* 9, 72, 97 ff.; cf. ibid., 13, 12). Although Magas, the viceroy of Cyrene, revolted from Egypt some time within the 270s, relations continued to be maintained between the two countries,[185] and bears may have been traded as part of the commercial traffic.

The next animals to appear are members of the cat family (201C; line 192). The παρδάλεις and πάνθηροι (an otherwise unattested plural of πάνθηρ; cf. πάνθηρες) have been identified as leopards and (possibly) cheetahs respectively.[186] Πάνθηρ more commonly means genet, but this small cat is perhaps out of place among the other large cats in this group. Both leopards and cheetahs are found in Asia and Africa and could have been obtained by the Ptolemies (both are represented in the painted tomb at Marissa (Mareshah) in Israel[187]). Their appearance here is noteworthy

---

[183] Tarn, *JEA* xiv (1928), 247.

[184] Jennison, 34.

[185] E. Will, *Histoire politique du monde hellénistique* (2nd ed., Nancy, 1979), i. 145 ff., 243.

[186] Jennison, 34; for a discussion of the problem of distinguishing the names of these cats see ibid., 183 ff.; Hull, 98 ff.

[187] Tomb I of the necropolis of Marissa contains a remarkable painted hunting scene which includes several animals, some identified by inscriptions. Ptolemaic influence was strong in Idumaea in the 3rd century BC, and the Hellenistic Sidonian colony shared the culture of contemporary Egypt. This is borne out by the resemblances between the art in these tombs and contemporary Ptolemaic funerary art. The animal painting in Tomb I reflects Ptolemaic interest in animals, and indicates some of the types of wild beasts which were known, if only by report, at that time. For the site of Marissa see F. J. Bliss and R. A. S. Macalister, *Excavations in Palestine during the Years 1898-1900* (London, 1902), 52 ff.; 67-70; for a description of the

since the leopard was sacred to Dionysus. The word λύγξ describes both
the spotted lynx (found only in northern Europe and Asia north of the
Caspian Sea) and the unspotted caracal (found in Africa and India), which,
because of its provenance, is probably the animal appearing here. The lynx
is often depicted yoked to the chariot of Dionysus and Ariadne, perhaps
because the spotted lynx was found in Macedonia and was associated with
the orgiastic rites of Dionysus.[188] The inclusion of the animal here may be
explained not only because of its place in Dionysiac ritual, but also because
of its associations with Alexander and India: in the *Alexander Romance*
(Ps.-Call. III 17, 20, ed. Kroll), Alexander writes to Aristotle that he has
seen λύγγες along with other wild animals in the course of his journey.
The caracal appears in reliefs from dynastic Egypt[189] as well as in the
Marissa tomb-painting (along with an unidentified animal which resembles
a lynx),[190] which suggests that the Ptolemies could have obtained it easily.
The meaning of the rare word ἄρκηλος is not certain since Aelian says that
leopard cubs as well as another kind of leopard both bore the name (*HA*
vii. 47). Although the word sounds as though it is cognate to ἄρκος (bear),
some type of feline is probably meant, given the place of this animal
among members of the cat family.

Like the white bear, the giraffe appears alone, which may be a reflection of the animal's rarity in Ptolemaic Egypt. This supposition is reinforced
by the depiction of a giraffe in the Marissa painting,[191] where the odd
representation suggests that the artist worked from a description rather
than from personal observation. Giraffes lived further north along the
Nile in antiquity than they do today. A graffito of a giraffe in the Great
Enclosure at Musawwarat-es-Sufra[192] in the Sudan may be later than the
period of the site's use, but its presence there indicates that the climate
was once temperate enough near Meroe for giraffes to be known in the
area. Giraffes appear on painted pottery from the Karanòg cemetery in
Nubia,[193] which dates from the early centuries AD, possibly inspired by
the artists' memories of the wildlife further south in their original home

---

necropolis and tomb see J. P. Peters and H. Thiersch, *Painted Tombs in the Necropolis
of Marissa* (London, 1905). For the leopard see ibid., 23–4 and Pl. VI; for the
cheetah, 24 and Pl. VII.

[188] W. F. Otto, *Dionysos*, 104 ff.; Keller, i. 84.
[189] Keller, i. 82; Figs. 28a–b.
[190] Peters and Thiersch, 28 and Pl. XV (caracal); 27 and Pl. XIII (other animal).
[191] Ibid., 25 and Pl. VIII.
[192] Seen by myself on the north side of the west wall of Room 202 in the Great
Enclosure.
[193] C. L. Woolley and D. Randall-MacIver, *Karanòg: The Romano-Nubian
Cemetery* (Philadelphia, 1910), iv. Pl. 41 No. 8183; Pl. 42–3 No. 8293; Pl. 53 No.
8154; Pl. 61 No. 8213.

(probably around the Dongola reach, much further north than Meroe).[194] Unlike those in the Marissa painting, these giraffes are life-like and suggest that their makers knew real giraffes. If giraffes did live in Upper Nubia in ancient times,[195] they would have been within easy access for the Ptolemies, especially if the Ptolemies exploited the route along the Nile in their search for elephants. Later, they may have been obtained from the Horn of Africa and shipped north via the Red Sea ports. Alexandria may then have been the source of many of the giraffes sent outside Africa; Varro mentions a giraffe which had recently arrived in Rome from Alexandria (*De Ling. Lat.* v. 100).

The final animal in the parade of beasts is a single Ethiopian rhinoceros, the two-horned variety (as opposed to the one-horned Indian type),[196] and certainly the White Ethiopian animal which is much more docile than the Black Ethiopian one. Found today in the southern Sudan, rhinoceroses, like giraffes, once lived further north; Pliny says that they came as far north as Meroe in his day (*HN* vi. 185), and thus they would have been accessible to the Ptolemies through trade or exploration. (Pliny, ibid., 173 says that rhinoceros horns were traded by the Ethiopians.) A peculiar representation of a two-horned Ethiopian rhinoceros in the Marissa painting[197] provides further evidence that this animal was known on the fringes of the Mediterranean. The one-horned Indian rhinoceros was encountered for the first time during Alexander's campaigns in India (Curt. Ruf. viii. 9, 16; ix. 1, 5); this suggests that its African counterpart may have had a special significance in the Indian triumph of Dionysus.

Many of the animals in this parade had an original connection with India, Alexander, and Dionysus, but many were African in origin and are specifically called 'Ethiopian'. Certainly African animals would have been more readily available to the Ptolemies than those from the East, but there may be other reasons why African animals appear in a triumphal train returning from India. Various mythological traditions associate Dionysus with Arabia, Libya, and Egypt, where he established himself over his defeated opponents as a divine king (D. S. iii. 62 ff., *passim*). Like Dionysus, Alexander also conquered Egypt before he went to India, and the letter of the Ethiopian queen Candace to Alexander, preserved in the *Alexander Romance* (Ps.-Call. III 18, 5 ff., ed. Kroll), records a list of animals sent as gifts to Alexander (parrots, elephants, παρδάλεις, rhinoceroses, πάνθηρες, and fierce dogs) as well as tribute, which is in striking similarity to that recorded in Kallixeinos (Ethiopian youths, ivory caskets and tusks, ebony logs, and gold). Although the letter of Candace is clearly fanciful, it may have stemmed from the tradition of Alexander as the

---

[194] B. G. Haycock, *JEA* liii (1967), 117.   [195] Ibid., n. 2.
[196] Toynbee, *Animals*, 125.   [197] Peters and Thiersch, 26 and Pl. X.

conqueror of the eastern desert and the inheritor of its fabulous spoils. The Indian triumph of Dionysus in the procession may be a composite triumphal train which by rights could have included African as well as Indian spoils, and which, on both counts, could symbolize a hypothetical triumphal train of Alexander. A further explanation for the appearance of African and Indian animals and spoils side by side may have been the fact that Alexander is known to have thought that the Nile was somehow connected to the Indus River or that both flowed from a common source (he believed that he had found the source of the Nile in India; Arr. *An.* vi. 1; Strabo 696). Consequently, Indian and African animals may have been considered more or less interchangeable if they were thought to originate from the same general geographical source. Arrian's remark that India and Ethiopia were similar geographically and in terms of their inhabitants (*Ind.* 6, 5 ff.) may derive from this belief in their geographical link.

7. *Dionysus at the Altar of Rhea* (201C)   The part of the Dionysiac procession which follows the triumphal return of Dionysus from India presents numerous textual, mythological, and historical difficulties which previous discussions have not completely disentangled. As the text stands in the manuscripts, the cart which appears after the rhinoceros apparently contains one large tableau: Dionysus at the Altar of Rhea, and a group of Alexander, Ptolemy Soter, Priapus, Arete, and Corinth preceding personifications of Cycladic, Ionian, and Asian cities (201C–D; line 194). It is clear that the characters of a more or less contemporary, historical nature have little to do with the mythological scene of Dionysus at the Altar of Rhea, and that two distinct tableaux have been run together because of a lacuna in the text after the description of the statue of Hera in the Rhea scene. Ehrenberg supplied the required sense of the missing words: ⟨μετὰ δὲ ταύτην εἵπετο ἄλλη τετράκυκλος (then the measurements), ἐφ᾽ ἧς ἦν⟩ ᾽Αλεξάνδρου . . .[198] This suggestion complies with the words used to introduce the other carts, satisfactorily completes the otherwise incomplete sentence beginning with ᾽Αλεξάνδρου, separates two scenes which are thematically distinct, removes the problem of Priapus appearing twice in one scene, and restores one scene to each cart in agreement with all the other carts.

The scene depicting Dionysus' absolution at the Altar of Rhea is yet one more in the series of tableaux illustrating events from the mythological life of the god, but its rarity in ancient art and literature requires some comment. According to a legend known as far back as the fifth century, Dionysus was afflicted with madness by Hera in revenge for her husband's infidelity with Semele (Eur. *Cyclops* 3 ff.), but the story of his absolution

---

[198] *Alexander and the Greeks* (Oxford, 1938), 6.

by Rhea after madness-induced wanderings is preserved only in the
Bibliotheke of Ps.-Apollodorus (iii. v. 1): Διόνυσος δὲ εὑρετὴς ἀμπέλου
γενόμενος, Ἥρας μανίαν αὐτῷ ἐμβαλούσης περιπλανᾶται Αἴγυπτόν τε καὶ
Συρίαν. καὶ τὸ μὲν πρῶτον Πρωτεὺς αὐτὸν ὑποδέχεται βασιλεὺς Αἰγυπτίων,
αὖθις δὲ εἰς Κύβελα τῆς Φρυγίας ἀφικνεῖται, κἀκεῖ καθαρθεὶς ὑπὸ Ῥέας καὶ
τὰς τελετὰς ἐκμαθών, καὶ λαβὼν παρ᾽ ἐκείνης τὴν στολήν, ἐπὶ Ἰνδοὺς διὰ
τῆς Θρᾴκης ἠπείγετο.[199] Dionysus was associated with Phrygia from the
time of Euripides, in whose poetry the Dionysiac orgiastic rites are compared to the equally frenzied Phrygian rituals in honour of the native
Phrygian goddess Cybele (*Bacchae* 58 ff.; 78 ff.). Cybele, the Asiatic
'Mother of the Gods', was frequently identified with Rhea, her European
counterpart (ibid.), a fact which explains the εἰς Κύβελα in the passage of
Ps.-Apollodorus as a garbled reference to the association between the
goddesses. It is the eastern goddess, Rhea-Cybele, from whom Dionysus
gains absolution. The editors of Ps.-Apollodorus have seen that this passage
is incomprehensible as it stands and that ἐπὶ Ἰνδοὺς is intrusive (see also
Ps.-Ap. iii. v. 2); if Dionysus is to be understood as being in Phrygia, it is
geographically meaningless to say that he then hurried through Thrace
(which is west of Phrygia) against the Indians, when the following passage
describes his encounter with Lycurgus, a Thracian king. Such convolutions
are more in the manner of the *Alexander-Romance*. Wagner (Teubner ed.,
1894, ad loc.) suggested either omitting ἐπὶ Ἰνδοὺς, or supplying a word
such as στρατεύσας (on the evidence of D. S. iv. 3, 1), to give the meaning
'and after marching against the Indians (i.e. from Phrygia), he hastened
through Thrace' (where he encountered Lycurgus, etc.). Given the pro-
liferation of legends about Dionysus (besides Ps.-Ap., see also D. S. iii.
62 ff.; iv. 1, 6 ff.), there exists no canonical order for his wanderings which
can be applied to elucidate this passage, nor, conversely, can the passage of
Ps.-Apollodorus be used as evidence for the sequence of the god's wanderings, both because of its textual difficulties and because of the nature of
the *Bibliotheke*, which is in essence an uncritical redaction of various
mythological fables taken from the poets and compiled about the middle
of the first century BC. All that can be said is that the Grand Procession
clearly preserves the legend whereby Dionysus was absolved by Rhea *after*
his Indian expedition, presumably upon his return from the East back into
Greece. The location of this 'altar of Rhea' is not given, but her traditional
association with the Phrygian Cybele argues that it is to be thought of as in

[199] There was an alternate version that Dionysus consulted the oracle at Dodona
in order to seek absolution from the madness induced by Hera. This tradition may be
based on a story in the *Catasterisms* of Eratosthenes; the sources are collected in C.
Robert, *Eratosth. Catast. Reliq.* (1878 [1963]), 90 ff. This association plays no
part in this scene of the Altar of Rhea, but see below, p. 131, for its possible relation
to the appearance of the 'precincts at Dodona' in the procession.

the East. This clear order of events should perhaps be used as evidence in support of the emendation of the passage in Ps.-Apollodorus; if the reading ἐπὶ Ἰνδούς is indeed regarded as an interpolation, the passage relates the same sequence of events as the Dionysiac procession.

In the tableau on the cart, Priapus appears as a fitting companion to Dionysus (as is emphasized by his ivy crown) on the assumption that he, the god's son, had shared his father's sufferings and was a fellow recipient of the absolution granted by Rhea.[200] The statue of Hera is dramatically necessary in the scene to indicate the reason behind the absolution which is depicted. This myth is extremely rare in Greek art; I am aware of no parallel either on classical Greek vases or on the numerous Imperial Dionysiac sarcophagi, although the scene has been unconvincingly identified on a relief from Cos.[201] Its appearance as a major feature in Dionysiac legend in third-century Alexandria is therefore all the more striking. Its rarity elsewhere leads to the speculation that the legend of Dionysus' absolution by Rhea derived from local Alexandrian traditions about the god, and that Ps.-Apollodorus took his account of this event from an Alexandrian source, perhaps from a lost tragedy or even from Kallixeinos. Whether or not the Coan relief is accepted as a representation of this scene (if indeed Cos is its original provenance[202]), an interesting link appears between Philadelphus (the organizer of the Grand Procession and presumably the arbiter of its mythological bias), Cos (his birthplace), and Rhea (who, along with the Great Mother, had a public cult and priesthood at Cos, and, so far as is known, only there[203]). Rhea's place in Dionysiac myth may have been deliberately emphasized by the king because of the goddess's Coan connections, which may in turn explain the local, Alexandrian importance of the scene. This tableau is the final illustration of scenes

---

[200] H. Herter, *De Priapo* (Giessen, 1932), 76.

[201] O. Benndorf and G. Niemann, *Reisen in Lykien und Karien, Reisen in Südwestlichen Kleinasien* i (Vienna, 1884), 13-14 and Pl. II, have identified a relief slab in the Castle at Cos as an illustration of this scene. From left to right, the sculpture consists of an altar with a snake on it, a female figure (who perhaps holds a thyrsos) facing it, a draped female in the centre who moves right with both arms outstretched, and, on the right, a (?) bearded male who supports himself against an unadorned altar, looking back at the central figure. Although it seems that this scene *could* portray Dionysus fleeing Hera, there are no distinctive iconographic features which clinch the identification, nor can the left scene be linked to the right scene. B. and N. identify the altar and the snake with 'die Schlangenfütterung der orphisch-sabazischen Mysterien', but this is clearly fanciful.

[202] B. and N., ibid., who took the word of other scholars quoted ad loc., have suggested that the provenance of this relief is not Cos, but that it came there with other sculpture found by Newton at Cnidus.

[203] Cf. S. M. Sherwin-White, *Ancient Cos, Hypomnemata* li (Göttingen, 1978), 324-5 and n. 315. The priesthood of the Great Mother is known in the early 3rd century, and that of Rhea in the 2nd, but little is known of these cults beyond the mere fact of their existence.

from the life of Dionysus (unless others have fallen out of the text), and it is noteworthy that the sequence seems to stop before the god's entry into Greece and return to Thebes. This is perhaps due to the wish to present the Indian Triumph as the culmination of the god's career, which is thematically necessary since it celebrates indirectly the glory of Alexander and through him of the Ptolemaic dynasty. Since this aspect of Dionysus has primary importance in the procession, the subsequent exploits of his life faded in comparison and were not depicted. The absolution of Dionysus can be seen as the appropriate end to the eastern saga in the life of the god.

8. *Statues of Alexander, Ptolemy I, Corinth, etc.* (201D–E)   The cart which follows does not belong to the same mythological context, and although its contemporary figures do not give it, prima facie, a Dionysiac character, the presence of Priapus, the cup-stand, and krater indicates that the scene belongs beside the others in the Dionysiac procession. However, no satisfactory interpretation of the composition of this tableau is evident: there are possible indications of further textual difficulties, and the reason for the presence of many figures is obscure. Many scholars have emended the text, as well as filling the lacuna already noted, because the several repetitions of phrases and motifs in this section may easily have led to errors of duplication: for example, it seems curious that Priapus appears on two successive carts, and Arete and Corinth are both said to be παρ-εστῶσα τῷ Πτολεμαίῳ although the thematically consecutive description of the two figures is interrupted by the intrusive mention of the second Priapus. It is also difficult to understand the scene as it stands in the existing, unemended text because the transmitted account is itself open to various interpretations (cf. the uncertain position of the second Priapus, who is described as συμπαρῆν αὐτοῖς, which could refer to Arete and Ptolemy, or, because Corinth is also said to be standing beside Ptolemy, to perhaps another combination of figures like Alexander and Ptolemy). Consequently, interpretations of this scene which are based upon the transmitted text vary according to the different arrangement of figures within it.[204]

Much of the general obscurity, and hence the subsequent emendation and discussion, surrounds the figure of Corinth, whose presence is not readily explicable. The presence of the city must have some historical implications, and it is probably to be understood as a personification of

---

[204] For the purposes of this discussion, the scene will be discussed as it is described in the transmitted account of Kallixeinos, on the assumption that he describes the figures in the order in which they appear to the observer: in this arrangement, Ptolemy is flanked by Arete and Corinth, and Priapus stands somewhere near Alexander, Ptolemy, or Arete (his position cannot be determined exactly). If raised platforms were used on the cart, all the figures would have been visible even if some stood behind others.

the Corinthian League (see below) over which Alexander presided after the death of its founder Philip II. Corinth's pre-eminence in the procession over the figures of the Greek cities of Ionia, Asia, and the Islands has been interpreted as evidence for a close relation between the League and the eastern Greek cities, and of the subordination of the latter to the former. Although Alexander's treatment of the eastern cities is an unsolved problem which hinges on their possible membership of the Corinthian League, this interpretation of the figures would endow the scene with a specific political meaning. Some have maintained that Alexander restored the freedom of these cities, which became his free allies probably united to the League, and that the procession provides evidence for this view. An emendation by Wilamowitz (noted by Kaibel, ad loc.) strengthens the connection between Alexander and Corinth by rearranging the position of figures in the text, which makes such a historical extrapolation more likely: Κόρινθος δ' ἡ πόλις παρεστῶσα ⟨τῷ 'Αλεξάνδρῳ⟩ instead of παρεστῶσα τῷ Πτολεμαίῳ.[205] (It has already been mentioned that the odd repetition of παρεστῶσα τῷ Πτολεμαίῳ may indicate a textual corruption, and the name of Ptolemy could have been mistakenly copied from the previous line, replacing the name of another.) Even the proponents of this view of Alexander's treatment of the eastern cities have expressed hesitation that this would be directly reflected in an Alexandrian procession some sixty years later.[206] This very improbability has been correctly taken by others as an indication that the scene could not in fact signify the eastern cities' membership in the League even if this were a historical certainty,[207] but no single satisfactory or comprehensive explanation for this scene has been proposed.

Two allegorical explanations of the figures on this cart must also be rejected, both based upon an incident told in the *Apology* of Prodicus (Xen. *Mem.* ii. 1, 21 ff.), where Herakles arrives at the crossroads of his life, and, forced to choose between the paths of virtue and vice, chooses the path of virtue.[208] In these interpretations of the scene, the 'triangle' is

[205] This interpretation of the scene was accepted by Wilcken, *SB Berl. Akad.* xvi (1922), 106-7; H. Berve, *Das Alexanderreich auf Prosopographischer Grundlage* (Munich, 1926), i. 250; P. Zancan, *Il Monarcato ellenistico nei suoi elementi federativi* (Padua, 1934), 12 and n. 2.

[206] Wilcken, *SB Berl. Akad.* xvi (1922), 107 n. 1.

[207] Ehrenberg, *Alexander*, 3-4, 8; W. W. Tarn, *Alexander the Great* (Cambridge, 1948), ii. 230. Wilcken, *SB Berl. Akad.* xxviii (1938), 302 n. 5, was later convinced by this argument and retracted his statements about Alexander and the East Greek cities.

[208] For an extraordinary interpretation of this scene with Ptolemy as Herakles facing the divergent paths of ἀρετή and ἡδονή (symbolized by a Corinth dressed in the guise of Aphrodite since Corinth was the seat of a cult of Aphrodite famous for its harlots), see G. W. Elderkin, *Klio* (n.F. xv) xxxiii (1940), 170 ff. Picard has written at length on the various representations of the *Apology* in art and literature, whether

composed of Ptolemy in the role of Herakles, Arete as 'virtue', and either Corinth or Priapus as 'vice'. Many factors argue against these identifications. Firstly, an allegory which publicly presents Ptolemy I, the founder of the dynasty and father of the current king, as poised between virtue and vice, is grotesque and inappropriate in the Grand Procession which elsewhere glorifies the virtue of the Ptolemaic house. Even if this objection can be overcome, these figures, appearing as they do in the company of other figures on the cart as well as in the wider context of the Dionysiac procession, cannot be interpreted as artificial triads of characters illustrating a specific myth as a fable within a fable. There is, moreover, an iconographical objection to the allegory. There must have been an unmistakable visual or written indication that 'Corinth' was meant to represent Corinth, or else Kallixeinos would hardly have called the figure by that name. If the statue was either labelled, or shown visually to be, Corinth, it could hardly stand for something else like 'vice', and furthermore, 'vice' could itself have been personified as Arete was. Finally, the suitability of Herakles as the main figure behind this allegory is doubtful in the context. Although the Ptolemies did at times stress a relationship to Herakles (cf. *FGrH* 631; Theoc. xvii. 13 ff.), the god appears nowhere in the Grand Procession, perhaps as the result of a deliberate, dynastic preference for an exclusive relationship with Dionysus. If, as seems likely, the appearance of Herakles in his own godhead was excluded for a particular reason,[209] the assumption that he is represented by another figure as the main character of an allegory, when this is nowhere made explicit, cannot be accepted.

The failure to discover a convincing allegorical interpretation of Corinth suggests that the figure does in fact have some contemporary significance even if it does not provide specific evidence about Alexander's possible inclusion of the eastern cities in the Corinthian League. Corinth wears a diadem, which is significant for the interpretation of the figure and of the

portrayed literally as the 'Choice of Herakles', or as an allegory; cf. *CRAI* 1951, 310 ff.; *Rev. Arch.* 6th ser. xlii (1953), 10 ff.; *REG* lxv (1952), xiv–xv. Hinks, *Myth and Allegory*, 114, is unconvinced that any artistic representation of this group survives. In *CRAI*, 1951, 313 ff., Picard also interprets Ptolemy as the Herakles of the scene who must choose between ἀρετή and κακία (in this case, Priapus depicted as the lascivious fertility god). These interpretations in terms of 'Herakles' Choice' seem quite unsuitable to the context, and are surely very fanciful.

[209] One reason for the genealogical bias in the Grand Procession may be that the family of Antigonus I also claimed descent from Herakles and the Argead house from a point as far back as the 5th century, perhaps beginning with Philip, the father of Antigonus I. His successors could claim dynastic legitimacy from a relationship to the house of Philip II and Alexander through their common ancestor, Herakles; cf. C. F. Edson, Jr., *HSCP* xlv (1934), 213 ff., and esp. p. 226. If Herakles was being claimed as the ancestral god of the Macedonian kings, the positive choice of the Ptolemies in favour of Dionysus may be explained.

scene as a whole. Given the current importance of the diadem in the Hellenistic world, Corinth's diadem must give her a political, or at least a contemporary, meaning, although one need not insist with Tarn that the diadem meant that Corinth had to symbolize a 'Sovereign State'.[210] Originally the prerogative of the Persian kings, the diadem was adopted by Alexander and was worn as a sign of kingship by several of his successors (Arr. vii. 22, 2; Justin xii. 3, 8; D. S. xvii. 77, 5; Plut. *Demetr.* xviii).[211] The assumption of the diadem, and hence the kingship, by various Diadochi had important political connotations. Antigonus I and Demetrius Poliorcetes took the title of king and wore the diadem after their successes against Ptolemy I in Cyprus in 306, and Ptolemy assumed the diadem in response when Antigonus and Demetrius failed to press their victory with a direct attack on Egypt. The rivalry between the opposing kings seems clear in this imitative action, even if Antigonus was laying claim to the whole heritage of Alexander while Ptolemy was only claiming sovereignty in Egypt, perhaps as a warning to Antigonus.[212] This rivalry became publicly polarized when each party claimed the diadem, and Corinth's diadem must be significant since the rivalry continued throughout the first decades of the third century.

The figure of Corinth, accompanied by Alexander, Ptolemy, Arete, and Priapus, appears on the cart which is followed by representations of the cities of the Islands, Ionia, and Asia which had been under the control of the Persians. The fact that these last figures are specifically described as ὅσαι . . . ὑπὸ τοὺς Πέρσας ἐτάχθησαν supports the view that this scene has some contemporary significance. (There must have been some sign or banner giving this information.) This precise phrase is unlikely to have had a mere geographical connotation in view of the fact that Alexander had conquered the Persian Empire in, even then, an almost legendary expedition, which could hardly be considered a remote event or a complicated political problem in the same way as his treatment of the eastern Greek cities.[213] The reference to the Persians must have been important or else the figures would not have been described in those exact terms. Since Corinth is also a city, it is a natural deduction that there is a relationship between her and the following cities, and although the other cities follow the whole cart and not any one figure on it, they must be somehow subordinate to it and its contents. Since Corinth alone of the cities appears on the cart, she must be pre-eminent among the cities, a hypothesis which is supported by her diadem. The reason for such pre-eminence can only be the League of Corinth which had been founded by Philip II, since one of

[210] Alexander, ii. 230–1.   [211] See also *RE* s.v. Diadema.
[212] Cf. Will, *Hist. pol.* i². 75 ff.
[213] *Pace* Ehrenberg, *Alex.* 7–8; cf. F. Miltner, *Klio* xxvi (n.F. viii) (1933), 43 n. 6.

the acts of this League had been a promise of support for him in his war of revenge against the Persians who had attacked various East Greek cities. Alexander was of course the inheritor and executor of this war. The reference to Persia seems to hark back to the founding of the League, which continued to exist (if only in theory) as an important medium of Greek freedom when the oppressors of the Greeks changed from the Persians to various of the Diadochi with designs on Greece. Given this continuing importance of the idea of the Corinthian League as the means by which the Hellenistic monarchs professed to liberate the Greeks and gain their support, Corinth may indeed symbolize the leadership of Greece (indicated by the diadem), and her appearance here beside Ptolemy and Alexander is relevant to the attitude both had towards Greece. By following the cart, the cities indicate that they had been freed by Alexander through the ideals of the Corinthian League, and that their freedom was being protected, if only symbolically, by Ptolemy. In view of these considerations, the scene publicly represents past Ptolemaic 'policy' as well as future goals.[214] As far as the past is concerned, the whole Dionysiac procession emphasizes the continuing tie of the Ptolemies to Alexander through Dionysus, and the achievements of Ptolemy become comparable with those of Alexander because of this legitimizing relationship between them. The mutual achievements of both regarding Greece are therefore relevant. Alexander was supreme over the Greek cities, having inherited this position and the hegemony over the Corinthian League from his father, and, in a sense, Ptolemy theoretically inherited this supremacy from Alexander even as he had actually acquired Egypt. Ptolemy I had publicly proclaimed himself as the *de facto* heir by his unsuccessful yet vocal attempt to refound the League of Corinth in 309/8 and by his intervention in the liberation of the Greeks.[215] If the Ptolemies appear as the legitimate heirs of Alexander in the Grand Procession, they likewise appear as the heirs of his hegemony in Greece since the idea of this hegemony was an important

---

[214] Ehrenberg, 4–5, believes that the scene can only refer to the present and future, while Tarn, *Alexander*, i. 229 ff., prefers the view that it refers to the past although he thinks that 'Corinth' cannot be explained.

[215] The historical background of this event is complex. Ptolemy made a hasty peace with Demetrius Poliorcetes in the East and set sail for Greece ostensibly to liberate the Greek cities (D. S. xx. 37, 1–3; Will, *Hist. pol.* i². 68 ff.: id., *REA* lxvi (1964), 320 ff.; see ibid., 322 for the date 309/8). Ptolemy called all the Greeks together at the Isthmus (Suda Δ 431), which probably refers to a proclamation of intent to renew the League (cf. Will. *Hist. pol.* i². 69; G. Moser, *Untersuchungen über die Politik Ptolemaeos I in Griechenland* (Diss. Inaug., Leipzig, 1914), 55–6; W. Kolbe, *Hermes* li (1916), 532; H. Bengtson, *Strategie*, i. 144). Ptolemy was unsuccessful; he retreated from Greece and patched up a peace with Cassander in which each retained the cities he was holding (D. S. xx. 37. 2). F. Miltner, *Klio* xxvi (n.F. viii) (1933), 43 and n. 6, and T. Lenschau, ib., xxxiii (n.F. xv) (1940), 216, also consider this event as the background to the scene on the cart.

instrument of Macedonian control and anti-Macedonian propaganda.[216] In this context, Ptolemy II was praised by Theocritus as the ruler of many Greek peoples (xvii. 85-90), among them the Ionians, Asians, and Islanders, who follow the cart in this scene. The cart represents the public aspect of past Ptolemaic interest in the mainland for some decades before the Grand Procession, although this interest was neither aggressive nor altruistic towards the Greeks but calculated to keep Macedon away from Egypt and her eastern possessions and entangled on the mainland (which was an area of vested interest to her) out of fear of Egyptian intervention there.

The view that the scene on the cart symbolized past Ptolemaic actions toward Greece is corroborated by the inscription of the Nesiotic League (*SIG*[3] 390) *c.*280 BC which stresses the importance to Ptolemy of all the Greeks and their liberation, and explicitly praises his successes regarding both, only a few years before the probable date of this procession. Although the cart may therefore, on the one hand, have celebrated the success of the Ptolemaic 'containment' policy regarding Macedon (especially since the feared Demetrius had recently died in 283), the scene at the same time represents political aims for the future, since it was a public statement that Greece and the revitalized Corinthian League would continue to play an important role in Ptolemaic strategy. Such claims may have been intended as a veiled warning to Antigonus Gonatas, who was currently trying to consolidate his position in Macedon, that ideological supremacy in Greece, and even the concept behind the League of Corinth, had by rights fallen to the Ptolemaic heirs of Alexander, not to the son of Demetrius. These future aims continue to be represented later by Theocritus, who praises Ptolemy II as the master of many Greeks (xvii. 85-90) only a few years after the procession, when Arsinoe II was queen. This encomium bears out the partial realization of the first Ptolemy's claims to be successor to Alexander in Greece, as witnessed by the scene on the cart. Ptolemy II is further celebrated, by following his sister's footsteps, as the champion of Greek freedom in an Athenian decree revealing Ptolemaic public policy on the eve of the Chremonidean War of the next decade (*SIG*[3] 434-5, 16-17). This evidence combines with the scene in the procession to reveal the consistent public policy of Philadelphus towards Greece.

Finally, a few words can be said about the individual figures in this scene. Alexander and Soter appear in this context as public cult figures, and Priapus, whose presence here is the god's earliest recorded appearance in Alexandria,[217] may be seen to have a comparable role. Even granting his traditional associations as a companion of Dionysus, a function which was

---

[216] See Ch. 5 below, and Will, *Hist. pol.* i[2]. 153 ff.

[217] *Ptol. Alex.* i. 207; see Herter, 14 ff., for the important and extensive role he later played in Alexandrian and Roman religion.

recognized in Alexandria because of his appearance in the Altar of Rhea tableau, Priapus must have emerged from his previous obscurity as part of the general Dionysiac entourage to assume a role in public Alexandrian cult since he here appears among contemporary, historical figures who were worshipped separately in their own right. He is better explained as an independent cult figure despite his, in this case, appropriate Dionysiac associations. It is not possible to establish his iconography conclusively at this date. He may already have been the ithyphallic fertility god who was so familiar later,[218] but several non-ithyphallic Priapi are also recorded[219] and there is no suggestion in any other contemporary Alexandrian reference that the god was always ithyphallic.[220] Even if Priapus could be proved to be depicted as ithyphallic in the procession, this feature cannot be shown to have been standard in the third century, nor to have been necessarily associated with lasciviousness as it came to be later.[221] Their individual cult associations aside, Alexander, Soter, and Priapus were related to Dionysus (Priapus was his son, and the others were related less directly through the Argead house). This tableau is therefore also a postscript to the scenes depicting aspects of the mythology of the god, since it publicly presents his posterity. Just as each of the cult figures receives individual glory, so they also honour by attraction their mutual ancestor Dionysus. The historical connections of Alexander and Ptolemy bring the mythological traditions into the contemporary sphere, illustrating to the spectators that the glory of Dionysus extends into their own day.

The appearance of Corinth and the other Greek cities has allegorical and iconographic, as well as historical, importance. Such local personifications began in the classical age, and, like all forms of personification,[222] became increasingly popular in the Hellenistic and Roman periods, and were current in Alexandria. The figures in the Grand Procession have later parallels in those statues from the Alexandrian Homereion built by Ptolemy IV, which personified cities claiming to be the poet's birthplace (Ael. VH xiii. 22), and in the depiction of Alexandria on the Sophilos mosaic, which, although dating from the second century BC, looks back to Eutychides' Tyche of Antioch of the early third century BC.[223] Since the Corinth of this

---

[218] Herter, 235, apparently believes that he was not ithyphallic in the procession.

[219] Ibid., 176, 178-9.

[220] *Ptol. Alex.* i. 207; ii. 351 n. 139.

[221] Since Priapus' early iconography is variable, even an ithyphallic Priapus in the procession would not be automatically associated in the minds of the spectators with κακία, as Picard suggests; cf. n. 208 above.

[222] For a full account of pre-Hellenistic personifications of places see Hamdorf, 25 ff., 90 ff. (for a list of all known representations); for some 4th-century and Hellenistic personifications of cities see J. M. C. Toynbee, *The Hadrianic School* (Cambridge, 1934), 7 and n. 7; P. Gardner, *JHS* ix (1888), 47 ff.

[223] Cf. Blanche R. Brown, *Ptolemaic Paintings and Mosaics and The Alexandrian*

scene is female, she must be an allegorical figure which represents Corinth, and not the eponymous male hero of the city who was a son of Zeus.[224] All the cities were no doubt abstractions, or idealized female figures who symbolized the cities they represented by attributes and dress, although they must also have had a more immediate means of identification since so many figures were moving past the spectators. The phrase προσηγορεύοντο δὲ πόλεις (201E; line 206) suggests that the cities, like other figures in the procession, were identified by some form of placard, or that their names were proclaimed in the stadium as the particular personifications marched past. A similar display of personified cities was common in Roman processions, both triumphs and imperial funeral cortèges.[225] These *simulacra oppidorum* may have consisted of painted or plastic repesentations of allegorical figures which symbolized the cities, instead of painted views of them. Their general role is similar to that of the figures in the Grand Procession, since both provided contemporary political information. In the case of the Roman personifications, they would have represented cities either captured by the Triumphator or ruled by the deceased Emperor.

The figure of Arete probably also either wore, or was preceded by, a label indicating that she was meant to represent Arete, and although there is no way of knowing what this figure looked like, the woman probably portrayed those features which the spectators naturally associated with a mental picture of Arete. Her appearance may have been similar to the allegorical figure of ἀρετή, whose path was one of the choices presented to Herakles in the *Apology* of Prodicus (Xen. *Mem.* ii. 1, 22); she is described there as a fair, noble figure with a pure complexion, respectful eye, and modest form, who is dressed in white clothing, all of which indicates that ancient readers conjured up the same mental associations about ἀρετή as modern readers might do about Virtue. *Arete* was personified in art as well as literature in the fourth century: the sculptor Euphranor produced a statue of 'virtus' and one of Greece (Pliny, *HN* xxxiv. 78) (although there is no known connection between the figures which might furnish an analogy for the group of Arete and Corinth), and the painter Aristolaus depicted 'virtus' (ibid., xxxv. 137) perhaps as part of a unified allegorical composition. The theory behind *arete* is vital to the understanding of the appearance and role of the personification in the procession and it is not adequately expressed by the narrow translation 'virtue'.[226] The *arete* of a man was an extremely complex and

---

Style (Cambridge, Mass., 1957), 67, No. 48; Martin Robertson, *A History of Greek Art* (Cambridge, 1975), i. 470 ff.; 579 ff.

[224] Paus. ii. 1, 1; *RE* s.v. Korinthos (2).
[225] Toynbee, *Hadrianic School*, 11 and n. 1.
[226] Cf. R. W. Livingstone, *Greek Ideals and Modern Life* (Oxford, 1935), 69 ff.

all-pervasive concept which changed through time as the Greeks evolved their philosophical ideas. Although every person or object had a particular *arete*, there existed a higher concept of universal, moral *arete*. One quality of *arete* which was familiar in third-century Alexandria can be seen in its association with kingship in the Alexandrian poets, by whom it is often cited as an essential royal attribute bestowed by the gods. Theocritus exhorts Philadelphus to seek *arete* from Zeus (xvii. 135 ff.), and Callimachus exhorts Zeus to grant *arete* as well as *olbos* (*Hymn.* i. 94-6). The concept of *arete*, and the appearance of its personification in the Grand Procession, must therefore have a special, contemporary connotation for the Ptolemies, and the exalted position of this royal Arete is indicated by her olive crown, the prize of the victor in the Olympic Games. Arete's position on the cart shows that she bestows special honour upon Ptolemy Soter, a king in whom *arete* was an expected attribute generally, but, given the over-all political implications of the scene, *arete* is surely meant also to embrace Soter's and Philadelphus' activities regarding Greece in the years preceding the Grand Procession.

D. *The End of the Dionysiac Procession* (201E–202A)

In the last part of the text, Kallixeinos does not describe the elements fully, or necessarily in the order in which they appeared in the actual procession (which he seems to have done earlier), but he here includes at random interesting items which either struck his fancy or were the only ones recorded in his sources. This part of the text cannot be understood, therefore, as a coherent narrative, and brief comment on matters of particular interest must suffice. The end of the fragment (203A-B; lines 275 ff.) provides special problems which will be dealt with separately.

The first uncertainty surrounds the unspecified end of the divisional procession of Dionysus (201E–202A; lines 210 ff.). One possible view is that the appearance of the phallos and other ritual objects of the god signals the end of his procession (201E; line 210); after the mythological tableaux, these attributes could be the final offerings to the god and a fitting conclusion to his procession even as the phallos signalled the end of the procession of the Country Dionysia at Athens (Plut. *Mor.* 527D). Furthermore, the text of the Dionysiac procession is fairly full and detailed before the appearance of these objects, but the following sections are severely excerpted and disjointed. This may be explained if Kallixeinos or Athenaeus had described the Dionysiac procession fully and chronologically until its end, but had abbreviated the rest of the Grand Procession. Finally, the sentence following the mention of the phallos explains the selection of the items which were included in the text (201F; line 215): πολλῶν οὖν καὶ ποικίλων εἰρημένων ἐν ταῖς πομπαῖς ταύταις μόνα ἐξελεξάμεθα ἐν οἷς ἦν χρυσὸς καὶ ἄργυρος. Although this statement contains important information about the type of subjects chosen for inclusion by Kallixeinos[227] (see below), it may be invoked as evidence for the end of the Dionysiac procession if the phrase means that the gold and silver objects have been chosen from all 'the separate divisional processions' which have already appeared in the Grand Procession, i.e. the procession of the Morning Star, that 'named after' οἱ τῶν βασιλέων γονεῖς, and the Dionysiac procession. If this is the case, it is implied that the description of the Dionysiac procession is completed at this point. The phallos must therefore have been the last item to appear in it.

The other possible ending for the Dionysiac procession is the mention of the next divisional procession, which occurs some lines after the appearance of the phallos (202A; line 226). If, as seems likely, the Grand Procession comprised only sectional processions dedicated to different honorands, the elements described after the phallos (assuming that it does mark the end of the Dionysiac procession) and before the following procession of Zeus would have no context since they are not part of any procession. Their appearance 'between processions' is hardly likely, and since many of the objects and participants in this intermediate section have Dionysiac associations, their most suitable context is probably the final stages of the procession of Dionysus. This view can be supported by another interpretation of the phrase ἐν ταῖς πομπαῖς ταύταις, which Jacoby took to mean 'although many and varied things have been said about these processions [sc. ἐν ταῖς τῶν πεντετηρίδων γραφαῖς] . . .' (*FGrH* 627 F 2 ad loc.). In this case, αἱ πομπαί could mean the various processions of the festivals whose descriptions were contained in the penteteric records, and Kallixeinos uses it in a general way to indicate that much more material was contained in the sources than he included in his text. If αἱ πομπαί does not refer to the divisional processions within the Grand Procession, there is no suggestion that the Dionysiac procession had ended by this point in the text.

A definite decision between these two possibilities cannot be made, but on balance it seems preferable that the description of the procession of Dionysus continues, although abbreviated, after the ritual objects until the appearance of the following procession of Zeus; the lack of context for the intermediate section is otherwise incomprehensible. The statement that the account has been abridged to include only gold and silver items shows

---

[227] Kallixeinos is no doubt the speaker here (although Gulick (Loeb) thinks that it is Athenaeus) since the 1st person plural verb form is used. This verb form, along with the 1st person singular, is used elsewhere in the text where it is clear that Kallixeinos is the speaker (196A; 197C, line 1). In the explicit abbreviations of the text made by Athenaeus, he uses the 3rd person singular form of the verb without exception (201B, line 189; 203A, line 274).

that much of the detail of the original Grand Procession has not been transmitted in the existing text. The omission of the less exciting objects may have given an unfair emphasis to the combined amount of gold and silver, the effect of which, if diluted by other materials, may not have been quite so overwhelming.

The remainder of the description of the Grand Procession, including the end of the Dionysiac procession as it is interpreted here, consists of items taken at random from the proceedings, an abbreviation which may have been made by Kallixeinos, Athenaeus, or both. If it was by Kallixeinos, he changed the previously consecutive treatment of his subject in midstream, perhaps so as not to spend an inordinate amount of time on the Grand Procession in a work which also had to include other aspects of Alexandria: once he had given an accurate impression of the whole procession by relating part of it chronologically and fully, he may then have included only the most spectacular parts of the rest. The verb ἐξελεξάμεθα, which interrupts the flow of the description, may indicate the moment of the change in his treatment of the material. On the other hand, Athenaeus may have abbreviated the rest of the account of the Grand Procession for similar considerations of length. He abbreviated Kallixeinos' text in other places (201B, 203A), but if he abridges it here also, he gives no indication that this has happened. It is consequently impossible to know whether or not this section of the text of Kallixeinos was fuller than the transmitted version.

The remaining elements of the Dionysiac procession seem to have included more tableaux (201F; line 217): διαθέσεις πολλαὶ ἀκοῆς ἦσαν ἄξιαι, which could have represented other scenes from the life of the god, if these did not conclude with the Altar of Rhea scene. In the next line, further carts containing images of kings and gods are mentioned, who, as part of the corpus of Dionysiac myth, may have been associated with the aforementioned tableaux (e.g. the figures of Hermes, the Nymphs, Hera, Priapus, Ptolemy Soter, etc., belonged to the tableaux drawn on previous carts), or else they may have appeared as isolated figures, such as Nysa. The kings may have been Macedonian ancestors of the Ptolemies, perhaps certain members of the Argead royal line who are traced in the official genealogy of Satyrus as far back as Dionysus (*FGrH* 631). The animals appearing in this final section are additional to those in the Indian Triumph, but their context is unknown. Lions would have been a natural part of the Dionysiac procession (cf. the lion in the Hellenistic Dionysiac procession in the dromos of the Memphian Serapeum; see p. 181) because of their role in his cult along with other large felines. The frieze of the Great Altar of Pergamon shows that the beast was part of the god's entourage in the Hellenistic Age; there Dionysus is himself accompanied by a

panther, but a huge lion between him and the next figure (usually identified as Nysa) successfully attacks a fallen Giant.[228] Lions are frequently
included on the later sarcophagi which depict Dionysus' Indian campaign,
either as part of the triumphal train or drawing the god's chariot. The
appearance of the lions reflects another aspect of the tie between Dionysus
and Alexander, since the lion had a particular association with the latter in
the East where the animal had an almost universal identification with
royalty. Alexander fought with a lion in Bactria and was given presents of
lions by the Babylonians (Curt. Ruf. v. 1, 21; viii. 1, 14). He was depicted
hunting lions on the Alexander Sarcophagus, and the inscription on the
Delphian statue of Craterus records that the latter saved Alexander's life
on a lion hunt (*FD* III (4) 137). Furthermore, when Alexander assumed
the guise of Herakles, as he frequently did, he wore the lion skin (Ath.
537F). The natural association of the animals with Dionysus in his procession may stem in part from their connection with Alexander and the East
even if they do not appear here in the Indian Triumph. Indian lions were
well known in antiquity; Aelian says that they were the largest of all lions,
and, although exceedingly wild and savage, were capable of domestication
(*HA* xvii. 26). These lions may have been Indian animals along with
various other beasts in the procession, but eastern lions would have been
less accessible to the Ptolemies than animals from Arabia and Africa,
which would have been available through trading routes to the east, west,
and south.[229] The lions in the procession were probably either present or
future inhabitants of the royal zoo and may have been partly tamed. Tame
lions were known in Alexandria, since an unspecified Queen Berenike is
said to have had one as a pet (Ael. *HA* v. 39).

The procession of Dionysus ends with the appearance of musicians, and
bulls with golden trappings who are the sacrificial offerings to the god
(201F-202A). The sacrificial animals did not always appear first in traditional Greek processions, but they rarely appeared last as they do here.[230]
This curiosity may be partly explained if one composite sacrifice was to be
held at the end of the Grand Procession (see p. 35), outside the context
of any one divisional procession. In this case the normal rules for the order
of the sacrificial animals and their attendants may not have applied. The
musicians consist of instrumentalists (kitharistai) and a chorus of singers
and probably dancers who perform as they march along the processional
route; although the verb συνεφώνουν refers technically to the kitharists, it
should probably be understood to refer to the chorus as well since the

---

[228] Cf. Evemaria Schmidt, *Der Grosse Altar zu Pergamon* (Leipzig, 1961), Pl. 27;
p. 35 and n. 175.
[229] Jennison, 35; Toynbee, *Animals* 61; Keller, i. 24 ff.
[230] Eitrem, *Gr. Rel.* iii. 79-80.

players are described as ἐν οἷς (i.e. the chorus). Greek religious processions and sacrifices were always accompanied by music, but there are two curious features about these groups. Firstly, wherever the victims and their accompanying musicians appeared in processions, the instrumentalists followed the animals, not vice versa as here in the Grand Procession.[231] There is no obvious reason for this anomaly, but it is perhaps comprehensible in view of the fact that the Grand Procession was not bound by conventions seen in religious ritual elsewhere in Greece at an earlier period. Moreover, this composite extravaganza honours several gods (albeit in discrete sectional processions), which may have exempted it from the same conventions as traditional cult ritual of even the same time and culture. The second curious feature is that kitharai are the only instruments mentioned in this ensemble, despite the fact that flutes provided the traditional accompaniment for processions and sacrifices (although other instruments such as kitharai could be added for an especially magnificent occasion[232]). If the principal instrument used to worship a deity was to a large extent determined either by the deity concerned or by the spirit of the ritual, as has been argued,[233] the use of the kitharai alone here may be understood on both counts. Although the aulos was the traditional accompaniment of the dithyramb in honour of Dionysus (the importance of the flautists elsewhere in the procession has been discussed above, p. 57), and, on the evidence of vases and literature, accompanied various Dionysiac processions and festivities in classical Greece,[234] the kithara appears in other Dionysiac associations especially when it is played by Satyrs and Silenoi.[235] Its use is also appropriate here in terms of the type of occasion since instruments besides auloi were added to processions in proportion to the splendour of the occasion; although the aulos normally accompanied the sacrifice after the procession, the kithara was sometimes added if the ceremony was elaborated to include dance and song at the altar.[236] Any of those considerations may explain the use of the kithara here, apart from the fact that the traditional relationship between music and religious festivals may have been less strictly observed in Ptolemaic Alexandria. The kitharistai could have appeared alone as a novelty. Finally, since there is some evidence that the altar hymn after the *prosodion* was thought to be accompanied by the kithara more than by the aulos in later days,[237] new types of processional music which required kithara accompaniment were perhaps in the course of development. Although these musicians

---

[231] Ibid., 87; cf. the Parthenon Frieze, north frieze, slabs II–VIII.
[232] J. A. Haldane, *G&R* 2nd ser. xiii (1966), 98 ff.; Eitrem, 94 ff.
[233] Haldane, 102.   [234] Ibid.; A. Frickenhaus, *JDAI* xxvii (1912), 61 ff.
[235] M. Wegner, *Das Musikleben der Griechen* (Berlin, 1949), 36, 210.
[236] Haldane, 101–2.   [237] Proclus, *Chrest.* 10; cf. Haldane, 102.

provided musical accompaniment for the procession and sacrifice, they probably had additional secular functions in the festival surrounding the procession. They may have participated in some of the dramatic contests (indicated by the appearance of the Guild of the Artists of Dionysus), since the kithara seems to have occasionally accompanied tragedy, if only for special effect.[238] Alternatively, the musicians may have performed in their own right, since musical competitions were probably part of this Alexandrian festival just as they formed part of the national games of Greece and of the other new festivals instituted by the Diadochi: Philadelphus decreed a musical contest to be part of the Ptolemaieia festival in honour of his father (*SIG*[3] 390, 21-2), and a kitharode listed along with a kitharist at Ptolemais-Hermiou as members of the Guild of Dionysiac Artists (*OGIS* 51, 41-4) suggests that musical performances were popular in Ptolemaic Egypt. If some of the kitharistai in this group were members of the Guild, Guild members here assumed roles traditionally performed by non-professional participants in religious processions, in addition to appearing elsewhere in their professional capacity as entertainers.

III. THE REST OF THE GRAND PROCESSION

A. *Other Processions* (202A)

After the conclusion of the procession of Dionysus come the other sectional processions in honour of Zeus, the other gods, and finally Alexander, who held the penultimate position in the Grand Procession before the procession of Hesperos, perhaps as a mark of special emphasis. The symmetrical arrangement of the divisional processions is now apparent: framed at the beginning and end by the processions of two stars, the major central section comprising the processions of the Olympian gods is flanked by processions in honour of deified or glorified mortals, namely those in honour of οἱ τῶν βασιλέων γονεῖς and of Alexander. The comparable positions of these two processions indicate that their respective honorands are somehow distinct from the Olympian gods, and this differentiation must stem from their mortal origin. Nevertheless, the prominent position of these two processions enhances the 'human' gods who are related to the Ptolemies. Nothing is said about the composition of these other divisional processions, but the analogy of the Dionysiac procession suggests that pageants and tableaux in honour of the religious cults and mythology of each god were included (cf. Kallixeinos' statement at the beginning of his description of the Grand Procession (197D; lines 5-7): μετὰ δὲ ταύτας αἱ

---

[238] *Dram. Fests.*[2], 165 ff.; H. Huchzermeyer, *Aulos und Kithara in griechischen Musik bis zum Ausgang der klassischen Zeit* (Diss. Münster, 1931), 55 n. 224.

τῶν θεῶν ἀπάντων, οἰκείαν ἔχουσαι τῆς περὶ ἕκαστον αὐτῶν ἱστορίας διασκευήν). The epiphany of the honoured god, represented by the appearance of his cult statue, was surely the main feature of each procession (it is in fact the only specified element of Alexander's procession), and priests, appropriate attendants, ritual objects, and sacrificial victims would also be expected.

B. *Miscellaneous Ritual Objects* (202B-F)

The remainder of the transmitted text, however, does not fit this pattern. Most of the objects described seem to be a random selection of items taken from various divisional processions, since, being divine attributes and ritual objects, they are best understood as belonging to individual gods even though they are all mentioned as if in a coherent group. Since the position, context, and (occasionally) the identification of these objects within any divisional procession cannot be ascertained, this part of the text is only comprehensible as a collection of disparate elements, chosen for their magnificence or extravagance. In this final section, Kallixeinos no longer uses the words which he had previously used to indicate sequential order, such as μετὰ δὲ ταῦτα, μεθ᾽ οὕς, etc., which argues that either his method of description or his sources changed. This catalogue-like section, which in its truncation is analogous to the account of gold and silver plate, may be partly explained by the tabular nature of his sources (see p. 173). There are, nevertheless, certain sequential items which form coherent groups, such as the empty thrones followed by incense (see below). Some of these objects and participants may belong to a grand finale of the Grand Procession after the appearance of the various divisional processions; the parade of armed troops certainly belongs in this category even if the other items do not.

The first objects to appear in this section are chryselephantine thrones, four with attributes resting on them, and one, which belongs to Ptolemy Soter, with an especially valuable gold crown (202A-B). The cult of the empty throne, whose origin and development can be traced from the ancient Near East through Greece and the Roman Empire, stems from the fact that the throne is a principal symbol of divine sovereignty which was adopted by kings with divine authority on earth, and thence by priests and magistrates who represented the authority of gods and kings respectively.[239] The empty throne was a similar symbol of authority of the absent deity or king whose imminent arrival was expected even as his invisible presence could be felt. The symbolism of the empty throne is clearly seen in the dream of Eumenes of Cardia (D. S. xviii. 60, 4 ff.;

---

[239] Cf. Picard, *Cah. Arch.* vii (1954), 1 ff.

Polyaen. iv. 8, 1–2), where the deceased Alexander orders that his royal tent be prepared with an empty throne holding his diadem, sceptre, crown, and other royal insignia before an altar smoking with incense. A similar manifestation of a throne cult appears also in Egypt; both gods and pharaohs appeared enthroned in dynastic Egypt (the throne itself perhaps being personified and worshipped),[240] and, in Ptolemaic Egypt, Theocritus describes a throne prepared for Ptolemy Soter in the temple of Zeus near the thrones of Alexander and Herakles (xvii. 16 ff.). Soter's throne is the only one in the procession with a specified owner, which argues that it is somehow different from the others. The natural explanation is that his throne is the only one belonging to a human. The other thrones must belong to their usual owners, the gods, especially since they are here clearly intended as divine votive offerings like the various divine attributes and cult objects which appear later in the text:[241] the numerous model thrones found in excavations prove that these objects were dedicated to the gods as an appropriate and necessary apparatus of divinity. The thrones in the procession are real cult objects because they are followed and honoured by *thymiateria*, altars, and *escharai* which either actually burn incense or symbolize this common ritual act.

The empty thrones all carry divine attributes, even if these are so generalized that their particular owners cannot be identified. The *keras* will be shown to be an attribute of Tyche or Isis, and the *dikeras* (if its appearance here can be textually substantiated) may perhaps be symbolic of the jugate divinities Isis and Sarapis (see Appendix II). The crescent-shaped *stephanē* is commonly found as an attribute of the goddesses Hera, Athena, Artemis, Aphrodite, Demeter, and others in art and literature, and although it was taken over by female mortals in Hellenistic times, there is no evidence that it was ever worn officially by a mortal before Arsinoe II, who is only shown wearing it on the large memorial coins issued after her death in 270.[242] Therefore, if the *stephanē* in fact belonged to Arsinoe, the Procession would have had to occur after her death, but this is unlikely on other grounds (see pp. 164–5). There is therefore no compelling reason to connect the *stephane* on the throne with any Ptolemaic queen since it is better known at this date as the attribute of a number of goddesses. The throne of Ptolemy Soter and another throne hold crowns, which were ubiquitous features of every aspect of cult ritual and therefore common dedications to the gods, occasionally made doubly suitable by the use of

---

[240] H. Frankfort, *Kingship and the Gods* (Chicago, 1948), 43; D. B. Thompson, *Ptolemaic Oinochoai and Portraits in Faience* (Oxford, 1973), 121.

[241] H. Herter, *RhM* n.F. lxxiv (1925), 168 ff.

[242] Thompson, *Oinochoai*, 29.

foliage, whether real or represented in precious metals, from trees particularly sacred to the honoured god. An extant 'siège d'honneur' on which a crown was placed shows that this combination of symbols was appropriate (Ny Carlsberg 817; *From the Collections of the Ny Carlsberg Glyptothek 1942* (Copenhagen, 1942), iii. 189 ff. and Fig. 1). The crown of Soter is described as ἐκ μυρίων κατεσκευασμένος χρυσῶν (202B; line 234). The number 10,000 may only be meant as an indefinitely large number to describe the seemingly countless leaves composing the crown, as in 'it was composed of 10,000 pieces of gold', but it is probably the precise number of gold coins required to pay for such a grand crown. This latter suggestion is supported by the fact that the exact worth or price of honorific crowns is often recorded in inscriptions, which indicates that a careful record of the cost was kept.[243] The cost of Soter's crown may well have been recorded in the official Alexandrian archives to which Kallixeinos had access; it is in any case clear that the value of the crown could not have been conveyed to him or to the spectators merely by its appearance in the procession. The *thymiateria* which follow the thrones appear to be standard processional objects like the votive *thymiateria* mentioned in the Delian inventory lists which are described by the adjective πομπικός.[244] These must have been used in processions and later dedicated to the gods. The *thymiateria* appearing in this procession may have been dedicated later to the gods of the thrones in whose honour the incense is being burnt. Altars wreathed with gold crowns follow the censers. The hundreds of marble altars with garlands and bucrania in relief show how common the practice of wreathing altars was, but the one altar with four torches affixed to its corners is unusual. The function of the torches may be primarily decorative, but it may, alternatively or concurrently, derive from an original ritual significance since fire was a well-known means of purification. As such, the fire may have appeared here in combination with the incense as an additional purificatory device. Yet again, the torches may have been attributes of gods, such as Hephaistos, Eileithyia, or one of the Eleusinian gods, to whom the role of cleansing was important; if one of these gods also 'owned' an empty throne in the procession, this altar may have been intended specifically to worship that deity. Two *escharai* are the final items in the parade of incense, which are normally 'hearths' or low altars (with sunken depressions) usually with chthonic significance. In view of their extreme height, they can hardly be considered 'low' altars, and must be exaggerated versions of their usual forms. The first *eschara* may resemble a *thymiaterion* because of its great height, but it is not stated whether the measurement of the second refers to its circumference or to its height.

---

[243] *RE* s.v. Kranz, 1599–1600.
[244] Cf. W. Deonna, *Délos* xviii. 371 and n. 20.

Like the *thymiateria* and the altars, these *escharai* may also have been dedicated to the gods after the procession.

Three different types of Delphic tripods follow the altars, which are additional to those earlier tripods intended as prizes for the victorious choregoi in the dithyrambic contests (198C). The primarily sacral function of the tripod (its valuable metal content may explain the origin of its ubiquitous use as a votive offering) doubtless explains its appearance here amid other divine dedications. Since these Delphic tripods follow the incense which honours the gods, they perhaps are also dedications to the gods whose thrones precede them, or to other gods. The size and elaborateness of these tripods argue against their use as personal prizes in the *agon* even though, in this case, they would have been dedicated to the gods later by the victors. In view of the fact that the following section of the text describes a parade of ritual objects sacred to various gods, these tripods may be the first in the series, and in honour of Apollo (to whom above all other gods the tripod was sacred because of its important role in Apolline mantic cult), especially since the palm tree which immediately follows the tripods also has Apolline connotations. Although votive tripods were frequently made of precious metals, these eighteen elaborate, valuable tripods reflect the contemporary trend of ostentatious decoration in tripods which became popular in the Hellenistic age: the largest tripod in the procession is encircled with a golden vine-wreath, a practice which began in the classical period and continued into the Hellenistic age, and the elongated shape of many Hellenistic tripods (seen in the representations of marble tripods on the weapon frieze of the Council House at Miletus) is found also in those which are six and nine feet tall in the procession. (The tripod measuring forty-five feet is comprehensible only in the context of the scale of the other gigantic objects appearing in the procession.) In the Hellenistic age, figures came to be attached to the tripod either on the legs or around the rim perhaps as a result of this elongation and the resulting problems of proportion,[245] a style which is seen in the seven-foot figures attached to the largest tripod here; although their position is not specified, the figures may be regarded as being attached to the legs as an extra means of support for the vessel instead of holding the crown around the rim.

The appearance of the tripods seems to initiate the parade of large objects (202C) which are best explained as attributes of various gods, whether the tripods are understood as offerings to Apollo or as generalized dedications to the gods. The palm trees may perhaps be symbols of Apollo, Apollo and Artemis, or Leto because of their associations with the

[245] *RE* s.v. Dreifuss, 1690; see, for example, E. Pernice, *Die Hellenistische Kunst in Pompeji* (Berlin and Leipzig, 1925), iv. Pl. X.

divine births at Delos, but there is no obvious explanation why they are seven in number. The gilded herald's staff may be a symbol of Hermes, and the thunderbolt of Zeus. The *naos* is presumably a portable shrine, or *aedicula*, carried in honour of one of the gods, and the *dikeras* may symbolize Tyche, Isis, or perhaps the jugate divinities Isis and Sarapis. The size of all these objects suggests that they were drawn on carts like the ritual objects of Dionysus in 201E. The following figures and animals may include statues of gods appearing in the various other sectional processions, and the appropriate animals sacred to them. Kallixeinos mentions that these figures are gilded, ἐπίχρυσοι, probably bronze, wood, or terracotta covered in gold. Eagles are the only specified animals, and they also appear as akroteria on the ornamental pavilion connected with the Grand Procession (197A). This bird was sacred to Zeus, and may have appeared in his divisional procession in connection with his statue, thunderbolt, or other ritual objects. The eagle was, however, also a symbol of the Ptolemies, no doubt because of its original connection with Zeus, and was an invariable emblem on their coinage from the time of Soter so that the kings are unmistakably associated with Zeus. The eagles in the procession may also be seen as symbols of Ptolemaic power because of the early association of the ruling house with Zeus through the symbol of the eagle.

The extraordinarily large number of crowns which are described after these figures may be interpreted as the private offerings of individuals to the various deities honoured by the Grand Procession; these donors are mentioned indirectly in 203B (line 279) when the combined cost of all of the donated crowns is reckoned. These appear in the procession in order to be displayed to the public before being dedicated later in the various shrines and temples. The so-called 'mystic' crown which is placed at the shrine of Berenike requires some comment. The symbolism of the mystic crown is understandable since crowns were standard ritual apparel for celebrants of all Mysteries, but this crown must have a special significance for Berenike because it is destined for her shrine, and the most natural interpretation may be that the queen had some connection with a mystery cult during her lifetime (for further discussion on this, see pp. 187 ff.). Some Mysteries were popular in the third century, but there is no independent evidence that the queen was an initiate in any of them. Nor can the hints which may be present in the Dionysiac procession about the possible existence of Mysteries of Dionysus at that date in Alexandria be taken as evidence for the explanation of this mystic crown because it appears outside the context of the procession of Dionysus. Although the mention of this crown may be a unique reference to the queen's participation in a mystic cult, the absence of corroborating evidence gives Kaibel's emendation of μυστικός to μύρτινος some merit. Crowns were standard apparel for initiates, but they were even more common as attributes of, and offerings to, the gods; myrtle formed the appropriate crown for Aphrodite (Ath. 676D), and although Berenike *may* have fostered the cult of Aphrodite during her lifetime as her daughter Arsinoe did, it is in any case clear that the queen was associated with the goddess after her death if not during her life.[246] Theocritus states that Aphrodite placed the dead queen in her own temple in order to deify her (xv. 106-9; xvii. 34 ff.), which indicates a very early association or identification of Berenike with Aphrodite. A myrtle crown may be hung around the door of Berenike's shrine as a symbol of this association, and, from the evidence in Theocritus, this otherwise unattested shrine of Berenike may have been a part of, or originally, a temple to Aphrodite. Whatever this crown signifies, its immense circumference, 120 feet, suggests that it was not a solid circle of gold, which would be not only awkward to carry along the processional route, but logistically impossible to place on, or around, the door of the Berenikeion. It seems more likely that the crown was a golden garland of sorts made of entwined gold thread, or perhaps even a real garland covered with gold foil, which, being flexible, could have been carried or drawn along the route in a shape and size befitting its vehicle or the width of the route. A crown of such a design could then have been wound upon itself several times in order to be placed on or near the door of the shrine.

The fact that the destination of this ritual object is stated by Kallixeinos has various ramifications. An observer of the Grand Procession could only know that the crown passing by was to be placed at the Berenikeion if there was a sign, banner, or announcement to that effect, but the detail as it appears in the text may have been proleptic in the sense that the eye-witness observer who later wrote an account knew that the crown had been placed in the shrine after the end of the procession. Kallixeinos himself, if he did not attend the procession, could have had the same information (even if his source for the account did not preserve it) if the crown remained at the shrine either as a permanent fixture or long enough for its existence to have passed into public memory. However, it is equally easy to imagine that Kallixeinos obtained this information from written records about the Grand Procession which stated that the crown had been made specifically for the Berenikeion.

The existence of a shrine in honour of Berenike at the time of the Grand Procession bears witness to the status of the queen, the date of her deification, and her place in the Ptolemaic dynastic cult. Since there is no evidence that the queen was deified before her death, it is clear that she

---

[246] *Ptol. Alex.* i. 240, 666; W. Meincke, *Untersuchungen zu den Enkomiastischen Gedichten Theocrits* (Diss. Kiel, 1965), 101 ff.

was both dead and deified before the Grand Procession, although the exact date of her death can only be inferred. The *terminus post quem* is probably 280/79 because there are no references to her deification in the decree responding to the announcement of the Ptolemaieia festival (*SIG*[3] 390; for the date of the establishment of the festival, see below, p. 182); this festival marked the establishment of a public cult and divine honours to Ptolemy Soter, and may have included the same for his queen had she already died. The *terminus ante quem* for her death is the death of Arsinoe II in 270, since Berenike's death and deification are referred to in *Idylls* xv and xvii of Theocritus, written when Arsinoe was still queen. Despite suggestions to the contrary,[247] one cannot conclude that the deification took place shortly before the time of the Adonia festival described in *Idyll* xv, although the process of deification is referred to in that poem, since the apotheosis of the first Ptolemaic queen was a remarkable event worthy of commemoration by a poet at any time thereafter, especially when Berenike was the mother of the currently reigning queen. If it is correct to maintain that the Grand Procession took place before the advent of Arsinoe II as queen, Berenike must have died and been deified between 280/79 and *c.*276 (the approximate date for the marriage of Arsinoe and Philadelphus). This is supported by the suggestion that Berenike was deified only by Philadelphus, which in turn implies that the event antedated his marriage to his sister: Theocritus states that Philadelphus founded shrines for his mother and father, but Arsinoe is only mentioned later as a worshipper at these shrines along with her husband (xvii. 121 ff.). Although this passage has usually been interpreted as evidence that Philadelphus and Arsinoe together established the joint cult of their parents as the Theoi Soteres (not to be confused with either's individual deification), it is not clear whether the poem refers to the joint cult of the Theoi Soteres or to the individual deifications of Soter and Berenike; in either case the emphasis is that Ptolemy alone was responsible for the deifications while Arsinoe was only a worshipper. Even if the marriage of Philadelphus and Arsinoe is indeed celebrated as a recent event in this poem, as has been maintained,[248] the deifications could still have occurred before the date either of the marriage or the poem when Philadelphus was the sole ruler. Theocritus may attest this deification by Philadelphus alone before his marriage as he does the later joint patronage of the cult by the king and queen.

Although Theocritus may or may not refer to the establishment of the joint cult of the Theoi Soteres, the joint cult does not appear within the context of the Grand Procession. Soter and Berenike are deified by

---

[247] Cf. Gow, *Comm. Theoc.* ii. 265, 326.   [248] *Ptol. Alex.* ii. 934 n. 388.

this time, but there is no evidence in the text of Kallixeinos that they are worshipped as the Theoi Soteres, which surely implies that this cult did not officially exist.[249] A case can therefore be made that the joint cult was established after the date of both the Grand Procession and the individual deification of each parent.

The next item in the procession is a golden aegis, which is the final ritual attribute presented in this section. The aegis could belong to any one of a number of gods, and, like the eagle, may also be symbolic of Ptolemaic power because of its association with Zeus, with whom the Ptolemies identified themselves on their coinage. There follows a parade of crescent-shaped diadems, including one exceptionally large one, carried by girls (202D; line 254). Like the *stephanē* which appears as a divine attribute on one of the empty thrones, these *stephanai* are appropriate offerings to the goddesses who traditionally wore them, being perhaps more ritually signifi-cant than the crowns which appeared previously, since crowns were a ubiquitous part of religious celebration and not particular pieces of divine apparel as *stephanai* were. The religious part of the Grand Procession ends with an extensive parade of gold and silver plate in no perceivable order (202E ff.), a miscellaneous treasure-display (distinct from that already presented in the Dionysiac procession) which probably comprised the offerings to the other gods by the worshippers on the occasion of the Grand Procession. The incredible volume of all this plate is conceivable only in the context of the rest of the ostentatious proceedings, and it may include the accumulation of all the divine dedications in the festival, both royal and private. Objects which are particular divine attributes appear also in this section, such as a breastplate (sacred to Ares?), another breastplate with thunderbolts and an oak crown (possibly an attribute of Zeus), and a solid gold *keras*.

C. *Parade of Infantry and Cavalry* (202F–203A)

The final feature of the Grand Procession is a parade of horse and foot soldiers with appropriate displays of arms and armour (202F; line 267). The exhibition of these troops in their enormous numbers can only be a deliberate show of military strength. Although the total of 57,600 foot and 23,200 horse has been considered pure hyperbole,[250] there is no in-dependent evidence for the size of the Ptolemaic army at this period. If, however, the numbers can be accepted as possible within the limits of either the standing or war strength of the Ptolemaic forces, their concen-tration in Alexandria requires some comment and may presuppose a set of

---

[249] This was pointed out by Tarn, *JHS* liii (1933), 60.
[250] Studniczka, 19 and n. 1.

extraordinary circumstances.[251] The numbers recorded for the troops are without doubt immense, but they are none the less precise, and hardly the type to be devised by one inventing or exaggerating the figure (as in *Gulliver's Travels* or Lucian's *True History*). Since Kallixeinos had access to official records for his account of the Grand Procession, the exact troop numbers may also have been taken from there. The only source for the size of the Ptolemaic army (at the end of the reign of Philadelphus) is found in Appian (*Prooem.* 10), whose account of the empire's military strength is taken from the βασιλικαὶ ἀναγραφαί: 200,000 foot, 40,000 horse, 300 elephants, 2,000 chariots, and a great number of arms. (Appian also includes a catalogue of the empire's naval strength which is in striking corroboration of another similar account probably included by Kallixeinos in *About Alexandria*; see below, p. 152). Appian's account of the armed forces has been considered gross exaggeration because the numbers 'seem' too large,[252] but this is a circular, subjective argument since there are otherwise no attested statistics. Appian's bona fides regarding the account of the navy is established because of the corroborating evidence for it, namely Kallixeinos, and there is no prima-facie reason to disbelieve his account of the army. However, even if his numbers are accepted for the army at the end of the reign of Philadelphus, it is impossible to know the size of the force some thirty years earlier at the time of the Grand Procession. At the other end of the scale, the number of Ptolemaic troops at Raphia in 217 has been calculated to be some 50,000 foot and 5,000 horse, which was gathered from various sources. This was all that could be mustered through extraordinary efforts on the government's part, which were necessitated by the army's bad condition after a peaceful twenty years during which Egypt's military strength had been reduced to insignificance.[253] The size of this force, therefore, is not analogous to the numbers available to Philadelphus some sixty years before when the army was in peak condition. Although nothing certain can be said about the size of Philadelphus' army in 280, a compromise between the high figure of Appian and the low figure of Raphia, and a reliance on the credibility of Kallixeinos, should allow for the total number of troops to be far greater than the 52,600 foot and 23,200 horse recorded in the Grand Procession.

Only part of the total Ptolemaic army could have been made available for participation in the festival, since many troops would have been stationed outside the country in Ptolemaic colonies and military bases.

---

[251] For the Ptolemaic armies in general see Lesquier, *Institutions militaires*; Griffith, *Mercenaries*, 108 ff.; for cleruchs see Rostovtzeff, *SEHHW*, 284 ff.; F. Übel, *Die Kleruchen im ptolemäischen Ägypten bis um die Mitte des 2. Jahrhunderts v. Chr.* (Diss. Inaug. Jena, 1959).

[252] Gow, *JHS* lviii (1938), 190 n. 49; Tarn, *Ant. Gon.* 456.

[253] Griffith, 118 ff.

There is no evidence for the percentage of troops normally stationed in Alexandria or spread among cleruchies, the chora, foreign garrisons, etc.[254] The standing garrison of the capital was the largest, most important garrison and contained the Household Cavalry and the Royal Bodyguard.[255] Since the garrison of Cyprus in 307 contained 12,000 horse and 800 foot, and was reinforced by 10,000 men when trouble began (D. S. xx. 47, 3 ff.; 49, 1 ff.; 52, 6; 53, 1), the standing garrison in the empire's capital may have been at least that size in later years, with many extra troops stationed permanently in the Delta (especially at Schedia) to be called up quickly in case of trouble. In addition, many thousands of troops would have been concentrated in the north of Egypt at any one time, especially since the Delta was the obvious marshalling place for troops to be sent overseas as replacements or reinforcements. Also, any cleruchs stationed in that area would have been available to be called up as necessary even if they were not part of the normal standing army there. It is impossible to know the military status or geographical origin of the troops in the Grand Procession, but it seems reasonable to suggest that their number is far greater than the normal standing garrison of Alexandria if not greater than all the troops available from all sources in the Delta.

It has generally been maintained that the occasion of the Grand Procession and its attendant festival was not a sufficient reason for so many troops to be concentrated in the capital, and that the procession was either a military triumph for a specific victory in war,[256] or a display of strength and a gathering of forces in preparation for war.[257] These arguments are connected with the alleged date of the procession, which must in this case have occurred immediately before or after a war in order to explain the troops (see Chapter 5 below). However, given the lack of information both about the external circumstances and date of the Grand Procession and about the size of the contemporary Ptolemaic army, one cannot insist upon the interpretation of the military parade as a victory celebration by troops recently returned to Alexandria from war, or as a general mobilization in the face of threatened hostilities. The number of troops could result from a combination of the city garrison, those stationed in the Delta, those called up from nearby cleruchies, and others imported to swell their ranks solely for the occasion of the Grand Procession. Hostilities were brewing in a general way at the time, both between the Ptolemies and the Macedonians, and between the Ptolemies and the Seleucids, and the army would naturally have been kept in an advanced

---

[254] For the location of the Ptolemaic garrisons see ibid., 131 ff.

[255] Ibid., 126–31; *Ptol. Alex.* i. 69; ii. 152–3 nn. 224–5.

[256] Tarn, *Alexander*, ii. 229.

[257] Otto, *Priester u. Tempel*, i. 153 n. 1.

state of preparation; the political atmosphere alone in those years could explain the presence and number of the troops. Such a deliberate display of military strength could not have failed to make a lasting impression upon the large number of official–and foreign–guests attending the festival in Alexandria. The march-past of the troops must have occupied several hours at least, or perhaps even a separate day, an amount of time which made their appearance emphatic and important; the impact of those solid ranks upon the spectators was calculated and desired. Special circumstances or pleading are not required to explain the presence, or even the number of troops, and the fragmentary knowledge of the circumstances surrounding the Grand Procession cautions against any fixed interpretation of this passage.

IV. CROWNING CEREMONY

The end of the text of the Grand Procession poses the most difficult problems in interpretation (203 A-B; lines 275 ff.):

> ἐστεφανώθησαν δ' ἐν τῷ ἀγῶνι καὶ στεφάνοις χρυσοῖς ΕΙΚΟΣΙ. Πτολεμαῖος δὲ ὁ πρῶτος καὶ Βερενίκη ΕΙΚΟΣΙ τρισὶν ἐφ' ἁρμάτων χρυσῶν καὶ τεμένεσιν ἐν Δωδώνῃ. καὶ ἐγένετο τὸ δαπάνημα τοῦ νομίσματος τάλαντα δισχίλια διακόσια τριάκοντα ἐννέα, μναῖ πεντήκοντα. καὶ ταῦτ' ἠριθμήθη πάντα τοῖς οἰκονόμοις διὰ τὴν τῶν στεφανούντων προθυμίαν πρὸ τοῦ τὰς θέας παρελθεῖν. ὁ δὲ Φιλάδελφος Πτολεμαῖος, ⟨ὁ⟩ υἱὸς αὐτῶν, ΕΙΚΟΣΙ χρυσαῖς δυσὶ μὲν ἐφ' ἁρμάτων χρυσῶν, ἐπὶ δὲ κιόνων ἐξαπήχει μιᾷ, πενταπήχεσι πέντε, τετραπήχεσι ἕξ.

These final lines have no apparent context since they begin, after an abbreviation indicated by Athenaeus, with an abrupt change of subject, and break off suddenly with no conclusion. There is no internal explanation of what is being described although various subjects are included and the narrative seems to jump among them: some kind of crowning ceremony, the dedication of statues to the royal family, and, in the middle, a seemingly extraneous section about the cost of crowns. These lines appear to have some connection, although an uncertain one, with the Grand Procession, since they refer to Soter, Berenike, Philadelphus, crowns, statues, and an *agon*, which, like a procession, formed part of a standard Greek religious festival. It is impossible to ascertain if these dedications are actually part of the Grand Procession (the statues at least may have been drawn along the processional route), or where or when these events are happening. After the Grand Procession, Kallixeinos may have described other notable features of the festival which were abridged but included by Athenaeus because of their magnificence. The most likely suggestion is that this section belongs to the crowning ceremony attached to the *agon* of the festival.

Some of the difficulties in this passage centre on the word ΕΙΚΟΣΙ, which, depending on the place of the accent, can be interpreted as either εἴκοσι, the indeclinable number '20', or the dative plural of the feminine noun εἰκών (εἰκόσι), 'statues', and the context leaves some room for disagreement about which should be read. Any interpretations must begin with the last sentence of this section, where the word εἰκόσι (statues) is clearly required because of the feminine adjective χρυσαῖς. A supplied verb such as ἐτιμήθη ('was honoured') or ἐστεφανώθη ('was crowned')[258] indicates that Philadelphus was honoured by dedications of two golden statues on golden chariots, analogous to the statue of Alexander which appears on a golden chariot (202A; line 227), and also by other statues on columns, a common practice in antiquity. These statues are not described, but may have been representations of Philadelphus, the two different types being dedicated by different donors.

The interpretation of ΕΙΚΟΣΙ elsewhere in this passage has been disputed, as well as the number of sentences into which this section should be divided. It is clear that a single sentence cannot be read from ἐστεφανώθη-σαν to Δωδώνη, regardless of the interpretation of ΕΙΚΟΣΙ, because the resulting word order (verb, first dative of agent, first subject, second subject, second dative of agent, third dative of agent) is completely at odds with the straightforward sequential word order invariably employed by Kallixeinos. To avoid this problem, the first sentence must end at the first ΕΙΚΟΣΙ, and the second begin with the subjects Ptolemy and Berenike, for whom a verb must be supplied. The analogy of the gold statues on chariots for Philadelphus indicates that statues should be understood with the chariots mentioned in connection with his parents. If the second ΕΙΚΟΣΙ is read as εἰκόσι, an acceptable meaning emerges: 'Ptolemy I and Berenike (were honoured) with three statues on golden chariots and with precincts at Dodona.' (If εἴκοσι were read here, 'twenty-three', the noun στεφάνοις would presumably have to be understood from the previous sentence, but chariots are not an appropriate vehicle for carrying and transporting crowns especially when they carry statues a few lines later.)

The first sentence presents no problems if εἴκοσι is read: 'And in the *agon* they were crowned with twenty gold crowns.' The subject is not specified, but this probably results from the fragmentary nature of this passage if Athenaeus began his quotation abruptly. Although Ptolemy I and Berenike could be understood as the subjects who were given honorary

---

[258] This verb is often used metaphorically in inscriptions with the meaning 'to honour'; for examples of honorands being 'crowned' with a statue see H. Engelmann, *The Delian Aretalogy of Sarapis* (*EPRO* 44) (Leiden, 1975), lines 9–10; L. Vidman(n), *Sylloge inscriptionum religionis Isiacae et Sarapiacae* (*RVV* 28) (Berlin, 1969), 102 lines 19–20; for an example of metaphorical 'crownings' with objects other than statues see Plb. xiii. 9, 5.

crowns in the *agon*, this is perhaps unlikely linguistically since their names are, in this case, repeated in the following sentence. If they are not the subjects, the unspecified parties may be the agonistic victors who are honoured with crowns, while the royal family received the higher honour of statues. (Εἴκοσι has been read in one translation as the subject of this sentence, 'twenty persons were crowned with gold crowns', but it cannot be right to take the last word in the sentence as a substantive. Kaibel reads εἰκόσι for all cases of ΕΙΚΟΣΙ and emends the first sentence to . . . στεφάνοις χρυσοῖς ⟨καὶ⟩ εἰκόσι. This is an unnecessary change given that the subject of this verb is unknown, and it removes the qualifying numeral from στεφάνοις although it is needed because Kallixeinos is always careful to record the number of everything.)

The mention of the precincts at Dodona in relation to a religious festival in third-century Alexandria is unexpected at first glance. If the phrase is correctly understood to mean that Ptolemy and Berenike were honoured with precincts at Dodona, it sounds as though a shrine was dedicated to them, or on their behalf, at that sanctuary and oracle of Zeus. A precinct had been dedicated to Ptolemy Soter by the Rhodians in thanks for his aid during the siege in 306 (D. S. xx. 100, 3-4; it is not known if this is the same as the 'temple of the Ptolemies' mentioned in Lucian, *Dem. Enc.* 2), and something of the kind may have been dedicated to the king and his wife at Dodona. Although no surviving inscription refers to this, and no such building has been identified, this would be explained if the form of the precinct was a defined plot of land (not a constructed shrine) which is the case with the Rhodian precinct. In any case, many of the buildings at the site of Dodona are not for the most part identifiable. The group of statues in honour of the family of Ptolemy III at Thermos in Aetolia shows that dedications to the Ptolemies did exist in western Greece.[259] Precincts may also have been dedicated to a god at Dodona 'on behalf of' Ptolemy and Berenike, which is a common form of Ptolemaic dedication; votive precincts, temples, statues, etc. are frequently specified in inscriptions recording such offerings to the gods.[260] The wording of the inscriptions show that a king was frequently honoured with this type of indirect dedication even if he might also be worshipped directly in his own right, which would have been the case with Soter and Berenike. Either type of dedication could explain the precincts at Dodona mentioned here, although it must be admitted that the phrase and historical context are alike obscure to the point of incomprehensibility.

This phrase is confusing in the context of this passage because it is not

---

[259] *IG* IX (1)² (1) 56; cf. *BE* 1959, No. 207 for a discussion of the possible arrangement of the statues.

[260] P. M. Fraser and A. Rumpf, *JEA* xxxviii (1952), 65 ff.

clear how the precincts are meant to be represented. The statues in honour of Soter, Berenike, and Philadelphus were probably displayed in public during the festival if not actually led along the processional route, perhaps on their way to a permanent site somewhere in the city, and within this group a model may have been displayed of the actual dedication to be established at Dodona (one portable shrine appears in the Grand Procession in 202C). Conversely, an inscribed plaque may have been displayed along with the statues recording that the precincts had been duly dedicated. Many such plaques exist, which were attached by a tang to a pillar or affixed to a wall, and this one may have appeared on a column along with the statues of Philadelphus in order to be displayed to the spectators.

Dodona was an ancient oracle of Zeus, and a large sanctuary whose importance did not decline in the Hellenistic period; although oracular inquiries from official state delegations may have decreased over the centuries, the large number of private inquiries of early Hellenistic date shows no diminution of the oracle's activity.[261] Even granting the prominence of the sanctuary, there must have been a particular reason why a Ptolemaic dedication was made so far afield from Egypt, since an offering to Zeus could have been made in an Alexandrian temple or elsewhere in Ptolemaic lands. Dodona's importance may lie in the fact that it was in the kingdom of Epirus, ruled at the time of the Grand Procession by Pyrrhus, who had a close tie with Ptolemy I. Ptolemy had restored the young prince to his throne from his Egyptian exile in 298 and the latter returned to Epirus married to one of Ptolemy's daughters, and established many reminders of his patron in his kingdom. This friendship was translated into a military alliance with Ptolemy and Lysimachus in the battle of the coalition against Demetrius in 288, and although Ptolemy did not help Pyrrhus in his later struggles against Lysimachus, his diplomatic need not to alienate Lysimachus was great. This lack of positive support did not end the friendship between Egypt and Epirus, and Soter's policy of general benevolence towards Pyrrhus seems to have been inherited by Philadelphus.[262] It appears that the Ptolemies never acted openly or directly against the aims of Pyrrhus; if they could not support him when he was acting against their own self-interest, or else be seen to support him, they maintained a neutral position, as with his struggle with Lysimachus. Pyrrhus was at least not hindered by Philadelphus in his Italian campaign, and may actually have been aided, if not merely supported, by Philadelphus in his later invasion of Macedonia which, strategically, could only have

---

[261] H. W. Parke, *The Oracles of Zeus* (Oxford, 1967), 120, 259 ff.
[262] For this reconstruction of events see P. Lévêque, *REA* lviii (1956), 83 ff.; id., *Pyrrhos* (Paris, 1957), 259 ff.

Egypt's blessing.[263] The sanctuary at Dodona was favoured by Pyrrhus: during his reign, it was extended and aggrandized, the main temple of Zeus was enlarged and refurbished, several smaller shrines were built, and an immense theatre was established.[264] In addition to his transformation of Dodona into an Epirote civic and cultural centre, Pyrrhus may have consulted the oracle about his own affairs, which would have been only natural (cf. *FGrH* 532 F 1 40 for a dedication made at Lindos on the advice of the oracle), and he used the sanctuary as a place of dedication for the spoils of his victories (*SIG*³ 392; Paus. i. 13, 3).

The Ptolemaic dedication may have had more immediate political connotations, since the Grand Procession probably occurred while Pyrrhus was absent in Italy. These newly dedicated precincts may have been a gesture of Ptolemaic support for Pyrrhus at home in the face of his many enemies who had been eager to remove him from Epirus. The symbolic presence of the Ptolemies would have recalled the fact that the parents of Philadelphus had once restored Pyrrhus to his rightful throne to the chagrin of Demetrius (the father of Antigonus Gonatas who was a current rival for the Macedonian kingship), and may have indicated continued Ptolemaic support for his position as king of Epirus. The public display and announcement of the precincts at Dodona in the festival connected to the Grand Procession would have been an emphatic statement of this support for Pyrrhus in face of the opposition to him by the other contemporary monarchs.

Apart from the political nuances of the Ptolemaic dedication, the Ptolemies may have felt a special tie with the sanctuary at Dodona for religious reasons which in turn may have strengthened the political significance of the precincts. In some traditions, the sanctuary had age-old ties with the oracle of Ammon in Egypt since the two oracles were believed to have a common source, being both founded by priestesses or doves from Egyptian Thebes (Hdt. ii. 52 ff.; Pind. *Paean* fr. 58 (Snell-Maehler).[265] Although this was not the traditional account of the founding of Dodona, it was evidently popular in classical times, and it is possible that the Ptolemies claimed some 'national' affinity with the Greek sanctuary. Another religious tie between the Ptolemies and Dodona may lie in the worship there of Dionysus,[266] with whom the Ptolemies wished to publicize their special relationship. The cult of Dionysus had connections

---

[263] Tarn, *Ant. Gon.* 445, suggested that Ptolemaic funds paid for the expedition, but see G. N. Cross, *Epirus: A Study in Greek Constitutional Development* (Cambridge, 1932), 120 ff.

[264] Cf. Parke, *Oracles*, 118 ff.; N. G. L. Hammond, *Epirus* (Oxford, 1967), 582 ff.; S. I. Dakaris, *Archaeological Guide to Dodona* (Ioannina, 1971), Pl. 13.

[265] For a discussion of this tradition see Parke, *Oracles*, 52 ff.

[266] Cf. an oracle of Dodona (which is perhaps genuine) ordering the Athenians to

with Dodona through certain variations in his mythology.[267] In one version of his childhood, Dionysus was entrusted to seven Nymphs who were the children of Dodon (e.g. Pherecydes, *FGrH* 3 F 90), and Dionysus was sometimes said to be either the son of Dione (the consort of Zeus at Dodona from early times; Schol. Pind. *Pyth.* iii. 177B; Hesychius s.v. Βάκχου Διώνης), or else her husband, and the father, by her, of Priapus (Schol. Theoc. i. 21). The adult Dionysus is said in some traditions to have consulted the oracle at Dodona in order to cure the madness inflicted upon him by Hera (see p. 100 and n. 199), and the Calydonians appealed to Dodona when they were afflicted with the madness of Dionysus (Paus. vii. 21). No one of these alternative versions would have been believed exclusively at any one time, but the variants may have merged into a general mythological picture of Dionysus' connection with Dodona, which may have been additional reasons for a Ptolemaic dedication there. If Dionysus was an important honorand in the Grand Procession because the Ptolemies ensured the legitimacy of their descent from Alexander through an alleged mutual relationship with the god, a dedication at a shrine in western Greece where Dionysus was also at home may have been another way of publicizing to the Macedonian kings the Ptolemaic claims nearer to the formers' homeland. The contemporary relevance of Dodona in Alexandria is perhaps seen in a reference in Callimachus, who mentions the sanctuary as the first stop of the Hyperborean Gifts on their journey from the north to Delos (*Hymn.* iv. 283 ff.).

The remaining sentence of this final section, which interrupts the account of the various dedications to the royal family, records the payment to officials of the very large sum of 2,239 talents and 50 minae. Kallixeinos must have copied such a precise amount from the official archives, and the amount must therefore have been recorded in Alexandrian currency, which obviates the suggested emendations of Kaibel (ad loc.), who assumes that Kallixeinos converted the sum to his native Rhodian currency. Kallixeinos records the cost in coinage because it was paid in by various private individuals, certainly in coin, from which crowns were purchased by some central authority. This politic gesture by those wishing to be seen publicly supporting the royal extravaganza is analogous to the practice of foreign states sending crowns to a host state on the occasion of an important festival (this was done, for example, at the

---

send dedications to Zeus Naios, Dione, Dionysus, Apollo, and Zeus Ktesios; the oracle is quoted in Demosth. *in Meid.* 53. For a discussion of its authenticity see Parke, *Oracles*, 84 ff.; 92 n. 12.

[267] For a more detailed discussion of Dionysus' tie with Dodona see Parke, *Oracles*, 150 ff.

Ptolemaieia; *SIG*³ 390, 42 ff.), except that here the price is paid instead of of the actual crown being sent.²⁶⁸

Although this sentence does not provide much information, a few further assumptions can be made. The sum of money appears to cover only the cost of the crowns and not the whole festival or Grand Procession, but it is not clear which crowns are meant. Thousands of crowns are mentioned throughout the text of the Grand Procession, some worn by participants, some carried along as divine offerings, one magnificent one dedicated to Ptolemy I, and some used in the agonistic crowning ceremony; but θέα may refer to the procession alone or to the whole spectacle of the festival. On the grounds of narrative proximity, which is not decisive in this confused section of the text, the sum may be intended to pay for the crowns used as prizes in the *agon*, since, judging from the scale and scope of the Grand Procession, the *agon* probably included thousands of participants and required many crowns as victors' prizes. On the other hand, it is possible that the crowns worn in the Grand Procession were reused as prizes in the *agon*, and that the sum here was the cost of all the crowns in the festival. More than 2,000 talents surely would have paid for thousands of crowns even of precious metal.

Oikonomoi were the officials in charge of the funds and presumably responsible for arranging the purchase of the crowns.²⁶⁹ These well-attested administrative officials were the stewards of the royal economic interests in the nomes of Egypt under the control of the *dioiketes*, the royal finance minister, and his assistants outside Alexandria. The *oikonomos* functioned as the local *dioiketes* of a nome, and was responsible for the economic life of his area, including all the state-controlled aspects of agriculture, husbandry, trade, and industry. With only the term 'oikonomoi' used in the text of Kallixeinos, it is impossible to know the level at which the collection of

---

²⁶⁸ Sending crowns, whether real crowns or sums of money equivalent to their cost, was an especially common practice in Ptolemaic Egypt during festivals and royal anniversaries; see Cl. Préaux, *L'Économie royale des Lagides* (Brussels, 1939), 39 ff. Later, the cost of a crown was required to be paid as a tax to the royal treasury in certain circumstances, as when, for example, holders of cleruchic land were promoted; see *PTeb.* 61 (b), 254 and note ad loc. Other gifts were also frequently sent from the chora to Alexandria for a festival: *PCZ* 59154, 59560 (presents sent to the king on the occasion of the Isis festival), 59820 (presents sent to the king for the festival of the Theoi Adelphoi), 59821 (presents sent for the royal birthday); *PLond.* 2000 (a variety of animals sent as a gift to the king for sacrifices at the Arsinoeia).

²⁶⁹ For the structure of financial management in Ptolemaic Egypt and for the duties of *oikonomoi* see Rostovtzeff, *Large Estate*, 148 ff.; idem, *SEHHW*, 269. For a study of the duties of *oikonomoi* as revealed in Zenon's correspondence see *PSorb.* 391 (M. Hombert, *Rev. Belge de Phil. et d'Hist.* iv (1925), 652 No. 8); *PTeb.* 703 contains a list of instructions on the management of various departments of the royal revenues, which the editors, ad loc., think is a letter from the *dioiketes* of Alexandria to an *oikonomos*; cf. *PPetr.* iii. 32 for a series of petitions to the *oikonomos* of the Arsinoite nome.

money for crowns was made. Since officials of this designation were spread around the nomes of Egypt, people throughout the chora may have made contributions to their local *oikonomos* who passed the funds into a central authority which purchased the crowns. *Oikonomoi* worked closely with the *dioiketes* in the third century,[270] so the invitations for contributions for the crowns may have come originally as a royal directive from Alexandria. The *oikonomoi* mentioned here may, however, have been those officials appointed by the *dioiketes* to administer Alexandria, in which case the inhabitants of the provincial nomes may not have been involved in this festival. If this refers to officials who were centred in Alexandria in addition to, or instead of, those in the chora, they may also have received the contributions of any foreign dignitaries who either sent or brought funds for crowns on the occasion of the Grand Procession.

[270] *PTeb.* 703, s.v. introduction.

4. Kallixeinos of Rhodes

The few biographical details which are known about Kallixeinos of Rhodes come from information provided by Athenaeus and cannot be amplified by additional facts from other sources. The name 'Kallixeinos' has a varied orthography in ancient texts, but Athenaeus uses the form Καλλίξεινος which is also the most usual version in Rhodian inscriptions.[1] The author's patronymic is unknown (which magnifies the difficulty of any attempt to identify the man with attested homonyms; see pp. 151 ff. and Appendix III), but he is occasionally given the ethnic Ῥόδιος in the *Deipnosophistai* (196A; 387C; 474E; 677D). Since Kallixeinos wrote a work entitled *About Alexandria*, he presumably spent some time in that city; movement from Rhodes to Alexandria was easy enough in the third century, and an educated man like Kallixeinos may have lived for a time in the Ptolemaic capital, naturally availing himself of the facilities of the Mouseion and Library. Indeed, it cannot be excluded that he was born there of Rhodian parents. If he was an eye-witness observer of some of the subjects of his descriptions, his presence at some point in Alexandria is assured, but even if he saw none of them himself, the records which he consulted for the details of the Grand Procession (197D; line 9) would surely have been preserved there. The date of Kallixeinos is anchored only by the accession of Ptolemy IV Philopator to the throne of Egypt in 221 BC, which furnishes a *terminus post quem* for the author's death since the boats described by him, the '40' and the Nile Barge, were constructed in the reign of that monarch. All other inferences about his life must come from internal evidence in the existing text of *About Alexandria*.

A. THE FRAGMENTARY TEXT

We possess four large fragments of *About Alexandria*, all preserved in the fifth book of the *Deipnosophistai*. Book I of the work contained the descriptions of the two ships of Philopator, and Book IV the account of the Grand Procession, preceded by that of the ornamental pavilion which was probably used in the festivities surrounding the procession. Kallixeinos is quoted elsewhere in Athenaeus in lexicographical discussions of unusual words, but all but two of these quotations (Appendix I F 3-4) come from the extant text of *About Alexandria*. These and other possible references to Kallixeinos and his works are discussed below (see Chapter 4 C and

[1] *Ptol. Alex.* ii. 738 n. 152.

Appendix III). The scant remains of *About Alexandria* indicate that the author described several impressive features of that city, and since these passages are quoted by Athenaeus as culminating examples in his digression on ancient luxury, the work may have been known primarily for accounts of such marvels. Since it consisted of at least four books, its scope may have been wide enough to encompass some permanent features of the city besides the ephemeral structures and events whose descriptions have been preserved. Since, however, the scope and arrangement of the work are unknown, it cannot be assumed that Kallixeinos wrote an ordered, discernible periegesis of the city. He clearly did not arrange his subjects chronologically since the ships of Ptolemy IV were described before the procession of Ptolemy II, but although the different books of *About Alexandria* may have treated individual topics (for example, naval matters in Book I, and religion in Book IV), this cannot be proved.

The fact that the fragments of Kallixeinos exist outside their original contexts in *About Alexandria* increases the difficulty in interpreting them. With any author whose work exists only in fragments, however substantial, it is vitally important to understand the nature and extent of the excerption from the original work (whether due to the chance of historical survival or to deliberate selection by other writers). Theories about Kallixeinos' work vary according to the views held on such questions. Four levels of selection are relevant to a study of Kallixeinos, the first of which concerns his choice of topic. Because the scope and content of *About Alexandria* are unknown, it is impossible to know what topics Kallixeinos chose for inclusion, or upon what basis he made his selection. Since the four preserved fragments describe subjects worthy of public admiration in terms emphasizing their ostentation and extravagance, one is tempted to suggest that Kallixeinos' interests may have been more paradoxographical than strictly periegetic or historical. Any such bias would have influenced his choice of subject-matter about Alexandria and affected his treatment of it. These considerations affect the interpretation of the account of the Grand Procession, whose context and the reasons for its inclusion in *About Alexandria* are alike unknown. It is impossible to determine, for example, whether Kallixeinos included the description because of the historical significance of the Grand Procession, or because its inherently fascinating ostentation captured his literary imagination. The many existing theories about the occasion of the Grand Procession stem from different hypotheses about such matters.

The second level of selection concerns Kallixeinos' choice of material within his topic. 'Penteteric records' are mentioned as the external source for his description of the Grand Procession. If he was totally dependent upon these sources for his information, his account could only have been as good as the source upon which it was based, but there is no way of knowing how accurately he used his sources. They were not reproduced verbatim, but excerpted, since they are recommended to readers wishing *more* details about the occasion. Kallixeinos may have selected from the sources only the most impressive items from all those whose descriptions were contained within. The information chosen for inclusion by Kallixeinos from all the available material on the topic was the result of a judgement made before composition from reasons unknown to his readers. His literary and artistic viewpoint determined what he chose from the sources and also perhaps from his memory (if he had been present at the Grand Procession), but his final choice is all that is visible in his work. The resulting descriptions may therefore be distorted versions of the subjects as they really were. Kallixeinos may have omitted large portions of material which he considered irrelevant to his particular purpose in writing, omissions which, in the case of the Grand Procession, may have provided the crucial clues to the identification and interpretation of the event, which cannot now be recovered. Conversely, if interested primarily in one particular aspect of his subject (such as the Dionysiac elements in the Grand Procession), Kallixeinos may have embellished and elaborated it so that in his text it had a disproportionate emphasis in relation to the whole event. A reader will hardly recognize this reduction or expansion of material and can never redress the balance; for this reason, theories about the occasion which depend upon the internal evidence in the transmitted text remain ultimately conjectural. The idea of the selection of information for the account of the Grand Procession (whether due to Kallixeinos' choice of material or to the limitation of his sources) leads, perhaps inevitably, to speculation about what the original Grand Procession 'must' have comprised. It is theoretically possible to maintain that it contained any feature whose description can be omitted, compressed, or expanded in order to concur, at least superficially, with the preserved account in Kallixeinos.[2]

   The third level of selection results from the artificial form of the dialogues in the *Deipnosophistai*, which forces the reader to consider both Kallixeinos and Athenaeus as possible-excerptors when the text is abbreviated explicitly or implicitly. In explicit abbreviations, the identity of the

---

[2] Otto's early interpretation of the Grand Procession, *Priester u. Tempel*, i. 145 ff., is a case in point. He begins with the conviction that the Grand Procession had some connection with the cult of the θεοὶ Σωτῆρες and explains the neglect of the cult of Soter as an indication that had become affiliated to, and eclipsed by, the cult of Alexander, which Otto sees as the climax of the Procession. He is thus forced to consider the over-all pre-eminence of Dionysus over Alexander throughout the text as a fortuitous result of Kallixeinos' selection of material from an original source which had emphasized Alexander. Otto later retracted this idea, but his error illustrates the freedom with which the text can be interpreted if the premise of distorted selection by the author is accepted.

speaker when a first-person verb is used may pose a problem. There may be no way of knowing absolutely when Athenaeus quotes Kallixeinos verbatim (in which case the first-person speaker is Kallixeinos), or when he abbreviates or paraphrases parts of Kallixeinos' text (in which case the first person is Athenaeus). Although a candidate for speaker can be suggested in most cases with reasonable certainty, the various opinions of the editors of Athenaeus when indicating *oratio recta* and *obliqua* bear witness to the possible differences of interpretation. Even when the identity of the excerptor is known for certain (as when Athenaeus interrupts the quotation and refers to Kallixeinos by name), it is impossible to recover the original text even if the general subject of the explicit abbreviation can be guessed from the surrounding context. Implicit abbreviations are more subtly misleading since there is no linguistic sign that the text has been shortened by Athenaeus. Just as when Kallixeinos selected information to include in his account from all that was available on the Grand Procession, material from the complete text of Kallixeinos may have been selected or omitted by Athenaeus so that his quotation is an irreparably distorted version of the original text. Without an independent textual transmission for Kallixeinos, this category of information, and even its general subject, can never be recovered.

The fourth and final level of selection which can never be overcome by the modern reader is the fact that the *Deipnosophistai* is not itself preserved in full, but has been handed down through several abridgements.[3] The original thirty books have disappeared irrevocably, and were at some unknown time reduced to the present fifteen books. In a second abridgement, the first two books and a part of the third were lost. (This stage is preserved in manuscript A.) A third abridgement is known as the Epitome (preserved in manuscripts C and E), which summarizes all fifteen of the remaining books and thereby restores part of the lacuna at the beginning as well as other passages which were accidentally lost. The present text of Athenaeus consists of the fifteen books (without the end of the fifteenth), and the parts of the first books which are supplied by the Epitome. Fortunately for the text of Kallixeinos, Book V seems to be complete and undisturbed by this series of abridgements, but it cannot be known for certain whether this part of Athenaeus' text was shortened by one of several ancient or medieval editors. Each and every abridgement of the *Deipnosophistai* may have increased our distance from the original text of Kallixeinos.

The reader of Kallixeinos is therefore caught in the centre of a series of concentric circles of information, which increase in size from the circle

---

[3] This process is reconstructed by A. M. Desrousseaux, ed., *Les Deipnosophistes* (Paris, 1956), i. *xxxi* ff.

of the Epitomator (although this can probably be safely discounted as far as Book V is concerned), through that of Athenaeus and his use of Kallixeinos for his own literary purposes, up to the outermost circle of the text of Kallixeinos, the nature of which is obscured further by the impossibility of knowing the author's conscious and subconscious literary methods.

B. THE CREDIBILITY OF ATHENAEUS AND KALLIXEINOS

Although the existing text of Kallixeinos has been distilled through several filters, the question of the credibility of the transmitted account must be considered on two main levels: the credibility of Athenaeus,[4] who quoted *About Alexandria*, and the credibility of Kallixeinos, who wrote it. The credibility of the former may be studied through a comparison of passages of authors quoted in the *Deipnosophistai* with the extant texts of those authors, a method applicable only to those works with a textual transmission independent of Athenaeus, which is not the case with *About Alexandria*. Nevertheless, the examination of such parallel texts suggests that Athenaeus quoted other authors with care and precision; many of the textual variations which do exist can be attributed to scribal errors or misunderstanding, and, in several cases, Athenaeus used texts of authors (Homer, Plato, Theophrastus, *et al.*) which preserved different readings often preferable to those obtained from a recension of the extant manuscripts of the authors in question. Athenaeus also appears to have been careful with the use of his sources throughout. A study of the word patterns used to introduce *oratio recta* and *obliqua* indicates that it is always possible to ascertain when Athenaeus quotes a text directly or paraphrases it. He furthermore gives occasional information about the limitation of his sources: he admits uncertainty about the identity of one of his sources (479F), he mentions that he cannot check the reliability of another source which names the author of a certain treatise (174E), and he acknowledges that parts of particular works may be spurious (166D). Such indications suggest that Athenaeus quoted his material carefully, did not change his excerpts wilfully or arbitrarily, and that reasonable credence may be attributed to his authority. This general picture of Athenaeus' literary method may be used with some confidence to illuminate his treatment of unsupported authors such as Kallixeinos, since there is no evidence that Athenaeus changed his scholarly standards throughout his work, assuming that a comparable standard of source

---

[4] These conclusions about Athenaeus' quotation of other authors and his methods of introducing *oratio recta* and *obliqua* are based on K. Zepernick, *Philologus* lxxvii (1921), 311 ff.

material was available to him. The literary purpose of the *Deipnosophistai* also argues for its over-all dependability. Precision in quotation must have been a desideratum to an author who was in fact compiling a compendium of ancient literature, and who included lexicographical discussions where comprehension depended upon exact quotation in order to explain a definition or syntactic usage. Athenaeus undoubtedly quoted from memory in several passages, as did all ancient authors whose formal education depended primarily upon the techniques of memorization, but he certainly had access to manuscript material since he mentions the large size of his own library (3A). Even if this claim is exaggerated, Athenaeus, a native of Naucratis in the Delta, may have had access to whatever remained during his time of the Library at Alexandria.[5] With such bibliographical resources at his disposal, he would have been able to check his references on specific points of quotation if he had deemed it necessary.

Athenaeus' excerpts from *About Alexandria* cannot be checked against an independent text to determine if they contain serious errors, but given his careful use of sources, there is no reason to suppose that he meddled with the text in an interpretative way, especially since Kallixeinos is quoted for the sake of the information he preserves. This holds true for the large fragments, whose importance to Athenaeus lay in the details of ancient luxury which they catalogue, as well as for the lexicographical references to the text of Kallixeinos elsewhere, where accuracy in quotation was essential. If all the excerpts from Kallixeinos had been quoted directly by Athenaeus from a text of *About Alexandria*, there are good grounds for supposing that he was as accurate as his circumstances permitted.

If reasonable confidence can be felt regarding the credibility of Athenaeus' account of Kallixeinos, the next question is the credibility of Kallixeinos himself. The discussion of the Grand Procession in the preceding chapter has shown that its component parts follow a logical progression, and that details which sound exaggerated may be comprehensible as they stand. A comparable standard of credibility emerges from an examination of the other three fragments of Kallixeinos, although they deal with subjects which sound equally, if not more, fantastic than some of the items in the procession because of their prodigious size, expense, and ostentation. A brief account of the ships and the pavilion, and the various views held about them, shows the sort of reliable detail which can be obtained from Kallixeinos' descriptions.

The interpretation of the descriptions of the two boats of Philopator is partly hampered by the modern world's incomplete understanding of

---

[5] For the later history of the Library see A. J. Butler, *The Arab Conquest of Egypt* (P. M. Fraser, ed.) (2nd ed., Oxford, 1978), lxxv.

ancient ships. Various theories have been advanced about the warship called the '40' (App. I, F 1, 203E ff.), and even if several details of its form remain obscure and disputed, recent theories at least assume that the ship can be explained from the information given by Kallixeinos. The account of the ship has been disbelieved by some scholars,[6] and the only other ancient evidence for the '40' comes from Plutarch who says that it was a cumbersome monstrosity which could barely move, much less manœuvre in battle conditions (*Demetr.* xliii. 4-5). Since, however, Plutarch does not give his sources, it is impossible to evaluate this remark which may only have been based upon his own understanding of ships built half a millennium before his own time, and a guess about the possibilities of ancient navigation. There remains Kallixeinos' observation that the '40' εὔρυθμος δ' ἦν καθ' ὑπερβολήν (204A). Although this speaks more for the pleasing lines and proportion of the ship than for its mobility, Kallixeinos' account of the methods used to launch the ship must mean that it was navigationally viable (204C-D): it is clear from this passage that the ship was used in successive voyages after being dry-docked and refitted,[7] and such an ambitious method of launching could hardly have been used for a ship so cumbersome that it was in danger of breaking up. Even if the '40' was slow and sluggish in the water, it may also have been unapproachable, unsinkable, and invincible because of its poliorcetic machines and the large complement of marines aboard.[8] Lightning ramming tactics had passed with the age of the trireme, and after Demetrius Poliorcetes warships were essentially floating battlegrounds. With the drastically changed naval tactics, great speed and manœuvrability were no longer a prerequisite of the great warships, and the design of the '40' may reflect these new tactics. With the benefit of hindsight, the assumption that the '40' was not an effective warship may seem consistent with Egypt's political decline throughout the third century, and with the belief that she was no longer a dangerous naval threat by the end of that century. It is, however, by no means clear that Egypt saw herself in this light. Despite grave defeats in the naval battles of Andros and Cos, Egypt maintained her fleet in Asia Minor, and since the Achaean League chose Ptolemy III as strategos on land and sea in 242/1 (Plut. *Arat.* xxiv), Ptolemaic naval power in the Aegean may still have been a force to be reckoned with, especially since possessions in Thrace had to be maintained (cf. the Adulis Inscription, *OGIS* 54, 14 ff., and *SIG*[3] 502, which attest renewed Ptolemaic activity

---

[6] G. S. Laird Clowes, *Sailing Ships: Their History and Development* (3rd ed., London, 1932), i. 28; Russell Meiggs, *Trees and Timber in the Ancient Mediterranean World* (Oxford, 1982), 138.

[7] See Landels, *Engineering*, 163, for the suggestion that it is a dry-dock (for repairing and refitting the vessel) which is described.

[8] Ibid., 153.

in Thrace in the first decade of the reign of Euergetes after the end of the Third Syrian War).[9] The next Ptolemy, Philopator, who had the same ambitious ministers (Agathokles and Sosibios) as his predecessor, may have been persuaded to see himself in a tenable position in the political triangle with Philip V and Antiochus III, who, it must be remembered, was severely defeated by Egypt at the battle of Raphia in 217. The construction of the largest warship ever known at that time may have been intended to announce that Egypt was far from finished as a naval power. This action would have been in keeping with the royal ministers' political designs and with the king's own megalomaniac preoccupations and flair for the grand gesture. In describing a ship whose details strain credulity (for example, the crew consisted of 400 sailors, 4,000 rowers, and about 3,000 marines), Kallixeinos may preserve the account of the ultimate development of a new trend in naval architecture in the power struggle of the third-century Hellenistic world.

The design of the '40' has posed problems since the number-name used to describe it is significantly greater than those naming the larger boats which came into fashion in the Hellenistic Age, among them '10s', '15s', '16s', '20s', and '30s'. It has been generally accepted that the number-names of these ships do not refer to the number of superimposed banks of rowers (there is no proof that boats were constructed with more than three such banks, and it is indeed improbable that any boat with more than four or five banks *could* have existed), but to the number of rowers per rowing unit, that is, the number of men in any one rowing position along the hull, spread out over the superimposed banks of oars.[10] Thus an '8' had eight men in each position along the hull, a '10' had ten, etc. Since it would have been impracticable to accommodate even as few as 10 rowers along a massive oar,[11] a new type of design or rowing system seems indicated in a ship with a number-name as large as the '40', although various arrangements of rowers spread over three levels could explain the number-names of the other large ships. Four thousand oarsmen, divided into groups of forty, could not have been distributed over a three-banked system[12] by the usual means of reckoning (assuming that the Greeks were consistent in the terminology used to name their ships), since Kallixeinos

[9] Cf. W. S. Ferguson, *JHS* xxx (1910), 199; Will, *Hist. pol.* i². 255 ff.; Beloch, *Gr. Gesch.* iv (2), 346–8; R. S. Bagnall, *JEA* lxi (1975), 168 ff. (on *PTeb.* 8).

[10] For a discussion about rowing arrangements on the larger ships see Casson, *Ships and Seamanship*, 99 ff.

[11] Casson, 100 and n. 20, reckons that 8 rowers were the maximum since this was the largest number ever accommodated on Venetian galleasses.

[12] The '40' must have had three banks, like a trireme, since Kallixeinos calls the longest oars αἱ θρανιτικαί, the term used for the topmost oars on triremes; cf. Casson, 83, 109.

states that the longest oars on the '40' were fifty-seven feet long, a length which could not accommodate many more than eight men on each.

The new, unusual form devised for the '40' may explain its large power-ratio number. Kallixeinos describes the vessel as δίπρῳρος καὶ δίπρυμνος (204A), 'double-prowed' and 'double-sterned', which must mean that the '40' was a catamaran consisting of two separate hulls joined permanently together.[13] Ancient ships were often lashed together temporarily,[14] a practice which was also used for special purposes in Ptolemaic Egypt (see below, p. 146), and the step from a temporary to a permanent pair is not a big one. The fact that the '40' had four steering oars when a usual Greek ship had two (one on either side of the stern) shows that one oar was placed on each side of the two sterns. Furthermore, the '40' carried twelve *hypozomata* (rope girders which passed horizontally from bow to stern around the hulls of ancient ships to give extra strength and support) when the usual number on a Greek ship was four. Six could have been intended for each hull of the '40' (with not all of them fitted at once), and it has been calculated that the length of these *hypozomata* (900 ft) was sufficient to encircle each hull singly, but not the whole vessel.[15]

If these unusual features of the '40' can be explained by the fact that it was a catamaran, its naming numeral may be twice the number of rowers spread over each rowing unit because there are two hulls to consider: the ship may really have been two individual '20s' called a '40' because it was one ship composed of two. Twenty oarsmen, not forty, distributed over three levels would be an acceptable number given the limitations of men per oar. This reason for doubling the naming numeral has not been universally accepted.[16] The use of the doubled numeral is certainly artificial, but if the '40' was an innovation as the first catamaran warship,[17] there would have been no precedent for its numerical rating, and if the designers had wanted to indicate that this ship was somehow different in form besides being the largest existing warship, the greatest possible numerical rating may well have been used for its name especially if there was some

[13] Ibid., 110 ff. Casson, however, ibid., 111, is seriously wrong in his interpretation of the rowing arrangements; see J. S. Morrison, *IJNA* i (1972), 232 (*sub* pp. 108 ff.).

[14] Polyaen. i. 47; iii. 11, 3; v. 22, 2; Livy xxiv. 34, 6–7; Hdt. vii. 35–6. See also Köster, *Ant. Seewesen*, 33 ff.

[15] For a discussion of *hypozomata* on Greek ships see Morrison and Williams, *GOS*, 294–8 (p. 296 for the '40').

[16] J. S. Morrison has told me privately that he disagrees with this suggestion.

[17] Casson, 112, 114, suggests that certain other Hellenistic warships were catamarans, and were the models for the '40' on the ground that Philopator was no naval innovator. There is, however, no evidence for the shape of the boats he adduces (only the number-names or number of rowers are known). Meiggs, 138, who makes no attempt to explain why the ship is called a '40', is unconvinced that it was a catamaran on the grounds that such a revolutionary change of design should have left some trace; but cf. n. 24 below.

slight numerical justification for it. Any detailed interpretations of the rowing arrangements rest on supposition, but must account for the 4,000 oarsmen accommodated in a ship 420 feet long by 57 feet wide (each hull being approximately 28 feet in width). Since the topmost oars were fifty-seven feet long, they must have had an inboard length of some sixteen to twenty-four feet, reckoning from the Renaissance limit of eight men per oar and two to three feet on the oar for each man, which would have taken up most of the space within the hulls. The number of rowing positions along the 420-foot hull is not stated, but, given the large number of men per oar,[18] about six feet would probably have been needed between tholes. On this reckoning, the maximum number of rowing positions along the hull of the '40' would be about sixty-five, allowing room for bow and stern projections. Twenty men in sixty-five positions in two hulls gives a full complement of some 2,600 rowers, but 1,400 still need to be accounted for. These may have been extras intended to take over when a fresh crew was needed, but if the inside oars took up as much as twenty-four of the twenty-eight feet available in the hulls, the extra crew could hardly have been stationed there, although they may have been on deck with the marines. Another solution may be inferred from Kallixeinos' statement that the numbers of the crew which he records were taken on a *trial* voyage (204B: γενομένης δὲ ἀναπείρας . . .). If these men were not the complement of regular crew, but a larger group taken on board as an experiment to find the maximum number which could be safely accommodated,[19] the recorded number of rowers can be explained in conjuction with the hypothetical rowing arrangement.

If it is an acceptable change in naval numerical terminology that the '40' is so called because it is a catamaran composed of two '20s', then the ship is comprehensible in design even if it is difficult to accommodate all the oarsmen in the space available if they are all rowing at the same time. The '40' cannot be a true '40', with forty men in each rowing unit, without accepting more people along an oar than is possible, given its length; the alternative would be to accept a push-pull system with men on both sides of the oar to make up the number of forty, but this system cannot be shown ever to have existed.[20] It remains to consider why the catamaran

[18] On Venetian galeasses of the 17th century (which had as many as 8 men per oar), the distance between tholes was *c.*5'9". Cf. A. Jal, *La Flotte de César* (Paris, 1861), 197; Meiggs, 138, who estimates about 180 oars in each bank, does not take this factor into account.

[19] Landels, 153.

[20] This is the suggestion of Morrison, *IJNA* i (1972), 232 (*sub* pp. 108 ff.), who reckons that rowers in groups of 14:13:13 were divided over 3 banks, and that the oarsmen were seated along both sides of the oar using a push-pull movement (this is not made clear in the article mentioned, but he has told me that this was his meaning). The only evidence that such a rowing arrangement was ever used at any period consists of a model of a 17th-century galeass, *La Royale*, the oars of which have

was developed as a naval innovation. The ships which were temporarily joined served tactical purposes (i.e. to carry large pieces of siege equipment), but in no case was their combination a nautical advantage. Since the boat was composed of two narrow hulls rather than a single wide one, it may have been able to attain a greater speed more easily because the water resistance would have been less than against one heavier hull sunk lower into the water, but, in any case, the double hull would have increased the stability of a ship which must have been decidedly high up out of the water and top-heavy. (The dangerous instability of modern multi-hulls is due to the fact that they are sailing boats which heel over from the force of the wind. This would not be the case with an oared ship.) It is possible that the design was used initially because of its novelty, but, nevertheless, the ship deserves a closer look as the ultimate example in a century of impressive naval developments. Kallixeinos' cursory description is comprehensible since enough can be inferred from it to allow for a plausible reconstruction of the ship. Allowing for the gaps in modern understanding of ancient naval technology, Kallixeinos remains a credible witness in his account of the '40'.

The Nile Barge, or Thalamegos, of Ptolemy IV is described by Kallixeinos after the '40' (Appendix I, F 1, 204D ff.). It has been studied by Caspari and Köster, who both attempt full interpretations and reconstructions of the vessel which differ from each other in many points, but still show that the boat has parallels in dynastic and Ptolemaic Egypt and is comprehensible in form and decoration. These conclusions give credibility to Kallixeinos' account of a ship which was undoubtedly the most magnificent vessel of its kind and whose description may seem the quintessence of fantastic luxury. Thalamegoi were in use on the Nile from early dynastic times, and, although less pretentious than that described by Kallixeinos, many of these river boats were large and elaborate, with spacious, pavilion-type cabins on their decks.[21] The Greeks adopted this effective mode of river

handholds on both sides. This vessel is drawn and discussed by F. E. Pâris, *Souvenirs de Marine* (Paris, 1884), ii. 65–71; cf. W. L. Rodgers, *Naval Warfare under Oars* (Annapolis, 1939), 238 Fig. 34. It is unlikely, however, that this ship was ever intended to be built, and its system of oarage is dubious in any case. Pâris, 71 (4), emphasizes the difficulties of co-ordination inherent in such a system, and R. C. Anderson, *Oared Fighting Ships* (London, 1962), 80–1, doubts that it was ever used.

[21] Cf. a cedar vessel of the 4th Dynasty said to be 172 ft. long, G. Bass, ed., *A History of Seafaring* (London, 1972), 16; for a thalamegos on a relief from Luxor (end of the 14th century BC) with a large, pavilion-type cabin with columns, doors, windows and a porch, see Caspari, 'Nilschiff', Pl. 1. See now the funerary boat of Cheops which is displayed beside his pyramid at Gizeh (140 ft. long with a cabin); a preliminary publication in N. Jenkins, *The Boat beneath the Pyramid* (London, 1980).

transport when they came to Egypt, and luxurious river craft performed both ceremonial and practical functions in Ptolemaic times. A thalamegos with a golden cabin bore the holy bull Apis on its river journey to Memphis (D. S. i. 85, 2), and in his royal archives Ptolemy II recorded 800 golden-prowed and golden-beaked thalamegoi which were used for royal transport on different occasions (Appian, *Prooem.* 10). Less ornate thalamegoi are widely attested for the transport and entertainment of civic officials (*PRyl.* 558; *PTeb.* 802; *PSI* 332, 9–10). In Strabo's day, the harbour of Schedia was τὸ ναύσταθμον τῶν θαλαμηγῶν πλοίων (800). (The Nile joined the Alexandrian canal-system at Schedia, some 20 miles from the capital, which was presumably the navigable limit of the large river boats before the entrance to the narrow canals). The many elegant river boats in Alexandria could have served as examples for Philopator's shipbuilders, who elaborated the design to form the ultimate example of a familiar type of boat. That boats of the level of luxury recorded by Kallixeinos, Appian, and Diodorus actually existed is shown by the Roman Nemi ships; although their date and purpose are unknown, their conception and execution attained a comparable level of magnificence.[22]

Kallixeinos makes a real or imaginary periegesis through the Nile Barge in order to describe it. After describing the outside, he enters the lower level at the stern, and moves forward to the bow, recording each room as he passes through it. Ascending to the upper level at the bow, he describes all the rooms there as he returns to the stern. The most lavish rooms are related in detail while the other mundane areas like storerooms, work-rooms, kitchens, servants' quarters, etc., are naturally omitted. The arrangement of the internal rooms is mostly self-explanatory since the floor-plan of the upper storey is obviously determined by the supports or lack of them in the lower storey. The floor-plans of both storeys are thus similar, and all the public rooms mentioned by Kallixeinos can be fitted into this hypothetical framework because it is clear how he is moving through the ship.[23] The decorative style of the barge is mostly Greek with a few added Egyptian elements; there are peristyles, propylaia, proskenia, symposia, courtyards, and even a tholos temple of Aphrodite. Kallixeinos describes in greater detail the few rooms decorated with an Egyptian motif, presumably for the benefit of his Greek readers. Caspari and Köster adduce many artistic and architectural parallels for features of the barge, and show that

---

[22] For an account of these ships and their finds see G. Ucelli, *Le Navi di Nemi* (2nd ed., Rome, 1950). For speculation on their date, purpose, and sinking see G. B. R. de Cervin, *Mariner's Mirror* xli (1955), 38 ff. The remains of these boats were destroyed in the last war.

[23] He also gives precise directions for the layout with phrases such as πλησίον τῷ προειρημένῳ, κατεναντίον δὲ τούτου, ἐν δὲ τούτῳ κατὰ τὴν δεξιὰν πλευράν, etc.

its decoration is stylistically consistent with its date and cultural context. Artistic representations and archaeological remains of other boats testify that the construction and conception of the Thalamegos would have been possible, and both the materials and technical skill for elaborate wooden structures and shipbuilding were available in third-century Alexandria.

The form of the barge below water-level has been a stumbling block to the interpretation of the description of the ship. Like the '40', the barge is called δίπρωρος καὶ δίπρυμνος (204E), which, on the analogy of the '40', seems to mean that the ship was a catamaran although neither Caspari nor Köster reach this conclusion.[24] Kallixeinos says that the ship was shallow, and *somewhat* different from the deep-bottomed war-galleys and merchantmen which had considerable draught for stability (204E); later he says that the hold of the boat contained many other rooms (206C). If the barge had a shallow keel, it copied the shape of the traditional Egyptian river boats, with their gently rounded keel and pointed bow and stern, which had in turn developed from the sickle-shape of the earlier papyrus rafts.[25] The Thalamegos may have consisted of a pair of sickle-shaped hulls lashed permanently together. This design may have served to increase the stability of a vessel with such a tall, top-heavy superstructure, but an additional point in its favour would be the flat platform, supported by the solid ridge of the joined inner sides of the two hulls, upon which the rectangular cabin was built. That wooden river boats supported weights comparable to the excessive weight of this cabin is shown by the obelisk barges of dynastic Egypt, which transported massive loads along the river and which also had a sickle-shaped hull with rounded bow and stern. The hulls alone could not bear the weight of the obelisks lying along the length of the deck, but were given extra supports beneath the deck by a series of crossbeams and vertical stanchions.[26] The change in the method of transporting heavy objects like obelisks in Ptolemaic times suggests that the catamaran design was structurally useful. Pliny describes a dynastic obelisk being transported by river for re-use in the reign of Philadelphus (*HN* xxxvi. 67 = Appendix I, F 5): two large ships were lashed together and weighed down with ballast in order to float under the obelisk, which

---

[24] Casson, 342 n. 67. The catamaran must have been a fairly common type of ship at least by Imperial times because Athenaeus (489B) describes the handles of the Cup of Nestor (*Il.* xi. 632-7) as παρακειμένως ἔχοντα τὰ ὦτα, καθάπερ αἱ δίπρωροι τῶν νεῶν. Casson, 115 n. 58, correctly points out that the simile would be meaningless unless such ships were familiar to Athenaeus' readers; *pace* Meiggs, 138.

[25] For examples of these early boats, see Casson Pls. 10-13; Bass, 15; G. A. Reisner, *Models of Ships and Boats* (Cat. Gen. Cairo Mus.) (Cairo, 1913), Pls. V-VI.

[26] For the obelisk barges, their strengthened internal structure, and their method of locomotion by towing, see C. V. Sølver, *Mariner's Mirror* xxvi (1940), 237-56; id., ibid., xxxiii (1947), 39-43; G. A. Ballard, ibid., xxvii (1941), 290-306; id., ibid., xxxiii (1947), 158-64; cf. Casson, 17 and n. 33.

lay horizontally across a canal hollowed out under it. When the boats were in position underneath, the weights were taken off so that the boats rose up in the water and took on the weight of the stone. The obelisk was then carried down the river, lying athwart both boats. This passage shows that river boats were lashed together temporarily in Ptolemaic Egypt, and that a 'double boat' provided additional support for extra weight spread horizontally across the hulls. Since Kallixeinos says that other rooms were found in the hold of the Thalamegos, its two hulls could not have contained internal crossbeams and stanchions of the type found in the obelisk barges since these would have used up the space required for additional rooms; the catamaran design, however, would have replaced this method of support for its heavy superstructure by the solid ridge formed by the joined inner sides of the two hulls, plus additional support from the dividing walls between the internal rooms in the hold.

The presence of a mast on the Thalamegos (206C), which may have been secured between the two hulls, shows that the ship moved at least partly under sail, but it is perhaps unlikely that this royal boat was left dependent on the mercy of wind and current. The formal superstructure would have left no room literally or aesthetically on the deck for the number of rowers needed to move such a large boat. Perhaps the Nile barge was towed when necessary by oar-powered 'tugboats' in the manner of the dynastic obelisk barges and the royal ship of the Roman Emperor Domitian, which was towed around Lake Albano at a distance by a galley to prevent the sound of nearby oars disturbing the emperor (Plin. Sec. *Pan.* lxxxii. 1-3).

Although Caspari finds fault with Kallixeinos' method of description because the exact points of many of his measurements are not given,[27] which hinders attempted reconstructions of the ship, he demands a greater level of precision than may reasonably be expected from an author whose purpose is not to verbalize a builder's scale diagram of the barge. Kallixeinos has, rather, the accuracy and amount of detail appropriate for a layman; for example, he says specifically that he measures the width of the boat at its widest part (204D). Whether Kallixeinos actually saw the boat or adapted the account of another writer, Köster maintains that records such as building manuals, accounts, and shipyard plans were not used in the compilation of the original account, which explains the lack of precision in some details, as well as the omission of technical features.[28] Neither Caspari nor Köster, however, seem fully to appreciate Kallixeinos' purpose in writing this description, which was surely to give an accurate impression of the size and magnificence of the Thalamegos. The ecphrasis becomes

---

[27] 'Nilschiff', 9 ff.   [28] Köster, 26-7.

completely comprehensible if one pictures Kallixeinos (or his source) walking around the ship, with or without an official guide, attentive to those extraordinary features which would naturally have impressed a non-sailor like himself. The technical details and measurements which are included could have been provided by a handy nauarch (the ὅ φασι in 204C, used in a story about the method used to launch the '40', may indicate that some third party provided verbal information about at least one of his naval topics, although it could equally indicate a general current tradition or a literary source), but equally many of them could have been estimated or roughly paced off. In relating a tour through a luxurious royal barge, Kallixeinos describes a construction that is technically possible, navigationally plausible, and culturally probable, given the level of achievement attained by ancient shipbuilders and Greek artistic conventions adapted to an Egyptian concept. The strong internal logic in the over-all design and arrangement of the ship is enhanced by the artistic details appropriate to its royal pedigree. The comprehensibility of the description gives weight to Kallixeinos' standard of reliability as a reporter.

The conclusions of Studniczka's excellent study of the ornamental pavilion need only be summarized here to indicate the credibility of Kallixeinos' description of the structure.[29] His account is accepted literally, and Studniczka uses the information provided to reconstruct the beauty and elegance of the marquee in all its details. Kallixeinos describes the pavilion while making a periegesis (whether real or imaginary) around it. In approaching the structure he mentions its isolated setting within an enclosed grove. Standing at the entrance to the pavilion, he notes briefly the basic over-all design, and then enters to describe in detail the interior decoration. He returns to the outside and describes the surrounding enclosure, which leads to a digression on Egyptian flora, and then the decoration of the exterior. The statues, paintings, woven cloaks, shields, and simulated grottoes are recorded systematically from the ground level upwards through the epistyle, ending with the acroteria in the form of eagles. Finally, he returns inside to describe the arrangement of dining couches and tables, and concludes his description by mentioning another display of gold plate. In this account, Kallixeinos follows the method of careful, consecutive reporting used consistently for the '40', the Nile Barge, and the Procession. He includes the most significant details and measurements to give an evocative impression of the scope and effect of the whole. Although many details are omitted in an account which is essentially ecphrastic, Studniczka uses

[29] The text of the description of the pavilion is given in App. I, F 2; for a discussion of the use of this pavilion see above, pp. 31 ff.

inference and common sense to reconstruct the pavilion in a convincing way.[30]

Studniczka interprets this pavilion in the same tradition as the series of ceremonial marquees from the tent in the *Ion* of Euripides (lines 1128–1166) to the marriage tent of Alexander in Susa (*FGrH* 125 F 4), which perhaps preserves some connection with the audience halls of the Great Kings of Persia.[31] On a smaller scale, this pavilion is related to the symposia, triclinia, and ἀνδρῶνες of ancient Greece, from which the concept of the large public dining room arose.[32] The numerous dining rooms on Philopators' Nile Barge show that this style of dining and entertainment was popular in Ptolemaic Alexandria. The functional context of the pavilion can be readily understood even though this one may have been the ultimate development of the type.

Studniczka concludes that the designer of the Ptolemaic pavilion took several features from the native architecture of Egypt, but for the most part used decorative elements which are purely Greek in style.[33] Many enlightening parallels for the decoration can be seen in Graeco-Egyptian tomb paintings[34] and Pompeian wall-paintings. (The over-all effect of this pavilion may perhaps be adduced from the lofty wooden structures seen in the second, third, and fourth Pompeian Styles.[35]) This structure reflects the luxury of the Ptolemaic court,[36] but although its roots may be seen in both Greek and Egyptian tradition, it is a new achievement in Ptolemaic architecture. This must be the basis of Kallixeinos' praise (196A): καλὴ γὰρ εἰς ὑπερβολὴν ἀξία τε ἀκοῆς ἐγενήθη.

The general impression created by the pavilion conforms to that received

[30] Diagrams of his reconstructions, including the interior arrangement, appear as 3 plates in his volume. Most have been republished by G. Grimm, 'Orient und Okzident in der Kunst Alexandriens' in *Alexandrien, Aegyptiaca Treverensia* i (Mainz, 1981), 13 ff., Ills. 1–3.

[31] Studniczka, 24 ff.

[32] Ibid., 30 ff., 133 ff.; R. A. Tomlinson, *BSA* lxiv (1969), 164 ff.; id., *JHS* lxxxix (1969), 106 ff.; id., 'Ancient Macedonian Symposia', in B. Laourdas and Ch. Makaronas, eds., Ἀρχαία Μακεδονία (Thessalonike, 1970), i. 308 ff.

[33] Studniczka, 106. Grimm, 23 n. 12, correctly dismisses the attempted reconstruction of the pavilion as an Egyptian building by G. Haeny, *Basikale Anlagen in der ägyptische Baukunst des Neuen Reiches, Beitr. z. ägyptischen Bauforschung u. Altertumskunde* ix (1970), 76 ff., Pl. 29b. The pavilion is clearly a Greek structure, and its Egyptianizing elements (as on the Thalamegos) were probably added for the sake of novelty and curiosity.

[34] More parallels have since come to light since 1914; cf. the remarkable early Hellenistic tomb of Petosiris; see G. Lefebvre, *Le Tombeau de Petosiris* (Cairo, 1923–4), 3 vols.

[35] Studniczka, 34, 116.

[36] Grimm, 17–18, emphasizes that this pavilion, like the Thalamegos, can be considered an example of 'Hofkunst', and that the incredible luxury of the structure is explicable on those terms.

from the other descriptions in *About Alexandria*; there is a comparable emphasis on lavish artistic decoration, an incredible wealth of precious metal and material, and a conception and design on a tremendous scale. Furthermore, the elements of the boats, pavilion, and procession are arranged with a calculated eye to their effect on the spectator (this is to be expected in the case of the pavilion, which must have been intended as the place of royal hospitality for the important foreign theoroi attending the festival of which the Grand Procession was part). Despite the immense height of the pavilion, its significant decorative elements are low enough down on the structure to be visible. The important artistic features such as the paintings, embroidered cloaks, and statues, form part of the exterior decoration and are thereby well lit and accessible to the general public as well as to the official guests, upon both of which groups this statement of Ptolemaic wealth and royal power would not be lost.

If the ornamental aspects of the pavilion can be shown to be credible, so too can its remarkable dimensions. The measurements which are recorded by Kallixeinos are accepted by Studniczka as within the known limits of the sizes of ancient trees, tapestries, etc. His reconstruction, based upon these measurements and a scale of proportion developed from them, was attested as tectonically possible,[37] although the transitory nature of the structure may have allowed it to be designed with considerable architectural daring. As a temporary construction which was perhaps removed after the festival in which it was used, the pavilion did not require the stability of a permanent building which had to withstand the stresses of weather and time. Hence, its material could have been less durable and more precious, and its conception more flamboyant. This transitory nature also removes any expectation of archaeological traces.

Studniczka's study illustrates what can be achieved in an interpretation of the fragments of Kallixeinos, and it is in striking contrast with the cursory treatment given to the pavilion by Franzmeyer.[38] Studniczka's conclusions, published in 1914, have withstood the test of time, a feat which puts him in a category of his own above all those who have studied the fragments of Kallixeinos.[39] Using only the information provided by the author, Studniczka offers a reconstruction of a satisfying, logical construction which conforms to the principles of Greek art, and which can be paralleled by both forerunners and successors. Kallixeinos' account therefore withstands close examination, and the resulting corroboration of artistic parallels from Greece and Egypt attests its credibility.

---

[37] Studniczka, 43.
[38] Franzmeyer, 6 ff.
[39] Grimm, 14, also praises Studniczka highly.

C. POSSIBLE LITERARY REFERENCES TO KALLIXEINOS

In addition to the four major fragments by Kallixeinos in Athenaeus, there are six lexicographical references elsewhere in the *Deipnosophistai* and one in Harpokration which either refer to the author, or quote short passages by him, to give examples of vocabulary and word usage. Of the references in Athenaeus, two repeat quotations from the text of the Grand Procession (387C–D; 483E–F), and two others discuss words used by Kallixeinos for objects carried in the procession (209F; 472A). (These four passages are inserted as parallel texts a–d into the text of the Grand Procession by Jacoby, *FGrH* 627 F 2, next to the phrases to which they either definitely or probably refer; passage d (= Ath. 387C–D) has already been discussed above, p. 94, as preserving a better version of the text of Kallixeinos.) These four references shed no light upon the author or his works, with the exception of the one probable textual improvement in 387C–D, since they only repeat information already known. Two further quotations come from *About Alexandria*, but the passages to which they refer cannot be specified; they may either be lost parts of the original text, or more complete versions of the preserved fragments, but since they discuss subjects familiar from the Grand Procession, neither is particularly helpful in providing a better understanding of other topics dealt with by Kallixeinos somewhere in *About Alexandria*.

The first of these latter references gives the definition of a karchesion (474E = Appendix I, F 3). It seems likely that this reference comes from the account of the Grand Procession where karchesia are mentioned: in 198B (line 40), a karchesion is carried by Satyrs bearing offerings to the god, and in 198C (line 47), the statue of Dionysus is posed pouring a libation from this type of vessel. Since, to judge from its appearance in his procession, the karchesion apparently had a special importance to Dionysus, an explanation of this fairly unusual type of vase may have been included. Gulick (Loeb edition, ad loc.) suggests that this reference in 474E originally formed part of the description of gold and silver plate in the procession at 199D. If it did come from a catalogue of plate, it could have come from anywhere within the section 199B–200A, or from another list of plate in 202E–F, if either section was originally fuller before being quoted by Athenaeus. If, as seems likely (since there is no indication to the contrary), the catalogue starting at 199B has been quoted verbatim from Kallixeinos, and even if the second passage was shortened by Athenaeus (the state of this part of the text has been discussed above, p. 116), in neither section does the catalogue-type list of plate seem to be interrupted by observations on a particular vase-shape. On these grounds, the description of the karchesion may rather belong to a part of the account which contains more information about the various objects appearing in the procession (such as 198B or C), or another section where the mention of the karchesion has fallen out. However, this passage appears nowhere in the preserved fragments of Kallixeinos, a proof that Athenaeus had access to a fuller text of *About Alexandria* than he recorded. If the reference was taken from the description of the Grand Procession and, for example, from section 198B or C, Athenaeus abbreviated the text of Kallixeinos without giving any sign in his quotation of it since both of these sections appear to be verbatim quotations from *About Alexandria*. If this type of 'invisible abbreviation' has occurred here, and therefore perhaps elsewhere, Athenaeus' version of the text of Kallixeinos is distorted in areas where it is never suspected. In any event, this reference deals with the same type of information available in the text of the Grand Procession, and does not extend our picture of Kallixeinos or his subject-matter.

The second unplaced reference mentions an Isthmian crown (677C–D = Appendix I, F 4). The actual verbatim quotation from Kallixeinos is lost, which makes it impossible to ascertain the context of the information given, but the passage may have been taken from the account of the Grand Procession, perhaps as a description of one of the various types of crowns which were used throughout the proceedings. As a type of crown indicative of victory, it could have been connected with the crowning ceremony in 203A–B, although the meaning of this particular passage is unclear; since this part of the text is severely truncated, any mention of the Isthmian crown may easily have fallen out when Athenaeus was excerpting a more complete version of the text of Kallixeinos. Even if the quotation concerning the Isthmian crown did not come from the Grand Procession, its disappearance from the text of Athenaeus in 677C–D makes it useless for illuminating the scope of *About Alexandria* or the interests of Kallixeinos.

Harpokration s.v. ἐγγυθήκη refers to Book IV of *About Alexandria* for an example of the use of this word. In his arrangement of the text of the Grand Procession (*FGrH* 627 F 2), Jacoby included this passage as fragment Bβ beside the appearance of these stands in 199C (line 96). It seems highly likely that Harpokration took this information from the text of the Grand Procession, and although Athenaeus may well have been Harpokration's source for Kallixeinos (depending upon the uncertain date of Harpokration), if he was not, parts of *About Alexandria* must have been available in the Imperial period in a form other than that of their quotation in the *Deipnosophistai*.

One other passage in Athenaeus may be the work of Kallixeinos of Rhodes. An account of the naval strength of Philadelphus (203C–D), which enumerates the number of each type of ship owned by the king, is interspersed between the accounts of the Grand Procession and the '40' which are quoted consecutively by Athenaeus out of the order in which they appeared in *About Alexandria*. This information is included at the end of *FGrH* 627 F 2 (see Appendix I, p. 200, 203B ff.), where it is indicated as a paraphrase by Athenaeus. This catalogue of the Ptolemaic navy forms part of an apostrophe made by one of Athenaeus' characters to his fellow diners, and it includes additional comments about the legendary wealth of Egypt. It seems clear that the account of Philadelphus' naval strength is included here not only to emphasize the power of the Ptolemaic kings, but also to form a convenient bridge to the subject of the ships of Philopator. (This is actually stated in 203E: ἐπεὶ δὲ περὶ νεῶν κατασκευῆς εἰρήκαμεν, φέρ᾽ εἴπωμεν. . . .) Several factors point to Kallixeinos as the source of this information. As the author of the fragments on either side of the naval passage, Kallixeinos may have been Athenaeus' one source for this whole section of the *Deipnosophistai*, where random sections which best seemed to illustrate the theme of ancient luxury were excerpted from *About Alexandria*. The information provided in this naval catalogue would be of the type likely to have been included by Kallixeinos since the navy of Philadelphus was certainly one more impressive feature of Alexandria. Since the descriptions of the ships of Philopator prove that Kallixeinos did include naval topics, Book I of *About Alexandria* may have compromised a brief, chronological account of the development of the Ptolemaic navy (concentrating upon its most remarkable elements), from which this list of Philadelphus' ships was taken. Moreover, the γραφαί mentioned by Kallixeinos in 197D as his source for the Grand Procession show that he had access to official archives dating from the reign of Philadelphus, and this precise enumeration of the navy may have been taken from the same group of records. The βασιλικαὶ ἀναγραφαί mentioned by Appian (*Prooem.* 10) were recorded by Philadelphus at the end of his reign, and furnished Appian's information about the king's navy, army, treasury, etc. The existence of Appian's analogous, though less detailed, account of Philadelphus' navy which was taken from the royal archives proves that the information was publicly available, and the similarity of the type of material recorded in the accounts of the navy points to a common source,[40] probably the βασιλικαὶ ἀναγραφαί. Since it is known that Kallixeinos had access to official royal archives, it is reasonable to suggest that he may also have written the account of the navy which was paraphrased by Athenaeus in this apostrophe.[41] If Kallixeinos was the author of this passage, a confirmation of his credibility comes from an inscription from

---

[40] This was noticed by Tarn, *Ant. Gon.* 465, although he denies that the common source can be the original, official source because he thinks that the figures are exaggerated.

[41] This view is accepted in ibid.; Bevan, *Hist. of Egypt*, 174.

Old Paphos in Cyprus (*BSA* 56 (1961), 9 No. 17 = *OGIS* 39) in which Philadelphus honours the builder of a '20' and a '30', the two most colossal
warships mentioned in the account of the navy preserved in Athenaeus. Although these ships have remarkably high number-names (larger than any
recorded except the '40'), the inscription proves beyond a doubt that they
did exist and were called by the names used for them in this passage.

Men named Kallixeinos are mentioned elsewhere in ancient literature, and
although none is stated to be Kallixeinos of Rhodes, the suggested identification of any of them with the author may expand our knowledge of the
man, his date, and his literary career.

A 'Callixenus' appears in Pliny's description of the transport of a large
obelisk down the Nile in the time of Philadelphus which was then set up in
the Arsinoeion at Alexandria (*HN* xxxvi. 67-8 = Appendix I, F 5; this
passage has been discussed in another context above, p. 146). Callixenus
attributes the ingenious method used to load the obelisk onto boats
to Phoenix, and not to the architect Satyrus, whom others considered
responsible. Since the known work of Kallixeinos of Rhodes concerns
Ptolemaic Alexandria, and includes material from the time of Philadelphus
as well as information about ships and engineering, Pliny's anecdote lies
within the Rhodian's field of interest. The mention of the Arsinoeion as
the destination of the obelisk may increase the likelihood that Kallixeinos
was the source of this information. Although the account of the transfer
of the obelisk by boat could have been taken from a larger piece on naval
matters in the time of Philadelphus (a subject which was probably dealt
with by Kallixeinos), it is equally possible that the information came
from a description of the Arsinoeion which formed another part of *About
Alexandria*. Judging from the inclusion of the ships and the pavilion, the
work comprised accounts of some of the noteworthy sites of the city, and
the Arsinoeion may well have been considered worthy to be ranked by
Kallixeinos as one of the marvels of Alexandria and described in his
work.[42] Constructed in honour of the deified Arsinoe Philadelphus,[43] the
temple was noted in antiquity for its marvellous features: the cult statue
was said to have been made of topaz (Plin. *HN* xxxvii. 108),[44] and the
roof was to be composed of magnetic material so that an iron image of

---

[42] For the Arsinoeion see *Ptol. Alex.* i. 25, 228-30. The use of the obelisk in the
Arsinoeion complex is not specified, but it seems likely that it was erected in the
temenos-surround.

[43] The Diegesis passage on the Apotheosis of Arsinoe by Callimachus (fr. 228
(Pfeiffer)) seems to connect the building of the shrine with the deification of the
queen.

[44] For the identification of this stone see *Ptol. Alex.* i. 25 and n. 170; *RE* s.v.
Topazus, 1717-18.

Arsinoe would float in mid-air (ib. xxxiv. 148). That a peripheral account of the obelisk would not be out of place in a description of the Arsinoeion is indicated by Kallixeinos' treatment of the '40', where he includes a digression on the ingenious method used to launch the ship. Another piece of evidence supports the suggestion that Kallixeinos of Rhodes was responsible for this information. The 'Phoenix' who is named as the engineer responsible for the transport of the obelisk cannot be identified. It may be significant that in Kallixeinos' description of the launching of the '40' 'ἀπὸ Φοινίκης τις' is the inventor of the most successful method (204C). The man named Phoenix in Pliny may be a garbled version of the same Phoenician engineer who worked on the '40'.[45] The identification of the two men appears reasonable since both were engineers concerned with similar technical problems, methods, and solutions; both worked with boats, applied mathematics, and physics, and had a flair for imaginative invention. Both were, furthermore, commissioned for important royal projects. The identification is not chronologically difficult since one man's working life could have spanned the years from about 250[46] to about 220 to include commissions from the second and fourth Ptolemies, and it is likely that an engineer in especial royal favour would have continued to work as long as he was able to do so. If these two men are the same, the likelihood that Pliny took the anecdote about the obelisk from *About Alexandria*, where the same engineer is mentioned elsewhere, is perhaps strengthened.

If Callixenus is identified with Kallixeinos of Rhodes, a wider picture of the scope of *About Alexandria* emerges. The work may have included some permanent, famous monuments of Alexandria besides the more transitory subjects of the preserved descriptions, which were only a temporary part of the city, and it may therefore have been at least in part a periegesis of the city, even if the permanent landmarks, like their transitory counterparts, were included in the work primarily because of their awe-inspiring features. If the account of the obelisk was included in *About Alexandria* (whether as part of a description of the Arsinoeion or not), Kallixeinos reveals the same methods and interests which are discernible in his other fragments: a catholic interest is shown in the background and construction of the objects which are fully described, especially when it

[45] For Phoenician engineers in general see *Ptol. Alex.* i. 429–30.

[46] The Arsinoeion was still being built many years after the death of Arsinoe, since Pliny says that Philadelphus died while construction was still in progress (*HN* xxxiv. 148). It is not known at what stage the obelisk was moved to Alexandria, and therefore in what year the Phoenician is known to have been working. The erection of the obelisk may have taken place at a fairly late stage so that, when in place, it did not hinder the rest of the heavy building work. In this case, the engineer need not have been working on the project before c. 250.

concerns engineering and mechanics on a practical level. Kallixeinos mani-
fests a continuing fascination with the unusual and the marvellous, which
also reflects contemporary Alexandrian interest in paradoxography. The
identification of this Callixenus does not help to determine the date of
Kallixeinos of Rhodes since the period of the Arsinoeion's construction
(which probably included the transport of the obelisk) spanned the years
from about 272/1 (if it was begun shortly after the queen's deification) to
after 246 BC, the year of Philadelphus' death. Kallixeinos may have seen
the obelisk being moved, arriving in Alexandria, or set up years later in
the Arsinoeion, if he was alive in about the middle of the third century,
but no such supposition is necessary to explain the inclusion of this
information. Such an ancedote may have existed in oral tradition and been
passed to him decades later by word of mouth. Conversely, an account of
the Arsinoeion could well have been included in the royal archives established by Philadelphus at the end of his reign, since the shrine was inti-
mately connected with his sister–wife and the royal cult. Kallixeinos says
that he had access to official records, and he could have taken the account
of the obelisk from them some time after the event.

If the identification of the two men can be accepted, this passage indicates that the works of Kallixeinos were extant, directly or indirectly, in
the first century AD in Rome when used by Pliny. The story of the obelisk
may have been included in the version of *About Alexandria* which was
available some one hundred years later to Athenaeus, who did not use it
in the *Deipnosophistai* since it was not particularly germane to his discussion of ancient luxury; but if Pliny and Athenaeus used different sources
for Kallixeinos, a more complete version of Kallixeinos' text may have
disappeared from circulation by the end of the second century AD.

The second reference to a Kallixeinos appears in the *Bibliotheke* of Photius,
where the Patriarch excerpts the twelve books of the *Eklogai Diaphoroi*
by the sophist Sopater, himself an encyclopaedist of earlier authors.
Photius records the sources used by Sopater in Book XII, which include
the ζωγράφων τε καὶ ἀνδριαντοποιῶν ἀναγραφή by a Kallixeinos (Codex
161, 104b 38 = Appendix I, T 1). No further information is given about
this Kallixeinos. The difficulty of a tentative identification with Kallixeinos of Rhodes is not mitigated by the distance from the source:
'Kallixeinos' excerpted by Sopater excerpted by Photius. The reference
can probably be trusted as far as Photius is concerned. The style of his
summaries of other works varies throughout the *Bibliotheke*; sometimes
only the title and author of the work are given, but elsewhere Photius gives
a detailed précis, often accompanied by a critical judgement of the worth
of the work. When his summaries can be checked against extant works,

they are extremely reliable, and studies of Photius' methods have accorded him a high degree of credibility.[47] There is no reason to suspect, therefore, that he erred on the sources of Sopater. The trustworthiness of Sopater is not so easy to determine since any of several homonymous candidates could have written the *Eklogai Diaphoroi*. The most likely author is Sopater of Apamea,[48] a sophist and philosopher who was admired for his erudition. A pupil of the Neoplatonist Iamblichus, he was a friend and confidante of the Emperor Constantine who was, however, instrumental in causing his death. If the suggestion is correct that the Suda entry Σ 848 is an interpolation from, and a gloss on, Sopater of Apamea's main entry (Σ 845), then the information in 848 also refers to him:[49] Ἀπαμεύς, σοφιστής, ἢ μᾶλλον Ἀλεξανδρεύς· ἐπιτομὰς πλείστων· τινὲς δὲ καὶ τὴν ἐκλογὴν τῶν ἱστοριῶν τούτου εἶναί φασι. If Sopater of Apamea wrote the *Eklogai Diaphoroi*, the ἐπιτομαί and ἐκλογαί of entry 848 may indeed refer to other works of similar type which he may have compiled, if they are not an implicit reference to the *Eklogai Diaphoroi* themselves. Since Photius states that Sopater used Athenaeus as one of his sources in the first book of the *Eklogai* (Codex 161, 103a 32), Sopater may have known of the quotations therein from *About Alexandria*, which may have led him to other works by Kallixeinos. Certainly the interests of Kallixeinos in marvellous and artistic objects in *About Alexandria* may have attracted Sopater, who is also said to have written Περὶ τῶν παρὰ τὴν ἀξίαν εὐ-πραγούντων ἢ δυσπραγούντων (Suda Σ 845) (which sounds like a collection of paradoxa[50]), and who reveals an unmistakable interest in marvels in the *Eklogai Diaphoroi*. The descriptions of artistic objects in Kallixeinos may also have intrigued Sopater, since he is known to have excerpted works on painting (Codex 161, 103a 31). Besides Athenaeus, Sopater used other writers from and about Egypt: he consulted an *About Alexandria* by Ailios Dios (161, 104a 12), a *History of Egypt* by Hellanikos (161, 104a 13), and *About the Mouseion in Alexandria* by Aristonikos (161, 104b 40). A familiarity with these authors suggests that Sopater was interested in Alexandria and had access to works about it, perhaps including the writings of Kallixeinos of Rhodes. (It is possible that the phrase ἢ μᾶλλον Ἀλεξενδρεύς in Suda Σ 848 contains a garbled reference to Sopater's tie

---

[47] *Ptol. Alex.* i. 540 ff.; T. Hägg, *Photios als Vermittler antiker Literatur* (Uppsala, 1975); G. Goossens, *Rev. Belge de Phil. et d'Hist.* xxxviii (1) (1950), 513 ff.; R. Henry, *Rev. Belge de Phil. et d'Hist.* xiii (1934), 615-27; id., ed., *Bibliothèque* (Les Belles Lettres, Paris, 1959-77), i. *xx-xxv*.

[48] F. Focke, *Quaestiones Plutarcheae* (Diss. Monasterii Guestfalorum, 1911), 65.

[49] Ibid., 64.

[50] Things happening 'contrary to expectation' were the basis of the genre of paradoxography.

with Alexandria.[51] If he spent some time in the city, he may have had access to the Mouseion and Library, and could have been acquainted with the works of Kallixeinos from that source.)

This passage furnishes the only suggestion that Kallixeinos of Rhodes wrote any work besides *About Alexandria*. From the fragments of *About Alexandria*, it is clear that he had an interest in art, even if it was inextricably tied to his interest in marvels. He describes in detail every artistic ornament, inside and out, on the pavilion, and not without some artistic sensitivity, for to Kallixeinos clearly the size and decoration of the structure makes it deserving of the accolade (196A): καλὴ γὰρ εἰς ὑπερβολὴν ἀξία τε ἀκοῆς ἐγενήθη. The same eye for artistic detail is seen in his minute descriptions of the costumes and objects in the Grand Procession; colours, materials, and types of decoration are specified. Critical appreciation may be seen in the remarks that the chased figures on one vessel are ἐπιμελῶς πεποιημένα (199E; line 111), as are the figurines on the shelves of the gold chest (199F; line 118). The ships are described with similar artistic interest: the exterior adornment as well as the structure of the '40' is recorded, and the account of the Nile Barge is packed with the minutiae of its decoration. The critical comment on the ivory frieze (205C) may have originated from Kallixeinos (this will be discussed below), but even if the remark is not an original aesthetic judgement, but one taken from another source, Kallixeinos' interest in the artistic worth of the frieze was still sufficient for him to include the criticism. The digression on the characteristics of Egyptian architecture (206B ff.) furnishes independent evidence that the author was qualified to appreciate the differences in artistic style. These observations perhaps support the suggestion that Kallixeinos of Rhodes wrote a separate work on art. The title used by Sopater suggests that the work is more anecdotal, biographical, and art-historical than paradoxographic (the approach to art seen in *About Alexandria*), but art and paradoxography were closely connected in the Hellenistic age in more than one way. Kallixeinos of Rhodes was only one of many authors who described objects which were 'marvellous' because of their lavish artistic features,[52] and in the first century BC, the artist Pasiteles wrote works on paradoxa and art (Pliny, *HN* xxxiv Index; xxxvi. 39). Furthermore, the connection between anecdotal art-history and paradoxography is made clear in the *Laterculi Alexandrini*,[53] a papyrus fragment containing lists of categories of famous things, including the names of both the categories

[51] Focke, 64.

[52] For others see P. Friedländer, *Johannes von Gaza und Paulus Silentiarius* (Leipzig, 1912), 1 ff. and esp. 38 ff.

[53] *Laterculi Alexandrini aus einem Papyrus ptolemäischer Zeit*, H. Diels, ed., *Berl. Abh.* (1904).

and their noteworthy examples. Categories II to V are artistic in nature: Ζωγράφοι, Ἀγαλματοποιοί, Ἀνδριαντοποιοί ('sculptors of gods' and 'sculptors of men', respectively; cf. adnot. ad loc.) and Ἀρχιτέκτονες. Category VI shows the transition from art to paradoxography with Μηχανικοί, since, although mechanical inventions may appeal to an artistic frame of mind, their execution is still due to the perfection of techniques wondrous to the layman. The remaining categories VII to XII are purely paradoxographical: the Seven Wonders of the world, the largest islands, the largest mountains, the largest rivers, the most beautiful springs, and finally Λίμναι(?) (presumably the largest or most beautiful). Since this papyrus can be dated to the second century BC,[54] these select lists and their relations to each other must have existed for some time to be so truncated and standardized here. (The fact that only three examples of each kind of sculptor are given must surely indicate the abbreviation of a much larger list.) The forerunners of this list, and the relation of the categories to each other, may date back to the third century at least. It is interesting to note that Categories II and IV of the *Laterculi Alexandrini* correspond to the given title of the work on art by a Kallixeinos, ζωγράφων τε καὶ ἀνδριαντοποιῶν ἀναγραφή. Kallixeinos of Rhodes may well have written about painters and sculptors, and several scholars have accepted his authorship of both works.[55] The possible identification of the two men does not affect the question of the date of Kallixeinos of Rhodes since the *terminus ante quem* for Sopater's Kallixeinos is the fourth century AD, but its acceptance gives a wider appreciation of the author's interests and literary output: Kallixeinos wrote more than one work, and did not confine his talents to the quasi-periegetic, paradoxographic literary genre. His interests in art and marvels seen in *About Alexandria* were expanded elsewhere, with emphasis given to the men responsible for their production. These two works, if written by one man, illustrate the conflation of the genres of paradoxography and art-historical, anecdotal writing in the early Hellenistic age.

The third reference to a Kallixeinos appears in Pliny's chapters on art. A chronological list of artists, dated to the Olympiad of their *floruit*, appears in the account of bronze statuary and continues down to the 121st Olympiad (296 to 293 BC). Pliny then comments that art ceased (the well-known phrase 'cessavit deinde ars') but came alive again in the 156th Olympiad (156 to 153 BC) under the auspices of Antaeus, Callistratus, Polycles Athenaeus, Callixenus, Pythocles, Pythias, and Timocles (*HN*

[54] Ibid., 4.
[55] Jacoby, *FGrH* 627 and *RE* s.v. Kallixeinos, 1751; Studniczka, 18; Henry (ed.) *Bibliothèque* ii. 128 n. 3; Susemihl, *GGL* i. 519.

xxxiv. 52 = Appendix I, T 2). He next catalogues the less famous makers of bronze statuary without any chronological context. The problems of this passage are manifold since it is by no means obvious what Pliny or his source means by this enigmatic statement. Since art did not 'die', in the sense of stopping completely, during the years in question, Pliny must be speaking metaphorically, and various opinions exist about the proper interpretation of the passage. The second problem is the identification of the artists mentioned in connection with the 'reawakening', the relation among them, and the reasons for their inclusion here. Finally, if this Callixenus is Kallixeinos of Rhodes, one must be able to connect him with this artistic reawakening and to date him without difficulty to *c.*156 BC. (See Appendix III for another identification of Callixenus.)

The identification of Pliny's Callixenus with Kallixeinos of Rhodes might seem attractive at first glance. Kallixeinos' interests in art require no explanation if he were himself an artist who thereby had the aesthetic basis for the critical judgements given in *About Alexandria*. He would in this case resemble other Hellenistic writers who were also artists, such as Xenocrates of Sicyon, Antigonus of Carystus, and Pasiteles. Moreover, since Rhodes and Alexandria were such thriving artistic centres in the Hellenistic age, Kallixeinos had a promising environment for his vocation if he was indeed an artist. Pliny's omission of any further information about this Callixenus (whether as a writer on art or as the author of *About Alexandria*) does not argue against a tentative identification because this information may have been unknown to him, for as in many other instances in his works, his chronological material was probably taken from a tabular source which gave no further details. Nor does the mention of the 156th Olympiad automatically preclude the identification, since it is only certain that Kallixeinos was alive some time after the accession of Philopator in 221 BC. If his descriptions were all taken from an independent source and depended neither on the author's autopsy nor personal knowledge, then Kallixeinos is not bound chronologically either by the earliest date possible for the Grand Procession or by the latest date at which he could have seen the ships of Philopator before they perished. On these grounds, he could have lived many years after the reign of Philopator, and well into the second century.

The interpretation of the passage in Pliny is the decisive factor for or against the identification. Some scholars have argued that 'ars' is the translation, or slightly misleading interpretation, by Pliny of a Greek term, since his dating by Olympiads shows that he was certainly using a Greek source for this passage. In this case, 'ars' may not mean 'Art' in the broadest sense, or even artistic skill, but may translate σοφία or even τέχνη and refer then to the theoretical precepts of professional artistic criticism which was applied to Greek art in the fifth and fourth centuries down to the end of the late classical style, and which was current among the contemporaries of Lysippos.[56] Since artistic production did not cease in the third century, Pliny's comment must be a critical judgement couched in metaphor about the style of art prevalent at that time. He implicitly criticizes a lack of something in other genres of art during that same period, which was rectified by a later revival; a lacuna in his account of painting (xxxv. 135) spans approximately the same years.[57] As far as sculpture is concerned, the third century saw the acme of the Pergamene school and the Athenian portrait school, as well as the development of the Rhodian school. If the Pergamene and Rhodian schools can be considered as nearly opposite to the Athenian school in terms of artistic style, Pliny's criticism may be aimed at one or the other. If 'ars' is the τέχνη of the high and late classical periods, Pliny may mean that the 'classical' style and its artistic precepts declined in the face of the popular so-called Pergamene or Rhodian 'baroque', whose florid, exaggerated manner was the antithesis of classical restraint. Pliny does not mention any Pergamene artists in his chronological account of bronze statuary (although they do appear elsewhere), and since bronze-working was a highly developed and popular art in Pergamon, the absence of Pergamene artists in this section should be significant. Pliny's source for this section was probably not unaware of the 'opposite' style of art prevalent in the Athenian school which continued the classical precepts if in a drier, more academic way; perhaps he considered it sadly overshadowed by the main 'baroque' trend in Hellenistic sculpture. If the argument can be accepted so far, it follows that the 'revixit' passage must signal a return to some kind of neo-classical influence. In terms of sculpture, the revival has been associated with the birth of neo-Attic art,[58] and various new trends need not be dated much before the 156th Olympiad.[59] The other genres which declined at the beginning of the third century also experienced a classical revival in their regeneration. The painters whom Pliny mentions after the gap in xxxv. 135 had neo-classical tendencies, and one of them, Metrodorus, worked for L. Aemilius Paullus at Rome, where neo-classical styles were appreciated and encouraged. This neo-classical revival resulted from various causes, the most obvious of which may have been an aesthetic reaction to the florid Pergamene style prevalent at the time. Also, a series of earth-

[56] O. J. Brendel, *MAAR* xxi (1953), 54 n. 111; J. J. Pollitt, *GBA* 6th ser. lxiv (1964), 324; see also A. W. Lawrence, 'Turning-Points in Hellenistic Sculpture', *Mel. Picard, RA* xxxi-ii (1949), i. 582–3; A. Stewart, *Attika, Soc. Prom. Hell. Stud.* Suppl. pap. 14 (London, 1979), 3 ff. and *passim.*

[57] Cf. C. Robert, *Archäologischen Märchen aus alter und neuer Zeit (Philologische Untersuchungen* 10) (Berlin, 1886), 135 n. 1.

[58] Pollitt, 324–5; for Athenian neo-classicism, see Stewart, 34 ff.

[59] Lawrence, 583.

quakes which damaged several Peloponnesian sanctuaries in the first half of the second century BC caused a flurry of building activity in mainland Greece.[60] Temples and cult statues, whose religious nature made them essentially conservative, would have been restored in the same classical style in which they had been made, thus stimulating the production of neo-classical works. The period of classical revival furthermore coincides with the beginning of Roman domination in Greece after the battle of Pydna in 168 BC. The Roman philhellenes encouraged the production for their own collections of classicizing works which appealed to the Roman taste, being reminiscent of the old masterpieces which were considered epitomes of artistic excellence by Greeks and Romans alike. A thriving industry arose to produce copies of old statues, and to create new statues in an old-fashioned style, for Roman markets.

The sculptors associated by Pliny with the reawakening of 'ars' should be among the originators of archaism in the neo-classical revival. The identification of many is uncertain: Antaeus and Pythocles are unknown, and although Callistratus may be the artist mentioned by Tatian (*Ad Graec.* ch. xxxiv; p. 36 l. 14, ed. Schwartz), there is no evidence of his date or style. Pythias is unknown, unless he is one of the several artists named 'Pytheas', the most likely candidate in this context being Pytheas of Argos, who signed a statue base at Ilion of a Metrodorus known to be an orator from the position of the holes for his feet (even if an orator's statue found nearby did not belong to this base).[61] The early editors of the inscribed base identified Metrodorus with Metrodorus of Skepsis, the orator friend of Mithridates Eupator of Pontus in the first century BC (Strabo 609). If this identification is correct, the early career of Pytheas may have dated back to the 156th Olympiad if he sculpted the orator at the end of his career, and this statue may then have had some connection with the classicizing Athenian portrait school. Frisch (ed. ad loc.) has, however, doubted the identification and has tentatively dated the base to the third century BC, which separates the sculptor from a neo-classical movement. In any case, the identification of 'Pythias' with Pytheas of Argos is purely speculative. The Polycles of Pliny's statement has been identified with the most famous of the many homonymous sculptors, and he may have been the artist to whom Pliny attributes a famous bronze Hermaphrodite (*HN* xxxiv. 80).[62] If this statue can be identified with the so-called 'Sleeping Type' which exists in several copies, it belongs to the classicizing movement of the second half of the second century BC,[63] as

---

[60] M. Bieber, 'Pliny and Graeco-Roman art', *Hommages à J. Bidez et à Fr. Cumont, Coll. Latomus* ii (1949), 39 ff.

[61] P. Frisch, *Die Inschriften von Ilion* (Bonn, 1975), No. 61 = Loewy, *IGB* 264.

[62] Lawrence, 583.   [63] Ibid., 583–4.

may a statue of Amyntas at Olympia which could also be attributed to the same Polycles (Paus. vi. 4, 5).[64] This artist may furthermore have been one of the sculptors of the cult statues in the temples which Pliny saw in the Portico of Octavia at Rome (*HN* xxxvi. 35), along with the statues by other members of his family, Timocles and Dionysius.[65] The temples of Juno and Jupiter which were adorned with Polycles' work were erected after 148 BC.[66] If the artist is the same Polycles who is mentioned in the 'revixit' passage, he was connected with the neo-classical revival in the second half of the second century, at least with the Roman element in it. The Timocles of the 'revixit' passage may then be the uncle of this Polycles who also worked on statues for the Roman temples. Nothing is known of his artistic style from the passages which refer to him in Pausanias, but if he worked with his brother and nephew at Rome, he may have practised a neo-classical style similar to theirs.

Only two of the artists mentioned in the 'revixit' passage (if they can be identified with the homonymous artists mentioned elsewhere in Pliny) can be connected with a neo-classical revival, although with one centred in Rome. This nevertheless lends some weight to the suggestion that Pliny *is* in fact referring to this new movement, since a neo-classical revival in sculpture, painting, and oratory is independently attested in the second half of the second century, but it is nevertheless curious that he mentions these unfamiliar artists instead of famous neo-classical sculptors such as Damophon and Euboulides. It is not, however, apparent that Kallixeinos of Rhodes was connected to any such neo-classical revival, even if he was an artist as well as a writer on art. His literary production is firmly rooted in the early Hellenistic tradition of ecphrastic-paradoxographic writing which developed early in the third century BC as a result of the mating of Peripatetic philosophy with Alexandrian scholarship, and which produced elaborate, descriptive set pieces which were very much in the same genre (see below, Ch. 4 F). As a prime member of that literary movement who is tied firmly to the Alexandrian tradition, Kallixeinos belongs intellectually and artistically to the third century even if his actual dates are later. His consistent literary style, with its highly sophisticated descriptive techniques which concentrated on the most lavish products of new technical finesse

---

[64] The only *terminus post quem* for this work is *Ol.* 145 (200–197 BC), when the boys' pankration (in which Amyntas was a victor at an unknown later date) was first introduced into the Games (Paus. v. 8, 11); cf. Loewy, *IGB*, p. 177 δ.

[65] For a stemma disentangling this family of artists see J. Marcadé, *Receuil de Signatures de Sculpteurs Grecs* (Paris, 1953–7), ii. 131; F. Coarelli, *Stud. Misc.* xv–xvi (1970), 75 ff.; Stewart, 42 ff.

[66] The temples were erected by Q. Caecilius Metellus Macedonicus after his triumph following the victory over the Macedonian pretender Andriscus in 148 BC (cf. Vell. Paterc. i. 11).

and royal luxury, could be considered in many ways the antithesis of classicism and neo-classicism. Despite the possibility that he wrote about art and lived during the 156th Olympiad, Kallixeinos of Rhodes cannot be tied to any part of the neo-classical revival except for the slim evidence of Pliny's statement. If Callixenus *is* Kallixeinos of Rhodes, another interpretation of the 'revixit' passage must be found, or else our estimate of Kallixeinos must be revised to include some connection with a classical revival. On balance, it is easier not to make the identification, and to relegate Callixenus to the unknown group of four or possibly five artists mentioned by Pliny; one is at a loss to know who they were, who put them in this category, or why. The removal of Callixenus from consideration allows the persona of Kallixeinos of Rhodes to be grasped fairly easily. The author of *About Alexandria* may be the Callixenus of the obelisk transport and the author of the ζωγράφων τε καὶ ἀνδριαντοποιῶν ἀναγραφή. All three pieces show the relation between art, anecdote, and paradoxography, but since this literary focus can be determined from *About Alexandria* on its own, little but independent corroboration is added to the characterization of Kallixeinos as a Hellenistic literary personality with perceivable interests and literary methods.

D. THE DATE OF KALLIXEINOS

The date of Kallixeinos of Rhodes is a difficult problem which can have no final solution without further information. Kallixeinos was alive after the accession of Ptolemy IV Philopator in 221, but the length of time the king ruled before constructing the ships which Kallixeinos describes is unknown. Various considerations could combine to date Kallixeinos many decades after this one *terminus post quem*, but these must be weighed against suggestions that his *floruit* was contemporary with the reign of Philopator.

The earliest topic described by Kallixeinos is the Grand Procession, which, since it occurred during the reign of Ptolemy II as Athenaeus says, took place between 285 BC (when Philadelphus was associated on the throne with his father) and 246, the year of his death. The date of this procession has already been discussed briefly in the preceding chapter, and will be considered more fully in the next chapter, but, to summarize, the self-confident, triumphant, and prosperous impression created by the Grand Procession suggests strongly that it occurred within the first two decades of the reign of Philadelphus, the so-called 'Golden Age' of Alexandria. A nearer approximation of the date depends upon more subjective issues such as the marital status of the king and the state of hostilities with Syria at the time of the festival. If it is correct that Arsinoe II does not appear in the text, then it is unlikely that the Grand Procession took place between *c.*276/5 (or whenever the royal marriage occurred) and a date well after the Chremonidean War, when the influence of the deceased queen may have waned to the extent that any reference to her in the procession would have been unnecessary. Although a later date cannot be positively excluded, one before 276 appears the more likely on the grounds that Egypt was then wealthy and victorious enough to stage a spectacle of such brilliance. The question of the date of the Grand Procession must influence our view of the date of the author if one accepts that the visual vividness of Kallixeinos' account resulted at least partly from the author's eye-witness observation of the procession. In this case, he must have been alive when it took place, although he may have written his description either directly after the event, or much later on from memory, notes, and other sources. The earlier one dates the procession, the corresponding probability that Kallixeinos could have been its observer decreases, and the supposition that it took place before the advent of Arsinoe II in *c.*276 raises the hypothetical age which Kallixeinos would have had to attain in order to have been a spectator who yet lived until the reign of Philopator. Many have maintained that the procession was held during the years when Arsinoe and Philadelphus were married.[67] Although a date in the second half of the 270s would be marginally easier to reconcile with the author's autopsy of the procession than an earlier date, the chronological considerations of his hypothetical longevity are still difficult. The opposite view is that Kallixeinos lived after the procession and used for his description only the outside sources of information which he mentions were available for it.[68] If sources similar to those for the procession were used by Kallixeinos also for his account of the boats (thereby removing the necessity of eye-witness observation of them as well), it is theoretically possible to date the author at any time after Philopator, regardless of the interpretation of the 'revixit' passage.

Kallixeinos has been dated much later than the reign of Philopator as the result of a complex linguistic argument concerning the verb tenses used by the author and a dissection of his literary style. The past tenses used by Kallixeinos in his descriptions of the boats have given rise to the view that the boats cannot have existed at the time when he wrote his account of them. According to this argument, if the boats were extant for some time after their construction, which seems likely, the length of their survival lowers the earliest possible date for Kallixeinos' writing. The scholars who have been mainly concerned with this problem have distinguished two

---

[67] *Inter alios*, Studniczka, 16; *RE* s.v. Arsinoe (25), 1281; Otto, *Beitr. z. Seleukidengesch.*, 7–8; id., *Philologus* lxxxvi (1931), 414–15 n. 27.

[68] Studniczka, 16–17; *RE* s.v. Kallixeinos, 1751–2; see below, pp. 171 ff.

types of literary style, which they describe as 'Beschreibung' (the literal, specific description of an existing object) and 'Erzählung' (an unsubstantiated story or narrative account of something which may or may not exist).[69] Pasquali and Jacoby interpret Kallixeinos' description of the Nile Barge as an 'Erzählung' (a story *about* the boat) rather than as a 'Beschreibung' (a description of the boat's actual state of existence).[70] If it can be categorized in this way, the account can be considered as a literary exercise only. Jacoby extends this premise to its logical conclusion: if the description is primarily a literary *tour de force*, no information about the actual condition of the boat, or its state of existence, can be gleaned from it. Studniczka, however, maintains that the account of the Nile Barge is a 'Beschreibung' and not merely an 'Erzählung'.[71] In his view, a proper 'Beschreibung' (at least in the German literary tradition) cannot be a stylistic device of the author but must reveal information about the subject of the description. He therefore insists that the verb tenses used by Kallixeinos in the description of the Nile Barge are not a function of literary style, but have a definite temporal significance. The temporal implications of the past verb tenses used in the passage imply to him that the boat no longer existed when Kallixeinos described it. Kallixeinos' description could in this case be dated during the reign of Philopator only if the boats were destroyed almost upon completion; since this seems unlikely, the date of Kallixeinos' account would be much later, according to this theory, probably well into the second century when the boats may very well have ceased to exist.[72]

However, any distinction between 'Beschreibung' and 'Erzählung' in Greek, with the respective implications for the truth of an account supposedly written in either style, seems to be artificial. In either case, a description could be a literary form which provides no evidence for the actual state of the object at the time it is described. Studniczka's extreme position on the verb tenses used in Kallixeinos is unwarranted. In the first place, he and his supporter Caspari are not specific in their terminology of verb tenses: 'das Präteritum' (the past) is juxtaposed to 'das Präsens' (the present). Since no differentiation is made among the various tenses in the past (imperfect, aorist, perfect, pluperfect), Studniczka bases his view on the fact that the Nile Barge is described in the 'past' tense and not the 'present', which indicated to him that the boat no longer existed at the time of writing. Since most of the main verbs in the account of the Nile Barge are either in the imperfect of the aorist tenses, it seems preferable to see them as simple narrative uses of the past, to be explained on the

[69] Cf. G. Pasquali, *Hermes*, xlviii (1913), 161 ff.
[70] Pasquali, 184–5; *RE* s.v. Kallixeinos, 1752.   [71] Studniczka, 17 n. 5.
[72] Ibid., 17 and n. 5; he is supported in this view by Caspari, 'Nilschiff', 7–8.

ground that the time is past relative to the time Kallixeinos saw, heard of, or studied source material about the boat. If his perception of his subject-matter occured some time in the past, he would naturally have used the past tense when writing about it later. In this case, the verb tense is temporal only in so far as the perception of the object or action is anterior to the actual moment of description, and cannot be interpreted as an indication of the continuing existence of the object.

In the description of the Grand Procession, Kallixeinos uses the aorist tense for most of the main verbs, which is a straightforward, narrative use of the past tense, given that the procession was an event which happened once in the past, and at any rate before the author wrote his description. The few pluperfect verb forms which appear indicate a completed action totally in the past, but even these have no bearing on the state of existence of the objects with which they are used. For example, in 198C (line 49), περιεβέβλητο gives the information that the statue of Dionysus is wearing a mantle. The force of this verb is surely that the purple, gold-spangled mantle *had been spread* over the statue when it was being dressed, and that it was still spread over it when the cart appeared in the procession. The pluperfect tense signifies a past relative to the main aorist past in the rest of the account; the action itself had occurred in the more distant past, but it brought about a certain state of being which continued into more recent past. It does not describe an action whose effect was entirely relegated to the past and is therefore irrelevant to the main action. An inelegant translation of this verb might be, for example, 'the statue had already been spread', or 'the statue was in a state of having been spread' with the mantle. It seems clear that Kallixeinos uses verb tenses in the same way in his other fragments; although these describe objects, and not a single event, their pluperfect verbs are past only in relation to the aorist and imperfect tenses used for the majority of the main verbs in the passage. In 204B, κατεπεποίκιλτο indicates that the exterior of the '40' *had once been physically painted*, but surely one must think of it as still covered in paint when Kallixeinos described it (whether or not it was extant at the time), or else he could not mention the paint at all. Again, the verb indicates a past action which caused a state of being which continued into the nearer past and was still perceivable. The pluperfect verbs ἐτέτακτο (205A), ἐπεποίητο (205A), κατεκεκόλλητο (205B), and ἐνετέτατο (206A) can be interpreted in exactly the same way. Since the main verbs used to describe the boats, like those describing the Grand Procession, are in the simple past tenses (which is a narrative use of the past giving no information about the state of existence of the thing described), the pluperfect verbs indicate only an earlier past relative to the time of the main verb and not to the present state of the objects. The state of the boats' existence cannot be calculated by the verbs used to describe them, or by any other internal evidence. If Kallixeinos need not have written his accounts of the boats when they had ceased to exist, his date does not have to be placed at the very end of the third century (at the earliest), or even later.

If this argument about verb tenses may be safely dismissed, one must return to indications of Kallixeinos' possible autopsy of his subjects as a better basis for conjecturing a date for the author. If there are signs of autopsy in his descriptions of the boats, Kallixeinos must have lived during the late third to early second century BC to have seen the boats himself (assuming they were extant for five to twenty-five years), even if he saw them early in life and wrote an account supplemented by other sources much later. Unfortunately, any decisions about possible autopsy are subjective. One piece of evidence is a critical comment made by Kallixeinos on the workmanship of a frieze in the main dining salon of the Nile Barge (205C): τῇ μὲν τέχνῃ μέτρια, τῇ χορηγίᾳ δὲ ἀξιοθαύμαστα. Studniczka admits that the remark has a personal ring to it which would not have come from any official source for the boats, but since he interprets Kallixeinos' verb tenses as a sign that the boats were no longer extant when described, his logical conclusion from a dubious premise is that Kallixeinos borrowed the critical judgement from an older source who had seen the frieze, unless he had once seen the boat himself but wrote his account later, when the Thalamegos no longer existed.[73] One could argue along similar lines that the comment and observation came from Kallixeinos, but were based upon some visual representation of the frieze which he saw long after the boats had ceased to exist.[74] If that were so, the artistic comment would be no help in determining the date of Kallixeinos. On the other hand, the hypothesis of another source for this criticism, be it literary or visual, is unnecessary. Since, as has been shown, the verb tenses are irrelevant to the question of the boats' existence at the time when their descriptions were written, there is no reason why the judgement on the ivory frieze could not have been his own personal observation. It is apparent that Kallixeinos had sufficient interest in art (seen in his choice of subjects for *About Alexandria* even if he did not write a separate work on art) to be capable of a critical opinion on a piece of workmanship. If the comment was based on the frieze itself and not upon a representation of it, Kallixeinos must have seen the Thalamegos. The digression on Egyptian architecture which is inserted into the description of one of the dining rooms in the boat (206B ff.) is another possible indication of autopsy by the author. This excursus is written in the present tense, in contrast to the surrounding narrative, and it is most naturally

---

[73] Studniczka, 17–18; Caspari, 'Nilschiff', 8.

[74] Cf. Caspari, 'Nilschiff', 8.

interpreted as a personal comment by Kallixeinos, inserted for the general information of his Greek audience about the Egyptian columns. Even if Kallixeinos used sources for his account of the boat (indicated by the many details he gives which he probably could not have known just by seeing the barge; cf. the ὅ φασι used in 204C), there is no reason to think that he did not include some of his personal observations, especially generalized comments on a topic like Egyptian architecture. This view is, curiously, denied by Jacoby, who believes that Kallixeinos did not see the boats but used only secondary sources as the basis of his account; he is forced to conclude, therefore, that the digression on Egyptian architecture must also have been taken from a secondary source. He maintains that this digression shows a mechanical interest in architectural technique more appropriate to an artist than to a writer about marvels, and then assumes an artistic source for Kallixeinos in this place alone, to account for the supposed lack of artistic observations elsewhere in his basically sensational descriptions.[75] This convoluted view is surely unwarranted. If this passage did originate with Kallixeinos, it still provides no evidence for the date of the author since his own observations on Egyptian architecture may have been included in an account taken otherwise from a secondary source. In that case, he could have lived years after the reign of Philopator. Conversely, if these general observations were inserted into an account based upon a combination of eye-witness evidence and secondary sources, Kallixeinos would have been alive during the period of the boat's existence. Nothing disproves the latter supposition, and the digression on Egyptian architecture, like the comment on the ivory frieze, may be an indication of autopsy on the part of the author which would place his date no later than about the last quarter of the third century.

Similar considerations apply to possible indications of autopsy in Kallixeinos' descriptions of the Grand Procession and the ornamental pavilion, and the conclusions reached are equally subjective. A passage on Egyptian flora appears in the description of the pavilion (196D ff.), which is written in the present tense as a general discussion arising from a point in the main narrative, which is written in the past tense. This digression, like that on Egyptian architecture, *may* have been a personal observation by Kallixeinos inserted into the description of the pavilion by way of explanation to his readers, but there is no way of knowing if this was written shortly after the festivities in which the pavilion was used, or years later when the author devised his account wholly from secondary sources. The same uncertainty extends to the account of the procession where two critical observations on objects carried along may be indications that

[75] *RE* s.v. Kallixeinos, 1752.

Kallixeinos had been an eye-witness observer of the proceedings. The figures on the shoulders of the Corinthian kraters are said to be ἐπιμελῶς πεποιημένα (199E; lines 111-12), and so are the golden statuettes on the shelves of the χρυσωματοθήκη (199F; lines 118-19). These remarks were probably not taken from the sources which Kallixeinos used for his description of the procession; such official sources, perhaps preserved in the state archives, would not have included critical observations about the artistic worth of the objects, which would hardly have been appropriate in the context. Even so, these first-hand opinions proffered by Kallixeinos do not necessarily mean that he was present during the Grand Procession, since many of the objects themselves, or at least visual representations of them, could have existed long after the event. Kallixeinos could have seen these years later, and have included various personal observations in a description taken otherwise from the official archives which recorded the Grand Procession. It would in any case be reasonable to suggest that such comments depended upon a closer examination of the objects than that afforded by a quick look as they passed by in the procession. If the Grand Procession is dated within the 270s (whether before or during the marriage of Arsinoe and Philadelphus), it is difficult chronologically to make Kallixeinos an eye-witness observer of it, and certainly the critical remarks inserted by the author into his text do not require this hypothesis. The view that Kallixeinos had been present at the procession cannot, however, be positively excluded.[76] If he had grown up during the reign of Philadelphus, he could have based his account (written up in later years) upon his own observations supplemented by other sources. Even if the critical remarks do not prove that Kallixeinos was an observer, it could be argued that his basic approach to the subject is personal, as seen in the first-person verb forms used here as well as in his other fragments, and in the fact that much of the description of the procession has a personal ring to it; for example, the vantage point for much of the description is the stadium (see above, p. 30), where it was actually suggested by Franzmeyer that Kallixeinos was seated as a spectator. If Kallixeinos had been a child or a very young man at the time of the procession (his presence may have been the cause of his later interest in the subject), he may well have survived to describe the boats of Philopator some fifty-five years later. Other men of the time are known to have lived to a comparable age: Hieron II of Syracuse lived from 306 to 215 BC, Hieronymus of Cardia lived from about 364 to 260 BC (and, it is said, retained all his faculties until his last day), Timaeus lived from about 356 to 260 BC, and the third-century court official Sosibios spanned the reigns of three Ptolemies.[77]

---

[76] This view was accepted by Franzmeyer, 28; Susemihl, *GGL* i. 519 and n. 23.

[77] P. Maas, *Kleine Schriften* (Munich, 1973), 100 ff.

Even though Kallixeinos would have lived to a greater age than the vast majority of the contemporary population, he *could* have been an eye-witness observer of the procession as well as of the boats. This view cannot be proved or disproved without further evidence, and it is by no means a necessary explanation for the style and the personal remarks in the texts of the pavilion and procession; these may have resulted from a combination of secondary sources, a conscious literary attempt to make his descriptions ring true in accordance with the aims of ecphrastic writing, and a personal view of many of the objects in existence years later. It will be suggested in section F below, however, that the literary outlook of Kallixeinos conforms exactly to an early Hellenistic date and that he was probably not a later imitator of a third-century literary style. If this view can be maintained, it remains highly likely that the author's *floruit* was in the third century.

E. THE SOURCES OF KALLIXEINOS

Kallixeinos refers anyone seeking more detail about the Grand Procession to αἱ τῶν πεντετηρίδων γραφαί (197D; line 9), but he does not explain what these *graphai* were. If the author lived late in, or after, the reign of Philadelphus and had no personal information about an event occurring several decades before, these records to which he had access, at first or remoter hand, were his only sources for the account of the procession. Even if Kallixeinos had seen the procession himself, or talked to eye-witnesses about it, he would still have been dependent on other sources for information on the numbers, weight, size, and cost of the objects which appeared, since precise particulars are often given which could not have been known by one merely watching the procession. One can only speculate about the identity of these *graphai*, and their form and content, although the phrase implies that they had some kind of formal arrangement.

The normal interpretation of γραφή is a visual representation of some kind, usually a drawing, painting, or picture, but it can have a connotation other than visual. In late classical and Hellenistic Greek, γραφή can be synonymous with ἀναγραφή which properly means 'written records'.[78] Jacoby (*FGrH* 627 ad loc.) tentatively suggested ἀναγραφαί as the correct reading in the text of Kallixeinos, but this is unnecessary if the words can be synonymous. It has been suggested that Kallixeinos indicates some literary source by his choice of words: λαμβάνειν, meaning physically to take up and hold, and ἐπισκοπείτω meaning to look into and read.[79] Some information about the Grand Procession may have existed in a civic

---

[78] Cf. Studniczka, 17.   [79] Ibid.; *RE* s.v. Kallixeinos, 1752.

religious calendar. Since the phrase αἱ τῶν πεντετηρίδων γραφαί proves the existence of several penteteric festivals and of records of many of them, an established system of regularly kept records of religious festivals must have existed in Ptolemaic Alexandria, at least for penteteric festivals. Detailed religious documents which were chronological and tabular in form existed at an earlier date, among them the Greater Demarchia inscription[80] and the Law Code of Nicomachus at Athens,[81] and the Coan religious calendar.[82] Similar records, if inscribed and set up in a public place, like these three calendars, could have been available to the public in Alexandria, but although Kallixeinos could have consulted such a catalogue, he seems to imply more than this; if one is advised to consult them for even more details than are contained in the minute description of the procession, these *graphai* must have been more extensive and comprehensive than any known ancient religious records. Although certain calendaric records on stone may have existed in Alexandria, records of another sort and purpose must have existed beside them.

The most likely suggestion is that these *graphai* are similar to, part of, or identical with, the βασιλικαὶ ἀναγραφαί mentioned by Appian as recorded by Philadelphus at the end of his reign (*Prooem.* 10: Ἐς γὰρ δὴ τοσοῦτο παρασκευῆς τε καὶ στρατιᾶς, ἐκ τῶν βασιλικῶν ἀναγραφῶν φαίνεται, προαγαγὼν τε καὶ καταλιπὼν ὁ δεύτερος Αἰγύπτου βασιλεύς . . .). If these records were extant in Appian's time in the second century AD in Alexandria, they would surely have been available to Kallixeinos who wrote shortly after the time of their compilation. Since Appian used these *anagraphai* for information about the navy of Philadelphus, one might expect Kallixeinos to have used them for the same information if, as seems likely, he wrote the passage in Athenaeus describing the complement of Philadelphus' navy (see above, p. 153). The form and content of these 'basilikai anagraphai' are unknown, but it is clear from Appian that they were official records compiled and maintained under royal auspices. Since these records included details of the royal fleet, army, and treasury (which Appian quotes), they may also have comprised accounts of some Alexandrian religious festivals which were arranged under close royal supervision. The records mentioned by Appian and Kallixeinos may refer to the same royal archive, or to different branches of an extensive system of royal record-keeping, part of which Kallixeinos used for his account of the naval strength of Philadelphus, and another

---

[81] S. Dow, *Historia* ix (1960), 270 ff.; id., *Hesperia* xxx (1961), 58 ff.; *SEG* 19, 28; 126.
[82] W. R. Paton and E. L. Hicks, *The Inscriptions of Cos* (Oxford, 1891), Nos. 37–43.

part of which he consulted about the details of the Grand Procession. It seems fairly clear from the type of information preserved about Philadelphus' navy in Appian and Kallixeinos that the 'basilikai anagraphai' contained, at the very least, numbers of ships, troops, and amounts of money, which suggests that they could also have contained exact measurements, weights, and prices of objects in the Grand Procession. The tabular nature of the information given by Appian, and also by Kallixeinos (especially in the parade of gold and silver plate (199B ff.) where the description is asyndetic and cursory in the extreme) suggests that lists of various categories may have formed part of these *anagraphai*, very much in the manner of the Delian temple inventories.

Other kinds of detailed literary sources for the Grand Procession could have comprised financial accounts for the objects as well as for the recruitment and payment of participants and artisans. There may also have been troop orders, and extant victory dedications or odes from the victors of the various competitions. All these may have been deposited in the 'basilikai anagraphai'.

It is also worth considering briefly a visual meaning for the word γραφή, since Kallixeinos refers specifically to the detailed character of his records, and some type of visual illustration would have been an ideal way for some of the details of the procession to be communicated quickly and accurately. Since the odds are against Kallixeinos having been an eyewitness observer of the procession, it is difficult to explain how he could have known many of the visual details which he records so vividly if not from some visual source. Most recent scholarship on the origin of the extensively illustrated medieval codices has seen its roots in classical antiquity.[83] Scientific manuscripts are known to have been illustrated in the last centuries before Christ, since diagrams exist on papyrus fragments from that time, and, although illustrated literary fragments are rare, some do exist. Some papyrus fragments are thought to illustrate historical subjects, and, although these date from after the fourth century AD, their sophisticated stage of development suggests that they were later examples of a type of illustration which must have begun at a much earlier date. If, by inference, the beginning of historical manuscript illustration can be put back in time much further than any of the papyri which have survived, such a medium may have been available in Ptolemaic Alexandria. Facilities for this type of illustration are suggested by the organized scriptoria which must have existed in the city at that time to

---

[83] For a review of relevant work in this field see K. Weitzmann, *Illustrations in Roll and Codex, Studies in Manuscript Illumination* ii (Princeton, 1947), Introduction; idem, *Ancient Book Illumination*, Martin Classical Lectures xvi (Cambridge, Mass., 1959).

serve the needs of the Library.[84] The dynastic Egyptians were prolific illustrators of papyrus texts, and their knowledge of the materials and technique were no doubt drawn on by the Alexandrians. If Philadelphus ordered a detailed literary account of the proceedings of the Grand Procession to be preserved in the archives of the Library for the sake of posterity and royal propaganda (whether or not it formed part of the 'basilikai anagraphai'), such a document may have been illustrated with sketches of some of the impressive ritual objects and scenes. Other kinds of visual sources can also be imagined. Although early Greek 'historical' paintings tended to represent events as epic sagas in idealized mythological garb, by the fourth century some paintings purported to be visual representations of historical events despite a certain amount of artistic licence. The Alexander Mosaic may mark the transition to a type of visual historical archive if it is a faithful copy of a painting which portrayed a real battle historically; although no judgement can be made about the truth of the details since the exact battle it represents cannot be determined, it has been thought to record some features accurately.[85] The few extant tomb paintings from Alexandria show that wall-painting was a current medium, and if by the third century the medium of accurate historical painting was in common use as a visual archive, some scenes from the Grand Procession of Philadelphus may have been preserved in this way (perhaps publicly displayed in a building like the Athenian Stoa Poikile). The whole procession, however, could hardly have been recorded even in a very long mural painting, given the length and complexity of the proceedings. A severely truncated version of the procession could have given Kallixeinos a visual impression and some visual details, but hardly an exhaustive account of the occasion, and the author would hardly have referred his readers to this sort of medium alone for *more* details about a particular one of a series of penteteric festivals. Similar reservations qualify the suggestion of sculptural reliefs as a possible visual source. Abbreviated representation is certainly characteristic of the extant sculptural reliefs of continuous historical subjects. The reliefs of Roman processions on triumphal arches, like that after the sack of the Temple in Jerusalem shown on the Arch of Titus in Rome, are necessarily truncated, and the long narrative reliefs on the columns of Trajan and Marcus Aurelius are subject to artistic whim in their representation of events.[86] The Parthenon frieze is perhaps the closest sculptural analogy to the procession of Philadelphus, but many participants in the Athenian procession are

---

[84] Cf. *Ptol. Alex.* i. 325 ff.
[85] Robertson, *Hist. Gr. Art*, i. 499.
[86] Weitzmann, 125 ff.

omitted from the frieze.[87] Even though a sculptured frieze could have given Kallixeinos some information, it could not have been his sole, or even main, source of visual information.

Other types of visual sources may have comprised plans and drawings of some of the ritual objects used in the procession. A selection of such designs could have been submitted for royal approval, and have been deposited in the archives of the Library. Even if there was not a formal collection of such plans, they must have existed at one time for the benefit of the builders and artisans. The scenes from the life of Dionysus would have required precise designs, as would some individual figures like Nysa with its automatic internal mechanism. Possibly clay or wooden models of the scenes and objects were made to ensure the sizing and spacing of all the figures. Even if these were not the primary sources to which *graphai* refer, such plans or models may have been supplemented by other types of information. Along similar lines, some of the statues and objects may have been preserved after the procession for public display. These may have been placed in the palace, in the Library or Mouseion, in a building comparable to the Athenian pompeion where ritual objects were stored between festivals (like the Panathenaic procession, this procession was part of a recurring festival), or, above all, in the various shrines of Dionysus and the other gods honoured in the procession. The temples were likely destinations for whatever gold and silver plate was intended as divine dedications.

Nothing final can be said on the form of Kallixeinos' sources. Apart from αἱ τῶν πεντετηρίδων γραφαί, which seem to have been part of the 'basilikai anagraphai' and to have comprised historical lists or nar-rative (perhaps partly illustrated), the most natural supposition is of a combination of secondary sources from different media: religious calen-dars, artistic representations of parts of the Grand Procession, as well as his own personal knowledge of the procession or someone else's account of it, and an acquaintance with any of the actual objects, or their models, which still existed in his day. The likelihood that many different sorts of records existed ought not to be underestimated since they furnished means of propaganda for the kings.[88] The Ptolemies were conscious of their public image, and took care to embellish it. Kallixeinos enhanced the glory of the dynasty by using, spreading, and therefore preserving details of royal majesty.

---

[87] For example, the ship-cart does not appear although it is attested in literature; cf. Paus. i. 29, 1; Photius, *Lex.* s.v. ἱστὸς καὶ κεραία; Strattis, *CAF* i. fr. 30; Robertson, *Hist. Gr. Art*, i. 307.

[88] Friedländer, 44.

F. THE LITERARY STYLE OF KALLIXEINOS

The writings of Kallixeinos reveal the conflation of genre which was prevalent in the Hellenistic age. His work combines many facets of Alexandrian scholarship, and the extant fragments show the interrelation of at least four literary genres, some new to the Hellenistic age, others familiar from classical literature although transformed by later writers.

About Alexandria is an example of historiographical writing, preserving an account of some past events and objects without, as it seems, any real historical analysis. Kallixeinos belongs with those writers of the fourth century and later who composed elaborate descriptions of objects which boasted several artistic features,[89] among them Moschion (the *Syracusa*), Ktesias (the pyre of Sardanapalus), Philistus and Timaeus (burial of Dionysius the Great of Sicily), Ephippus and Hieronymus of Cardia (the catafalque of Alexander), and Chares and Phylarchus (the marriage tent of Alexander). Whether these preserved fragments of set-piece descriptions stood alone or were parts of larger historiographical works does not affect their literary techniques or generic conventions. If the ecphrases were part of a larger narrative, the whole work may have comprised a series of such pieces loosely linked around a central theme, which appears to have been the case in *About Alexandria*, or else the descriptions may have been peripheral to the main narrative but were included to provide background material or extra information. Others may have stood on their own, such as Moschion's account of the *Syracusa* (Ath. 206D ff.), and may be considered special topics rather than as part of more general histories. Similar techniques can be traced in these detailed ecphrastic accounts. The surroundings and the immediate setting are treated first, and then the objects are described piecemeal to present them vividly and clearly to the reader. This progressive technique may take the form of a pretended reconstruction of the object (which follows the hypothetical, consecutive process of construction), or else the parts may be described by means of a periegesis in a way that an observer would see them. The writers of such descriptions are coherent generically in terms of theme, aim, interests, and techniques, and seem to have seen themselves as dependent upon each other for literary stimulus. The idea of rivalry and emulation among the historiographers in the choice of topics for description reveals a common tradition behind them. (Instances of interdependence may be seen in Philistus and Timaeus with the burial of Dionysius, in Ephippus and Hieronymus with the catafalque of Alexander, and in Chares and Phylarchus with the tent of

---

[89] For a discussion of these writers and their techniques of composition see ibid., 38 ff.

Alexander.) Kallixeinos may be considered a part of this group both because of his choice of topic and his treatment of it.

Many of the formal, descriptive historiographical writings can also be considered examples of paradoxography, another literary genre which became especially popular in the Hellenistic age.[90] This study of marvels grew out of the studies of natural sciences by Aristotle and Theophrastus in the fourth century. Natural laws as well as their exceptions were noted, and the latter became an equal part of the study of science. The Greek world, unlike the modern one, accepted the concept of paranormality even in physical objects. Interest in 'paradoxa'—things contrary to expectation— spread to Alexandria, where its popularity was perhaps due to the attraction which recherché and recondite scholarship had for the Alexandrian mind. Callimachus may have been among the first in Alexandria to translate these interests into a literary form through the composition of a 'Wonder-Book': among the corpus of his encyclopaedic writings was included a collection of wonders, Θαυμάτων τῶν εἰς ἅπασαν τὴν γῆν κατὰ τόπους ὄντων συναγωγή (Suda K 227). After Callimachus, the study was no longer part of the larger scientific inquiry of the philosophers, but became a distinct pursuit on its own merits. Callimachus gave the study the form which became traditional in the Hellenistic age and later. From these para-scientific beginnings, interest grew in man-made objects which surpassed normal expectations of size and magnificence and which could therefore be considered to flaunt natural laws in the same way that physical phenomena may do. Many ecphrases belong to the genre of paradoxography since they describe an awe-inspiring subject and concentrate on the spectacular, almost incredible, aspects of it. This interest in the unusual and wonderful combines with the highly sophisticated 'Beschreibungstechnik' to produce ecphrases different in effect from the descriptive passages of Homer, Hesiod, and even the Hellenistic poets Theocritus and Apollonius of Rhodes. Whereas the poets concentrated on the mundane in order to make it seem wonderful (although vivid and immediate) by their descriptive methods, the historiographers like Kallixeinos chose topics which in themselves surpassed normal expectation, but were made credible, although no less awe-inspiring, by the accumulation of precise detail in their descriptions.

Such historical-paradoxographical works are closely tied to a third literary genre, that of art-historical writing. Many 'marvels' which were attractive to writers were either works of art, or larger objects which included works of art, which became increasingly elaborate with the wealth

---

[90] For the history of this genre see *RE* s.v. Paradoxographoi; A. Giannini, *Inst. Lomb. (Rend. Lett.)* xcvii (1963), 247-66; id., *Acme* xvii (1964), 99-140; id., ed., *Paradoxographorum Graecorum Reliquiae* (Milan, 1966).

and love of ostentation which the Hellenistic monarchs poured into their production. Art and paradoxography were in this way closely related in the early Hellenistic period. The paradoxographical interest apart, writings on art at this period had a biographical, anecdotal, or historical emphasis rather than a truly analytical approach. Writers on art were anecdotal historiographers who happened to choose an artistic subject for consideration rather than 'professional' writers on art, like the earlier artists who wrote about form and techniques for achieving it. A 'non-professional' approach may be seen in the fact that the writers of artistic ecphrases, although often detailed in their descriptions, are not so accurate and precise that their objects could be reconstructed on the basis of the descriptions; this is so with Kallixeinos' accounts of the pavilion and the boats. A more graphic approach would pertain rather to the architects or builders of the objects, not to writers whose purpose was to give a comprehensible impression of the artistic whole. The Kallixeinos who wrote the ζωγράφων τε καὶ ἀνδριαντοποιῶν ἀναγραφή reflects this type of art-historical writing exactly, if, as the title suggests, this work was a biographical–anecdotal study of the artists rather than a technical, aesthetic analysis of the art they created. Even if this Kallixeinos is not Kallixeinos of Rhodes, a similar approach to art can be seen in *About Alexandria* with its basically tabular account of all the artistic elements of the subjects considered. Only the remarks on the workmanship of the ivory frieze in the barge and of the figures in the procession, and the digressions on Egyptian flora and architecture, begin to reflect aesthetic sensibility, but even they are banal and factual respectively, rather than analytically critical.

The fourth genre which becomes inextricably related to this type of scholarship is pinacography, the classification of other subjects either in a catalogue or index, be they literary genres, marvels, famous men, etc. Such work stems from the reconsideration of past knowledge more than from an interest in the discovery of new knowledge; in this way it can be considered typical of the retrospective nature of Alexandrian scholarship in general. Callimachus again appears in the forefront of the development of this genre with his Πίνακες τῶν ἐν πάσῃ παιδείᾳ διαλαμψάντων καὶ ὧν συνέγραψαν (Suda K 227), which attempted to organize biography and bibliography according to subjects.[91] List-making became a popular and widespread literary activity throughout the Hellenistic age.[92]

---

[91] For differing views on whether or not the *Pinakes* were meant to be the catalogue of the Library of Alexandria, see R. Pfeiffer, *History of Classical Scholarship* (Oxford, 1968), i. 127 ff.; *RE* s.v. Πίναξ (2), 1420.

[92] For the history of the genre and an indication of its popularity see *RE* s.v. Πίναξ (2); F. Schmidt, *Die Pinakes des Kallimachos* (Klass.-Phil. Stud. i, F. Jacoby, ed.) (Berlin, 1922).

Paraoxographical topics furnished good material for pinacographers, and lists of marvels and para-normal objects were some of the favourite topics to be indexed. Kallixeinos and the historiographers may be considered partly as pinacographers in so far as they organized, listed, and preserved historical paradoxa in their works. In apparently periegetic works like *About Alexandria*, the format may be a veneer for grouping topics of varying nature. If Kallixeinos of Rhodes was the author of the ζωγράφων τε καὶ ἀνδριαντοποιῶν ἀναγραφή, which sounds like a tabular account of artists and perhaps a list of their works, he was a pinacographer in its proper sense. If this work was a comprehensive catalogue in the style of the *Pinakes* of Callimachus, its date of composition should have been earlier than the beginning of the truncation of the lists, which is seen in the second century with the *Laterculi Alexandrini* (see above, p. 159).

All of the literary genres which have been discussed in this context reveal a typically Alexandrian preoccupation with the past—past events, past phenomena and creations, and lists of the above. This re-examination of former scholarship may be indicative of the often lamented lack of original creativity in various fields of Alexandrian scholarship, but such reconsideration reveals an impressive capacity for organization and synthesis and an ability to recreate new from old. Historiography, 'non-professional' art-historical writing, paradoxography, and pinacography are all aspects of this basically antiquarian approach to learning. As an author in whom all these genres are combined, Kallixeinos may be considered an Alexandrian antiquarian. His literary coherence shows the difficulty of separating from each other the threads of the different studies which overlap broadly in subject, treatment, and technique, and the work of Kallixeinos is thus a useful focus for study because it reflects the interests of the author's age and shows how they could be synthesized. Furthermore, Kallixeinos represents a further stage of this type of 'para-scholarship' begun by Callimachus and his pupils. His importance in Alexandrian literature may lie in the preservation of this fusion of genres, which is a crystallized stage in the process of literary development in the third century BC, and his literary achievement testifies how much could be accomplished within a basically antiquarian framework.

5. Conclusion

Although the preceding commentary has discussed some individual historical issues which arise in the text and has offered certain tentative conclusions about them, the Grand Procession has also to be considered in a larger context, despite the fact that many uncertainties cannot at present be resolved without further information which at present seems unlikely to be forthcoming. Firstly, in the general context of early Ptolemaic religion, the two changes which occurred in Greek religious processions after the time of Alexander (outlined above, pp. 26-7) are relevant in the case of this particular procession and its festival. The emphasis on the armed troops, although they appear at the end of the proceedings and may even have occupied a separate day of the Grand Procession, creates an undeniably secular atmosphere which is enhanced by the sensationalism inherent in the unremitting concentration on wealth, extravagance, and ostentation throughout the procession. Moreover, the Grand Procession comprises divisional processions in honour of many gods as well as deified mortals, and the festival to which the procession belonged must therefore also have had a group of honorands, not a single patron god. These two factors indicate that the festival was in all likelihood not merely one, or a simple combination of several, classical religious festivals transferred to Alexandria, while the Dionysiac procession included in the Grand Procession is similarly unlikely to have been a transplanted traditional Attic festival in honour of the god, such as the Lenaia or the Anthesteria. The diverse contents of this sectional procession point to the same conclusion even if some features may have taken their basic iconographic stock from the older, traditional celebrations of Dionysus (i.e. the cart-drawn phallos, the orgiastic thiasoi, various aspects of mystic cults, etc.); they appear to be removed from any narrow ritual context within a particular cult celebration, and are instead recombined into an anomalous amalgam of Dionysiac worship.

The Grand Procession must also be considered against the native religion of Egypt, a country of ancient civilisation on to which the Ptolemies grafted their Graeco-Macedonian culture. The native Egyptian religion, which was remarkably conservative by nature, had existed for millennia and continued to be practised alongside the Greek cults which were introduced at a comparatively late stage. Processions played an important role in the native celebrations: the great, week-long festivals of the Egyptian gods included processions of the deity, usually on an annual progress from one shrine to another.[1] For example, in the Opet festival of Ammon at Karnak the image of the god travelled upriver in an elaborate procession by sacred barque from his home at Karnak to another temple at Thebes. These processions provided the sole opportunity for public focus in a religion whose primary means of worship was otherwise restricted to the daily rituals of priests in private ceremonies within the inner halls of the temples, isolated from public view and participation.[2] The Ptolemaic kings assumed the role of the pharaoh in relation to the Egyptian popu-lace,[3] and regularly performed the religious and royal birthday celebra-tions whose rituals had been prescribed from dynastic times (cf. *OGIS* 90, 38 ff.). They likewise participated in the purely Egyptian annual religious festivals, including the processions. At the annual New Year's festival at Edfu, the Ptolemaic king and queen took part in the carefully regulated ritual procession from the various halls of the temple to the roof and back again. This ritual is preserved in a series of reliefs carved along the stair-way, commemorating the processional journey of the 'Greek pharoah', Ptolemy III.[4] The elements of the Grand Procession as they are described by Kallixeinos are wholly Greek in iconography and religious significance. No Egyptian elements appear in the preserved parts of the text, and it seems therefore unlikely that there were any Egyptianizing features in the rest of the Grand Procession. Such a purely Greek religious occasion in a native environment is paralleled by a similar juxtaposition at the Serapeum at Memphis, a dynastic temple-precinct dating from the Old Kingdom, where early Ptolemaic sculpture of Dionysus and his associated animals, which are wholly Greek in iconography, adorn the dromos to the shrine in which the sacred Apis-bulls were interred in accordance with dynastic ritual.[5] None the less, the Grand Procession may have served as an ideal syncretism of the public aspects of Greek and native religion in Egypt. Although this Olympian extravaganza was a Greek festival designed to appeal to Greeks, the magnificent occasion may well have attracted the Egyptian population of Alexandria, which was in any case accus-tomed to attending the processions of its own native festivals. The festive atmosphere and anticipation of a lavish spectacle would have been familiar

---

[1] A. Erman, *Die Religion der Ägypter* (Berlin and Leipzig, 1934), 198 ff.; W. M. Flinders Petrie, *Religious Life in Ancient Egypt* (London, 1924), 28-9; H. Bonnet, *Reallexikon der Ägyptischen Religionsgeschichte* (Berlin, 1952), s.v. Prozession.

[2] Bonnet, 610; H. W. Fairman, *Bull. John Rylands Library* xxxvii (1) (1954), 174.

[3] *Ptol. Alex.* i. 214.

[4] For an account of this festival and its procession see M. Alliot, *Le Culte d'Horus à Edfou au temps des Ptolémées* (Cairo, 1949-54), i. 303 ff.

[5] *Ptol. Alex.* i. 255; see Lauer and Picard, op. cit. (p. 94 n. 174 above) for illus-trations of this sculpture.

and attractive to Egyptians as well as to Greeks, and natives may have been among the onlookers in the streets of Alexandria.

The primary issue which must still be considered is the occasion and interpretation of the Grand Procession. In the preceding chapters frequent reference has been made to the Ptolemaieia festival which was established by Ptolemy II in honour of Ptolemy I. The once hypothetical date of the first celebration of the festival in 279/8 (the penteteric anniversary of the death of Soter) has recently been confirmed by an Athenian decree in honour of Kallias of Sphettos,[6] with the result that the decree proclaiming the announcement of the festival by Philadelphus (now lost) was probably made *c.*280/79 to allow time for preparations, travel, etc. This festival was the formal announcement, with attendant recognition, of the deificiation of Soter, even though he was not included in the dynastic cult until the end of the third century (see p. 44). The coincidence between the existence of this description of the Grand Procession and the independently attested Ptolemaieia festival has led to many assumptions of a connection between the two; most scholars have interpreted the Grand Procession as the procession of the Ptolemaieia and have concentrated on identifying the particular celebration to which it belongs. Two decrees recording the replies of the Nesiotic League (*SIG*[3] 390) and the Delphic Amphictyony (*SEG* 13, 351; cf. *HTR* liv (1961), 141 ff.) to the original lost establishment decree outline the essential features of the Ptolemaieia festival and are thus vital to the alleged connection between the festival and the Grand Procession. According to the decrees, the Ptolemaieia is to be attended by theoroi from other Greek cities and federal institutions, and is to include a sacrifice and an *agon* comprising gymnastic, musical, and equestrian events. The fe tival is to be isolympic in its periodicity and in the prizes given to the vic rs. Above all, Ptolemy I is to be honoured with honours equal to those of a god. The Nesiotic League, whose reply is the more complete, approve the king's measures as decreed, and agree to send theoroi to each celebration of the festival, and a crown worth 1,000 staters to Philadelphus. Most of these provisions are also alluded to in the Athenian decree for Kallias of Sphettos, who attended the first celebration of the Ptolemaieia as the head of the Athenian delegation.[7] Additional information about the festival may be provided by an inscription mentioning the victory won in a Ptolemaieia by a Tegean actor (*SIG*[3] 1080); if, as seems likely, this refers to the same Alexandrian Ptolemaieia, dramatic

---

[6] H. von Prott, *RhM* n.F. liii (1898), 460 ff.; T. L. Shear, Jr., *Kallias of Sphettos and the Revolt of Athens in 286 BC, Hesperia* Suppl. xvii (1978), 33 ff.; (cf. M. J. Osborne, *ZPE* xxxv (1979), 181 ff.); C. Habicht, *Untersuchungen zur politischen Geschichte Athens im 3. Jahrhundert v. Chr.*, *Vestigia* xxx (Munich, 1979), 61 n. 66.

[7] Shear, 33 ff.

competitions were also part of the *agon*. No procession is mentioned in any of these decrees, but Greek religious practice suggests that one would have been included since the other three parts of a standard four-part festival are specified (the sacrifice, which entails the feast, and the *agon*). The Ptolemaieia seems, then, to have had the usual form of a Greek religious festival. The omission of the procession from the decrees may perhaps be explained by the fact that it was the one feature of the festival which would have been staged by the Ptolemaic authorities alone, and which would not have required the acknowledgement or participation of the other Greeks attending, unlike the sacrifice, *agon*, dedicatory honorific crowns, or honours for Soter, with which, according to the specifications in the decrees, the theoroi would have been involved.

Attempts to identify the Grand Procession as part of the Ptolemaieia must therefore be confined to suggested similarities between the former and to that part of the latter which is not mentioned in the decrees which provide the only certain information about the festival. Nevertheless, the few known details of the Ptolemaieia have a certain similarity to features in the text of the Grand Procession, which includes a few hints about the rest of its festival although it cannot be expected to describe in detail other parts of the celebration of which it was one discrete component perhaps occurring on a separate day. It is clear that this festival is isolympic, both because the figure of Penteteris (who must refer to the periodicity of the festival) appears in the procession and because Kallixeinos states that his sources for the procession were included in the penteteric records. The 2,000 bulls which march in the Dionysiac procession show that a huge sacrifice was part of the Grand Procession, the scope of which would be expanded if the other sectional processions also had complements of sacrificial victims. The ornamental pavilion which was used in festivities connected with the Grand Procession was undoubtedly the setting of a magnificent banquet, most likely the feast upon the sacrificial offerings, and its separation from the place where the ordinary populace was entertained shows that it was intended for the official guests, namely, the theoroi who attended the festival. An *agon* is referred to at the end of the text along with the mention of a crowning ceremony, which, despite the many difficulties of this final section, indicates at least that some kind of competition was included. There is no mention of any athletic events (although the cavalry would have been obvious participants in any equestrian events), but musical performances may lie behind the presence of the kitharistai and the chorus, and the presence of the Guild of the Artists of Dionysus and the Delphic tripods for the choregoi indicate the inclusion of dramatic contests. Moreover, large numbers of crowns appear throughout the text as articles of apparel and as dedications (either to various members of the royal family or to the gods, some perhaps as victors' prizes), and some crowns at least were paid for by individual contributions collected by the *oikonomoi*. Finally, Soter is granted honours 'equal to those of a god' because his deification is apparent: he is one of the honorands of the procession 'named after' οἱ τῶν βασιλέων γονεῖς, he appears upon a cart in the company of Alexander and other gods, and he is honoured with an empty throne adorned with an especially large crown.

A case can therefore be made that the provisions of the decrees of the Nesiotic and Amphictyonic Leagues are reflected, however indirectly or superficially, in the description of the Grand Procession. This, however, is hardly surprising in view of the formalized nature of Greek religious festivals and the fact that the Ptolemaieia and the festival of the Grand Procession both contain these standard elements. Considerations which have been invoked to connect the Grand Procession with the Ptolemaieia also revolve around the identification of the particular celebration which the text is supposed to record. The likelihood of the various dates suggested depends upon different interpretations of the text's internal evidence regarding the marital status of Philadelphus and the reason for the congregation of so many troops in Alexandria. Since the first celebration of the Ptolemaieia occurred in 279/8, the next penteteric dates for the festival were 275/4, 271/70, and so on. The different interpretations of the contemporary external circumstances suggested by the text of the Grand Procession can be variously reconciled with the first three celebrations of the Ptolemaieia. The year 279/8 accords best with the belief that Arsinoe II was not the wife of Philadelphus at the time of the Grand Procession, which makes the acceptance of a date early in the decade inevitable. The foreign intrigues of this year may also explain the great number of troops in Alexandria if a concurrent military involvement is thought necessary to explain their presence; they could, for example, have been gathered in the capital in 279 in order to celebrate the victory which could be claimed after the Carian War of that year. A further subjective argument in favour of 279/8 may be that the particular magnificence of this celebration indicates the inauguration of the Ptolemaieia festivals.[8] The second isolympic celebration of the Ptolemaieia in 275/4 is the easiest to reconcile with differing views regarding Arsinoe II, who was probably back in Egypt by that date but may or may not have been married to her brother. This date therefore suits the view that she was indeed queen at the time of the Grand Procession as well as the belief

---

[8] If Fraser, *Ptol. Alex.*, ii. 381 n. 335, 814 n. 151 (cf. p. 48 n. 39 above), is right to connect the 'first large procession' mentioned by Athenaeus (415A–B) with the procession described by Kallixeinos, then this festival (whatever it was) *was* the first celebration in the series.

that she was not, depending on one's interpretation of οἱ βασιλεῖς and the *dikeras*. In this year, the troops could have been massed in Alexandria in preparation for the expected hostilities of the First Syrian War. The third date, 271/70, can only be supported by those who either believe that the text shows that Arsinoe II *was* queen at the time (as she was, although she had not long to live), or accept the anomaly that, although queen, she is not referred to in the text. This year best suits the interpretation of the troops as participants in a military triumph, since they could then have been celebrating their recent victory in the First Syrian War, a success which inaugurated the 'Golden Age' of Philadelphus and Alexandria.

All these arguments are clearly subjective. Since it has been argued throughout the commentary that there is no direct or indirect reference to Arsinoe II in the text of the Grand Procession, the most suitable date for the procession on these grounds is *c.*280–275, when she was not yet married to her brother. If the troops can be explained equally as victors, as forces mobilized for some threatened hostility, or merely as an exceptionally large force mustered for the occasion of the Grand Procession (no matter what it was), their presence causes no difficulty either in that period. If we consider only the chronological evidence provided by the absence of Arsinoe and the presence of the troops, the text of the Grand Procession might be a description of part of the first or second celebration of the Ptolemaieia except that the identification of the Grand Procession and the Ptolemaieia is precluded by the former's lack of any particular emphasis on Soter, in whose honour the latter was established.[9] The references in the text to the deified king are indeed clear but hardly sufficient if the festival which included the Grand Procession was created specifically in his individual honour. Arguments that more significant, decisive references have fallen out of the text (perhaps even an account of a very grand sectional procession, dedicated to Soter alone) are not very convincing, albeit irrefutable on account of the fragmentary nature of the evidence. Given that Kallixeinos admittedly includes in his account only the most magnificent elements of the Grand Procession (he states, for example, that he describes only the gold and silver objects, 201F; line 216), and that Athenaeus in his turn chose from these only the most spectacular excerpts to crown his examples of ancient luxury, it is difficult to believe that any particularly marvellous honours given to Soter in the Grand Procession were omitted by both Kallixeinos and Athenaeus, and that neither gave the information that the festival was in Soter's honour if this was the most singular feature about it. The silence of the sources on this central point is

---

[9] Fraser, *BCH* lxxviii (1954), 57–8 n. 3, and *Ptol. Alex.*, i. 231–2, has already pointed out that the identification of the Grand Procession and the Ptolemaieia is tenuous.

impossible to accept, fragmentary though the text is, and despite our ignorance as to the details of the actual celebrations of the Ptolemaieia. The burden of proof must still lie with those who maintain that the description of a procession belonging to a festival in honour of the deified founder of the Ptolemaic dynasty did not concern him ritually, thematically, or iconographically to any significant or identifiable extent.[10]

Although the identification of this festival with the Ptolemaieia can then be rejected, no other certain interpretation of its occasion can be offered. The amalgamated nature of the Grand Procession, with its individual processions in honour of various gods, precludes the suggestion that the festival honours any one god in preference to any other (despite the fact that the preserved text is weighted in favour of Dionysus), or that it reflects rituals copied directly from his or her annual civic worship. From the collection of honorands presented in the Grand Procession, the festival seems to have been some kind of Olympian extravaganza in honour of all the gods and the deified mortals important to the Ptolemaic dynasty.[11] As such, it was surely a new festival instituted by the Ptolemies in their capital, not one brought to Alexandria from the traditional religion of mainland Greece or Macedonia. For all that is known, the festival may have been established in the earliest years of Alexandria by Soter, and the text may describe one of its many successive penteteric celebrations which continued into the reign of Philadelphus (but see n. 8 above). This festival may have been popularly called the 'Penteteris' (the appearance of the personified Penteteris perhaps supports this notion), but festivals in Greece were regularly called by names specifying their periodicity even though

[10] A further argument against this identification is the papyrus fragment *POxy.* 2465, fr. 2, col. i, which contains part of an Alexandrian decree specifying public participation in a procession of the Kanephoros, probably upon the occasion of the inauguration of the cult of Arsinoe II; see *Ptol. Alex.* i. 229. Although described by the historian Satyrus (cf. *FGrH* 631), which probably attests the importance of the occasion, the provisions of the festival mention only private sacrifices on individual altars, and a procession consisting of some of the magistrates of the city and officials responsible for maintaining public order. If this celebration is the inauguration of the public cult of Arsinoe (and therefore arguably analogous in importance to the first celebration of the Ptolemaieia), one would perhaps expect an especially magnificent occasion, but the provisions mentioned in the papyrus are not comparable to the scale of the celebration depicted in the Grand Procession. If the event described in the papyrus fragment is indicative of public celebrations (and processions) in the dynastic cult, it seems unlikely that the Grand Procession (which took place some years earlier) celebrated the deification of Soter with such unparalleled magnificence.

[11] Cf. *Ptol. Alex.* i. 232. Fraser, ib., ii. 381 n. 335, who thinks that the passage of Athenaeus 415A-B (see n. 8 above) refers to the Grand Procession, believes that the actual wording used by Poseidippos to describe the procession indicates that it was not for one particular deity, because, as he tells me, he feels that a procession for a single, specific deity would not simply be called, even in a curtailed form, ἡ μεγάλη πομπή.

they had official names as well; for example, the Athenian Apollonia festival at Delos is occasionally called the 'Penteteris' (*ID* 104-10, 13 = *IG* II² 1639 (355/4 BC)), and the decrees of the Guilds of the Artists of Dionysus often refer in similar, colloquial terms to festivals which must also have had official titles (see p. 57). Although the official name of the festival of the Grand Procession can only be surmised, possible suggestions may include something along the lines of 'The Festival of the Olympian Gods'. It is clear, however, that more than one penteteric festival existed at the time, since Kallixeinos refers to the official αἱ τῶν πεντετηρίδων γραφαί. Any of these penteteric festivals may be seen behind the mention of one or more festivals called 'the Penteteris' in various papyri (*PMich. Zen.* 46; *PRyl.* 562 = *SB* 7645; *PGrad.* 6 III; *PSI* 409 a). Also, the Ptolemaieia was itself entitled to be called the Penteteris (whether or not it ever *was*) because it was isolympic. Since the papyri give very little information about these various Penteterides, none can be certainly identified with the festival of the Grand Procession, or indeed with the Ptolemaieia as it is attested in the decrees concerning the celebration of 279/8.[12] The successive dates of the celebration of Kallixeinos' 'Penteteris' with its Grand Procession cannot therefore be calculated, since no one year of its occurrence is known, but there is no external objection to a celebration of this 'Penteteris' within the years *c.*279-275, the date which accords best with all the evidence provided by the text.

Certain 'mystic' aspects of the cult in the Grand Procession, to which attention has already been called, may here be discussed collectively in order to shed some light, however dim, upon the existence of mystery-cults in early third-century Alexandria even if none of the elements in question can be assigned to any particular set of Mysteries. Most of these so-called 'mystic' elements appear within the sectional procession of Dionysus, except for the 'mystic' crown which is intended for the Berenikeion and which seems to appear in another, unspecified, part of the Grand Procession. If the text is sound (see p. 120), the most natural interpretation of this phrase is that the queen had been an initiate in some Mysteries during her lifetime, even though we are in no position to trace the

---

[12] An additional reference to a Penteteris may be seen in the conjectural supplement τὸν [πεντετηρικὸν] ἀγῶνα in the *Dikaiomata*, line 262; see ibid., ii. 380 n. 326. For opposing views on whether or not festivals called 'the Penteteris' in papyri can be identified with the Ptolemaieia, see ibid.; E. Visser, *Götter und Kulte im Ptolemäischen Alexandrien* (Amsterdam, 1938), 10-11; Otto, *Beitr. z. Seleukidengesch.*, 88; H. Braunert, *JDAI* lxv-lxvi (1950-1), 251 ff., n. 5; C. C. Edgar, *Mélanges Maspero* (Cairo, 1934), ii. 53 ff. (Edgar identifies the Penteteris with the Ptolemaieia, and both with a later celebration (in 251 BC) of the festival to which the Grand Procession belongs.)

development of any such cults in early third-century Alexandria, and we know nothing of any participation by the queen in them. Mysteries of Sarapis do not seem to have existed before the Imperial period and may not in any case have had an Egyptian origin.[13] There is a tradition about the possible celebration of a version of the Eleusinian Mysteries at Alexandria, but although a religious festival with musical contests (perhaps involving the Eleusinian legend) was held at the Alexandrian suburb of Eleusis in the third century, Mysteries as such are not attested.[14] Ptolemy I, who consulted the high-priest of Eleusis about the cult of Sarapis (Tac. *Hist.* iv. 83) may have had the unfulfilled intention of establishing an Alexandrian version of these Mysteries; Berenike may have furthered his plans by lending them her support, and the 'mystic crown' of the Berenikeion could have had some connection with this. Equally uncertain is the existence of Mysteries in honour of Adonis. The Alexandrian Adonia festival is described in Theocritus xv, and it is clear that it had the royal patronage of Arsinoe II. Berenike may also have been a devotee of this cult since she was associated with Aphrodite, with whom Adonis was worshipped at the festival (the singer of the Adonis song in the poem relates that Aphrodite had made Berenike divine, lines 106-8).[15] The existence of Mysteries in this cult has been inferred from a papyrus fragment (*PPetr.* iii. 142) even though they do not appear in Theocritus' account of the festival.[16] If Berenike was devoted to the cult of Adonis, she may have been concerned with such Mysteries if they existed, but that is all that can be said. Perhaps the most likely Mysteries into which Berenike may have been initiated were those of the Great Gods of Samothrace, which are well attested as early as the fifth century BC.[17] The sanctuary on the island was patronized by the Ptolemaic kings, and Philadelphus and Arsinoe II (as wife of Lysimachus of Thrace and daughter of Ptolemy I) both funded large building projects there, while *PCZ* 59296, 30-3, shows that the Gods of Samothrace were worshipped in the mid-third century BC in a shrine at Philadelphia (named after Arsinoe II) in Egypt. Although there is no evidence that any member of the royal family was ever initiated into these Mysteries, the hypothesis has certain attractions both because the Ptolemaic building projects may conceivably have been in honour of the respective initiations of Philadelphus and Arsinoe II, and in terms of

[13] Fraser, *Op. Ath.* iii (1960), 4 n. 1; *Ptol. Alex.* ii. 419 n. 620.

[14] *Ptol. Alex.* i. 200-1; but see *PAnt.* 18, discussed in ibid., ii. 341 n. 95, §1 (ii).

[15] *Ptol. Alex.* i. 197.

[16] G. Glotz, *REG* xxxiii (1920), 169 ff., but against this view see W. Atallah, *Adonis dans la littérature et l'art Grecs* (Paris, 1966), 136 ff., 274 ff., 289 ff.; Gow, *Comm. Theoc.* ii. 262 ff.

[17] For all ancient literary sources for these Mysteries, see N. Lewis, ed., *Samothrace I: The Ancient Literary Sources* (London, 1959).

geographical likelihood: Arsinoe stayed on the island before her return to Egypt, and Berenike may have gone to Samothrace on a visit to her daughter then, or earlier if she had stopped there *en route* to her daughter in Thrace. It may have been her original interest in the cult which was inherited and transformed into tangible contributions by her children.

Its context being uncertain, the 'mystic' crown may nevertheless refer to Berenike's connection to the mystic aspects which are seen in the Dionysiac procession. Mysteries of Dionysus certainly existed in Ptolemaic Egypt and are well attested by the time of Ptolemy IV, himself an eager devotee of the religion of this god, especially in its wild, orgiastic aspects.[18] Philopator passed a series of regulations for the registration of those celebrating the mystery-rites in the chora (*BGU* 1211),[19] and, whether this edict should be interpreted as a measure of repression or encouragement to the partici-pants, it probably has to be assumed, in order to account for the regula-tion, that popular Mysteries of some long standing existed at the end of the third century. The establishment and development of the Mysteries of Dionysus must by implication have occurred some decades before, per-haps in the earliest Ptolemaic period, close to the date of the Grand Proces-sion.[20] This edict is the strongest piece of evidence for the early existence of these Mysteries, but it is supported by other pieces of indirect evidence. *Idyll* xxvi of Theocritus has already been discussed as a possible indication of some kind of mystic rites which included Dionysus and Semele in Alexandria (see above, p. 79), and the poem is dated early in the reign of Philadelphus, contemporary with the Grand Procession. Finally, a papyrus fragment from Gurob (*PGurob* 1) of the early third century contains part of a Ritual of Mysteries, and although the fragmentary condition of this papyrus and the disjointed nature of its utterances preclude any definite interpretation, various Dionysiac elements appear in the text among those which seem to belong to other Mysteries, such as the Orphic ones.[21] A popular version of Orphic Mysteries may therefore have existed in Alexandria (they were certainly extant in classical Greece) which, like the earlier Orphic rites, contained various Dionysiac elements.[22] This

---

[18] *Ptol. Alex.* i. 203 ff.

[19] = *SB* 7266 = M.-T. Lenger, *Corpus des ordonnances des Ptolémées*[2], *Mém. Acad. Roy. Belg.* 2nd sér. lxiv (2) (1980), No. 29 (with bibliography). For a discus-sion of the decree, the meaning of whose provisions has been disputed, see ibid.; *Ptol. Alex.* i. 204 and n. 114; for a new discussion of the date, see now E. G. Turner, 'The Ptolemaic Royal Edict *BGU* VI 1211 is to be Dated Before 215/4 BC' *100th Anniver-sary of the Austrian National Library* (Vienna, 1983)), forthcoming.

[20] *Ptol. Alex.* i. 204; O. Kern, *Die Religion der Griechen* (Berlin, 1926–38), iii. 197. For the Mysteries of Dionysus in general see Nilsson, *Dio. Mysts.*

[21] J. G. Smyly, ed., *Greek Papyri from Gurob* (Dublin, 1921), 1 ff.

[22] For the Orphic Mysteries in general see Harrison, *Prolegomena*, 455 ff.; M. P. Nilsson, *Opuscula Selecta* (Lund, 1951–60), ii. 628 ff.; W. K. C. Guthrie, *Orpheus and*

papyrus may even attest that various mystic cults had already been syn-
cretised to some extent by the early part of the third century BC.[23] This
body of Orphic ritual and myth perhaps furnished the base from which
the Dionysiac Mysteries proper developed in the third century. The
Grand Procession may reflect an early stage of this development, but the
suggestion is better left as a question than as an answer, in the hope that
the text may be studied further in connection with other evidence for
'mystic cults' in early third-century Alexandria.

It is hardly necessary to summarize either the elements or the themes of
the Grand Procession, and most 'conclusions' have already been given in
the body of the commentary where their discussion is most relevant. However, a few conjectures may usefully be made about the intentions which
Philadelphus may have had regarding this festival, and about its effect
upon those who witnessed it. Clearly, the staging of any festival by a
central authority, especially when it was a new festival initiated by that
authority, would be interpreted as an act of general benevolence towards
the populace because of the free entertainment and food provided. The
Alexandrians, who must have formed the majority of the spectators,
would have been the main beneficiaries of this aspect of the festival. The
over-all magnificence of the festival must have been equally calculated to
impress the large number of foreign theoroi, who, as we have seen (p. 33),
attended it. The extreme ostentation and extravagance which predominate
throughout the Grand Procession emphatically communicate the wealth
and success of the Ptolemaic kingdom to the rest of the Greek world, and
give support to the statement of Theocritus (xvii. 95 ff.) that Ptolemaic
riches were legendary. The obvious conclusion must have been that Alexandria claimed to be the new capital of the Greek world. Along the same
lines, the lengthy march-past of the troops can only be interpreted in a
contemporary, if not specific, context as demonstrating the military
strength of the Ptolemaic empire in the face of any threat. These two
aspects of the Grand Procession must be seen in the light of the current
political situation. The discussion of the tableau which contained the
representations of Corinth and the Greek cities has indicated that a general
state of watchfulness existed at this period between the Ptolemies and the
rulers of Macedonia as a prelude to the open hostilities of the Chremonidean
War about a decade later (see above, p. 107). The two parties manœuvred
for position using 'weapons' such as the Corinthian League and the freedom

Greek Religion (London, 1935); id., *The Greeks and Their Gods* (London, 1950),
309 ff.

[23] Smyly, 2.

of the Greeks, which, as far as the Ptolemies were concerned, may have been designed to divert Macedonian attention towards the mainland and away from the more vested Ptolemaic interests in the Aegean, Asia Minor, and North Africa.[24] Ptolemy I is depicted on this cart in his avowed role as the champion of Greek freedom according to the ideals of the Corinthian League, in stark contrast to the kings of Macedonia, whose proclaimed philhellenic policies had in the past years turned to brutality in their public actions in Greece. The public propaganda spread by the Grand Procession may have been intended to suggest to Macedonia that the Ptolemies were still a force to be reckoned with in Greece, primarily a sphere of Macedonian influence. Similarly, the presence of Alexander on the same cart could be interpreted to mean that the Ptolemies claimed a legitimate inheritance of Greece, the islands, and Asia Minor. Even if Philadelphus had no actual designs on Greece, any doubts to the contrary implanted in the mind of Antigonus Gonatas may have helped to keep him occupied on the mainland, away from the islands and Asia Minor. The public position regarding the Seleucids at the time of the Grand Procession is even more germane since the hostility between Egypt and Syria was soon to develop, if it had not already done so, into the open warfare which was bitter enough to flare up sporadically for more than a century in six Syrian Wars. The presence of the troops must have been a pertinent deterrent to those neighbours who were in a position to attempt to threaten the Ptolemies on their home ground. The presentation of Dionysus and Alexander as the conquerors of the East and as gods with a special relationship to the Ptolemies places the Ptolemies metaphorically in the position actually occupied by the Seleucids in the eastern stretches of Alexander's empire. The Ptolemies at this time surely had no intention of usurping eastern Asia from Antiochus I, but their indirect claim to it here as part of the inheritance from Alexander can hardly be interpreted otherwise than in the context of their current struggles with Syria over Coele-Syria and, to a lesser extent, Caria. The great number of elephants in the Grand Procession surely had important military connotations in those years (see p. 92). Their presence may have been intended to inform the Seleucids of the potentially vast supply of Ptolemaic elephants, especially if these were the first African beasts to appear in Alexandria and, as such, the first challenge to hitherto total Seleucid control over the supply of Indian elephants to the West. Finally, the importance of the emphatic presentation of Alexander as the Neos Dionysos who followed in the footsteps of the god and succeeded as an equal conqueror in the East can hardly be overestimated. These scenes from the Dionysiac procession give support to the claims

[24] For a similar, more detailed interpretation of Ptolemaic foreign policy at this period (esp. regarding Macedon), see Will, *Hist. pol.* i[2]. 153 ff.

that this picture of Alexander had an Alexandrian origin. Whether this was invented by Cleitarchus or not, the fact remains that the Ptolemaic kings adopted and publicized this view of Alexander, and shared in the glory of this vision themselves through their claim to a blood-relationship with both Alexander and Dionysus. This in turn enhanced their position as the legitimate heirs of Alexander in Egypt and endowed them with a convenient legitimisation of the divine status of their dynasty.

Appendix I

Text of other fragments of Kallixeinos

The following text is reproduced from F. Jacoby, ed., *Die Fragmente der griechischen Historiker* (Berlin and Leiden, 1923–58), III C (1), No. 627, pp. 161–7, 177–8, with the kind permission of E. J. Brill, Leiden.

627. KALLIXEINOS VON RHODOS

T

1 (III 55) Phot. *Bibl.* 161 p. 104 b 38: ὁ δὲ δωδέκατος αὐτῶι (*scil.* Σωπάτρωι 20 σοφιστῆι) λόγος συνήθροισται ἐξ ἄλλων τι διαφόρων καὶ ἐκ τῆς Καλλιξένου ζωγράφων τε καὶ ἀνδριαντοποιῶν ἀναγραφῆς . . . .

2 Plin. *N.H.* 34, 52: cessavit deinde ars (scil. *statuaria*) ac rursus olympiade *CLVI* (156/5) revixit, cum fuere longe quidem infra praedictos, probati tamen, Antaeus, *Callistratus, Polycles Athenaeus, Callixenus, Pythocles, Pythias, Timocles.*

25

F

1. ΠΕΡΙ ΑΛΕΞΑΝΔΡΕΙΑΣ Α̅–Δ̅

Α̅

1 (1) Athen. 5, 37–39 p. 203 E-206 C: (F 2) ἐπεὶ δὲ περὶ νεῶν κατασκευ- 203 E

---

23 *CLV* V   *fluere* VR   24 *pythias* h *pytas* d *pitas* VR om. B
timocles h *timoles* VRd om. B   Jacoby, Fragm. Griech. Hist. III C

ἧς εἰρήκαμεν (F 2 c. 36), φέρ' εἴπωμεν (ἀκοῆς γάρ ἐστιν ἄξια) καὶ τὰ ὑπὸ τοῦ
Φιλοπάτορος βασιλέως (222/06) κατεσκευασμένα σκάφη, περὶ ὧν ὁ αὐτὸς
Καλλίξεινος ἱστορεῖ ἐν τῶι πρώτωι Περὶ Ἀλεξανδρείας, οὑτωσὶ λέγων·
   ‹‹τὴν τεσσαρακοντήρη ναῦν κατεσκεύασεν ὁ Φιλοπάτωρ τὸ
5 μῆκος ἔχουσαν διακοσίων ὀγδοήκοντα πηχῶν, ὀκτὼ δὲ καὶ
τριάκοντα ἀπὸ παρόδου ἐπὶ πάροδον, ὕψος δὲ ἕως ἀκροστολίου 203 F
τεσσαράκοντα ὀκτὼ πηχῶν· ἀπὸ δὲ τῶν πρυμνητικῶν ἀφλάστων
ἐπὶ τὸ ‹ὑπὸ› τῆι θαλάσσηι μέρος αὐτῆς τρεῖς πρὸς τοῖς πεντήκοντα πήχεις. πηδάλια δ' εἶχε τέτταρα τριακονταπήχη, κώπας
10 δὲ θρανιτικὰς ὀκτὼ καὶ τριάκοντα πηχῶν τὰς μεγίστας, ‹αἳ› διὰ 204 A
τὸ μόλυβδον ἔχειν ἐν τοῖς ἐγχειριδίοις καὶ γεγονέναι λίαν εἴσω
βαρεῖαι κατὰ τὴν ζύγωσιν εὐήρεις ὑπῆρχον ἐπὶ τῆς χρείας.
δίπωιρος δ' ἐγεγόνει καὶ δίπρυμνος, καὶ ἔμβολα εἶχεν ἑπτά·
τούτων ἓν μὲν ἡγούμενον, τὰ δ' ὑποστέλλοντα, τινὰ δὲ κατὰ
15 τὰς ἐπωτίδας. ὑποζώματα δ' ἐλάμβανε δώδεκα· ἑξακοσίων δ'
ἦν ἕκαστον πηχῶν. εὔρυθμος δ' ἦν καθ' ὑπερβολήν. θαυμαστὸς
δ' ἦν καὶ ὁ ἄλλος κόσμος τῆς νεώς· ζῶια μὲν γὰρ εἶχεν οὐκ
ἐλάττω δώδεκα πηχῶν κατὰ πρύμναν τε καὶ κατὰ πρῶιραν, καὶ 204 B
πᾶς τόπος αὐτῆς κηρογραφίαι κατεπεποίκιλτο, τὸ δ' ἔγκωπον
20 ἅπαν μέχρι τῆς τρόπεως κισσίνην φυλλάδα καὶ θύρσους εἶχε
πέριξ. πολὺς δ' ἦν καὶ ὁ τῶν ὅπλων κόσμος· ἀνεπλήρου δὲ
‹πάντα› τὰ προσδεόμενα τῆς νεὼς μέρη.   γενομένης δὲ ἀναπείρας ἐδέξατο ἐρέτας πλείους τῶν τετρακισχιλίων, εἰς δὲ τὰς
ὑπηρεσίας τετρακοσίους, εἰς δὲ τὸ κατάστρωμα ἐπιβάτας τρισ-
25 χιλίους ἀποδέοντας ἑκατὸν καὶ πεντήκοντα· καὶ χωρὶς ὑπὸ τὰ
ζύγια πλῆθος ἀνθρώπων ἕτερον, ἐπισιτισμοῦ τε οὐκ ὀλίγον.
καθειλκύσθη δὲ τὴν μὲν ἀρχὴν ἀπὸ ἐσχαρίου τινός, ὅ φασι 204 C
παγῆναι πεντήκοντα πλοίων πεντηρικῶν ξυλείαι, ὑπὸ δὲ ὄχλου
μετὰ βοῆς καὶ σαλπίγγων κατήγετο. ὕστερον δὲ τῶν ἀπὸ Φοι-
30 νίκης τις ἐπενόησε τὴν καθολκήν, τάφρον ὑποστησάμενος ἴσην
τῆι νηὶ κατὰ μῆκος, ἣν πλησίον τοῦ λιμένος ὤρυξε. ταύτηι δὲ
τοὺς θεμελίους κατωικοδόμησε λίθωι στερεῶι πρὸς πέντε πήχεις τὸ βάθος, καὶ διὰ τούτων φάλαγγας ἐπικαρσίας κατὰ
πλάτος τῆς τάφρου διώσας συνεχεῖς, τετράπηχυν εἰς βάθος
35 τόπον ἀπολειπούσας. καὶ ποιήσας εἴσρουν ἀπὸ τῆς θαλάσσης 204 D

1 εἴπομεν A   8 ‹ὑπὸ› Kaibel ἐπὶ τὸ τῆι A ἐπὶ τὸ πρὸς τῆι C   10 [τὰς
μεγίστας] Kaibel   ‹αἳ› add. C   14 ‹καὶ› κατὰ Graser   22 ‹πάντα› Schwei
26 ἐπισιτισμοῦ Cas -ούς A   28 ξυλείαι C -λίαι A   ὄχλου ‹πολλοῦ›?   31
ταύτης? Kaibel   35 ἀπολειπούσας C -λιπ- A

ἐνέπλησεν αὐτῆς πάντα τὸν ὀρυχθέντα τόπον, εἰς ὃν ῥαιδίως ὑπὸ
τῶν τυχόντων ἀνδρῶν εἰσήγαγε τὴν ναῦν· <εἶτα> τὸ ἀνοιχθὲν
κατ᾽ ἀρχὰς ἐμφράξαντας μετεξαντλῆσαι πάλιν τὴν θάλασσαν
ὀργάνοις. τούτου δὲ γενομένου, ἑδρασθῆναι τὸ πλοῖον ἀσφαλῶς
5 ἐπὶ τῶν προειρημένων φαλάγγων.

  (38) κατεσκεύασεν δ᾽ ὁ Φιλοπάτωρ καὶ ποτάμιον πλοῖον, τὴν
θαλαμηγὸν καλουμένην, τὸ μῆκος ἔχουσαν ἡμισταδίου, τὸ δὲ
εὖρος ἧι πλατύτατον λ̄ πηχῶν· τὸ δὲ ὕψος σὺν τῶι τῆς σκηνῆς 204 E
ἀναστήματι μικρὸν ἀπέδει τεσσαράκοντα πηχῶν. τὰ δὲ σχῆμα
10 αὐτῆς οὔτε ταῖς μακραῖς ναυσὶν οὔτε ταῖς στρογγύλαις ἐοικός,
ἀλλὰ παρηλλαγμένον τι καὶ πρὸς τὴν χρείαν τοῦ ποταμοῦ τὸ
βάθος. κάτωθεν μὲν γὰρ ἀλιτενὴς καὶ πλατεῖα, τῶι δ᾽ ὄγκωι
μετέωρος· τὰ δ᾽ ἐπὶ τῶν ἄκρων αὐτῆς μέρη καὶ μάλιστα τὰ κατὰ
πρῶιραν παρέτεινεν ἐφ᾽ ἱκανόν, τῆς ἀνακλάσεως εὐγράμμου
15 φαινομένης. δίπρωιρος δ᾽ ἐγεγόνει καὶ δίπρυμνος, καὶ πρὸς ὕψος
ἀνέτεινε διὰ τὸ μετέωρον ἄγαν ἵστασθαι πολλάκις ἐν τῶι ποτα- 204 F
μῶι τὸ κῦμα. κατεσκεύαστο δ᾽ αὐτῆς κατὰ μὲν μέσον τὸ
κύτος τὰ συμπόσια καὶ οἱ κοιτῶνες καὶ τὰ λοιπὰ τὰ πρὸς τὴν
διαγωγὴν χρηστήρια. πέριξ δὲ τῆς νεὼς περίπατοι κατὰ τὰς
20 τρεῖς πλευρὰς ἐγεγόνεσαν διπλοῖ, ὧν ἡ μὲν περίμετρος ἦν πέντε
πλέθρων οὐκ ἐλάττων, ἡ δὲ διάθεσις τοῦ μὲν καταγείου περιστύ- 205 A
λωι παραπλήσιος, τοῦ δ᾽ ὑπερώιου κρύπτηι φραγμοῖς καὶ θυρίσι
περιεχομένηι πάντοθεν. πρώτη δ᾽ εἰσιόντι κατὰ πρύμναν
ἐτέτακτο προστὰς ἐξ ἐναντίου μὲν ἀναπεπταμένη, κύκλωι δὲ
25 περίπτερος, ἧς ἐν τῶι καταντικρὺ τῆς πρώιρας μέρει προπύλαιον
κατεσκεύαστο δι᾽ ἐλέφαντος καὶ τῆς πολυτελεστάτης ὕλης γε-
γονός. τοῦτο δὲ διελθοῦσιν ὡσανεὶ προσκήνιον ἐπεποίητο τῆι διαθέσει κατάστεγον ὄν, ὧι πάλιν ὁμοίως κατὰ μὲν τὴν μέσην πλευρὰν προστὰς ἑτέρα παρέκειτο ὄπισθεν, καὶ τετράθυρος ἔφερεν 205 B
30 εἰς αὐτὴν πυλών. ἐξ ἀριστερῶν δὲ καὶ δεξιῶν θυρίδες ὑπέκειντο
εὐαερίαν παρέχουσαι. συνῆπτο δὲ τούτοις ὁ μέγιστος οἶκος·
περίπτερος δ᾽ ἦν εἴκοσι κλίνας ἐπιδεχόμενος· κατεσκεύαστο δ᾽

---

  1 ὑπὸ C ἀπὸ A   2 <εἶτα> Cas 'quod non sufficit' Kaibel   11 τι Cramer
τε A   16 ἀνέτεινε<ν ἱκανὸν> Kaibel   20 ἐγεγόνεισαν A   22-23 κρύπτηι –
περιεχομένηι Schwei -τη -νη A   23 πρῶτον Kaibel   24 προστὰς Villebrun
πρὸς τὰ A   ἐξ ἐναντίου μὲν Cas ἐξεναντιούμενα A   28 κατάστεγον ὄν, ὧι Kaibel
κατάστεγον· νωι A   29 προστὰς Villebrun πρὸς τὰ A   30 ὑπέκειντο vel
ἐπέκειντο Kaibel   31 εὐαερίαν Cas εὐαγείαν (sic!) A εὐαύγειαν Dobree συνῆπτο
Schwei συνήγετο A   32 κατεσκεύαστο C κατεσκευάσθη A

αὐτοῦ τὰ μὲν πλεῖστα ἀπὸ κέδρου σχιστῆς(?) καὶ κυπαρίσσου
Μιλησίας. αἱ δὲ τῆς περιστάσεως θύραι τὸν ἀριθμὸν εἴκοσι
οὖσαι θυΐναις κατεκεκόλληντο σανίσιν, ἐλεφαντίνους ἔχουσαι
τοὺς κόσμους. ἡ δ᾽ ἐνήλωσις ἡ κατὰ πρόσωπον αὐτῶν καὶ τὰ
5 ῥόπτρα ἐξ ἐρυθροῦ γεγονότα χαλκοῦ τὴν χρύσωσιν ἐκ πυρὸς
εἰλήφει. τῶν δὲ κιόνων τὰ μὲν σώματα ἦν κυπαρίσσινα, αἱ δὲ   205 C
κεφαλαὶ Κορινθιουργεῖς, ἐλέφαντι καὶ χρυσῶι διακεκοσμημέναι,
τὸ δὲ ἐπιστύλιον ἐκ χρυσοῦ τὸ ὅλον, ἐφ᾽ οὗ διάζωσμα ἐφήρμοστο
περιφανῆ ζώιδια ἔχον ἐλεφάντινα μείζω πηχυαίων, τῆι μὲν
10 τέχνηι μέτρια, τῆι χορηγίαι δὲ ἀξιοθαύμαστα. ἐπέκειτο δὲ καὶ
στέγη καλὴ τῶι συμποσίωι τετράγωνος κυπαρισσίνη· γλυπτοὶ δ᾽
αὐτῆς ἦσαν οἱ κόσμοι, χρυσῆν ἔχοντες τὴν ἐπιφάνειαν. παρέκειτο δὲ τῶι συμποσίωι τούτωι καὶ κοιτὼν ἑπτάκλινος, ὧι   205 D
συνῆπτο στενὴ σῦριγξ, κατὰ πλάτος τοῦ κύτους χωρίζουσα τὴν
15 γυναικωνῖτιν. ἐν δὲ ταύτηι συμπόσιον ἐννεάκλινον ἦν, παραπλή-
σιον τῆι πολυτελείαι τῶι μεγάλωι, καὶ κοιτὼν πεντάκλινος.
καὶ τὰ μὲν ἄχρι τῆς πρώτης στέγης κατεσκευασμένα τοιαῦτ᾽
ἦν.   (39) ἀναβάντων δὲ τὰς παρακειμένας πλησίον τῶι προει-
ρημένωι κοιτῶνι κλίμακας οἶκος ἦν ἄλλος πεντάκλινος ὀρόφωμα
20 ῥομβωτὸν ἔχων, καὶ πλησίον αὐτοῦ ναὸς Ἀφροδίτης θολοειδής,
ἐν ὧι μαρμάρινον ἄγαλμα τῆς θεοῦ. κατεναντίον δὲ τούτου ἄλλο   205 E
συμπόσιον πολυτελὲς περίπτερον· οἱ γὰρ κίονες αὐτοῦ ἐκ λίθων
Ἰνδικῶν συνέκειντο. παρὰ ⟨δὲ⟩ καὶ τούτωι τῶι συμποσίωι
κοιτῶνες, ἀκόλουθον τὴν κατασκευὴν τοῖς προδεδηλωμένοις
25 ἔχοντες. προάγοντι δὲ ἐπὶ τὴν πρῶιραν οἶκος ὑπέκειτο Βακχικὸς
τρισκαιδεκάκλινος περίπτερος, ἐπίχρυσον ἔχων τὸ γεῖσον ἕως
τοῦ περιτρέχοντος ἐπιστυλίου· στέγη δὲ τῆς τοῦ θεοῦ διαθέσεως
οἰκεία. ἐν δὲ τούτωι κατὰ μὲν τὴν δεξιὰν πλευρὰν ἄντρον κατ-   205 F
εσκεύαστο, οὗ χρῶμα(?) μὲν ἦν ἔχον τὴν πετροποιίαν ἐκ λίθων
30 ἀληθινῶν καὶ χρυσοῦ δεδημιουργημένην· ἵδρυτο δ᾽ ἐν αὐτῶι
τῆς τῶν βασιλέων συγγενείας ἀγάλματα εἰκονικὰ λίθου λυχνέως.
ἐπιτερπὲς δ᾽ ἱκανῶς καὶ ἄλλο συμπόσιον ἦν ἐπὶ τῆι τοῦ με-
γίστου οἴκου στέγηι κείμενον, σκηνῆς ἔχον τάξιν, ὧι στέγη μὲν

---

1 σχιστῆς: Συριακῆς Mei   18 ἀναβάντι Schwei   22 οἱ γὰρ: οἱ δὲ?
23 ⟨δὲ⟩ Cas   28 οἰκεία Cas οἰκία A   29 χρῶμα: 'i.e. species externa' Kaibel
χῶμα ('fornix') Mue   30 δεδημιουργημένην Cas -μένον A   31 συγγενείας: A.
Wilhelm *Beiträge*, 1909, p. 162   33 ὧι στέγη Emperius ὥστε τῆι A ὥστε τῆι
μὲν οὐκ ἐπῆν* * Mue

οὐκ ἐπῆν, διατόναια δὲ τοξοειδῆ διὰ ποσοῦ τινος ἐνετέτατο 206 A
διαστήματος, ἐφ' ὧν αὐλαῖαι κατὰ τὸν ἀνάπλουν ἁλουργεῖς
ἐνεπετάννυντο. μετὰ δὲ τοῦτο αἴθριον ἐξεδέχετο τὴν ἐπάνω
τῆς ὑποκειμένης προστάδος τάξιν κατέχον, ὧι κλῖμάξ τε ἑλικτὴ
5 φέρουσα πρὸς τὸν κρυπτὸν περίπατον παρέκειτο καὶ συμπόσιον
ἐννεάκλινον, τῆι διαθέσει τῆς κατασκευῆς Αἰγύπτιον· οἱ γὰρ
γεγονότες αὐτόθι κίονες ἀνήγοντο στρογγύλοι, διαλλάττοντες
τοῖς σπονδύλοις, τοῦ μὲν μέλανος, τοῦ δὲ λευκοῦ παράλληλα 206 B
τιθεμένων. εἰσὶ δ' αὐτῶν καὶ αἱ κεφαλαὶ τῶι σχήματι περιφερεῖς,
10 ὧν ἡ μὲν ὅλη περιγραφὴ παραπλησία ῥόδοις ἐπὶ μικρὸν ἀνα-
πεπταμένοις ἐστίν. περὶ δὲ τὸν προσαγορευόμενον κάλαθον οὐχ
ἕλικες, καθάπερ ἐπὶ τῶν Ἑλληνικῶν· καὶ φύλλα τραχέα περί-
κειται, λωτῶν δὲ ποταμίων κάλυκες καὶ φοινίκων ἀρτιβλάστων
καρπός· ἔστι δ' ὅτε καὶ πλειόνων ἄλλων ἀνθέων γέγλυπται
15 γένη. τὸ δ' ὑπὸ τὴν ῥίζαν, ὃ δὴ τῶι συνάπτοντι πρὸς τὴν κεφα-
λὴν ἐπίκειται σπονδύλωι, κιβωρίων ἄνθεσι καὶ φύλλοις ὡσανεὶ
καταπεπλεγμένοις ὁμοίαν εἶχε τὴν διάθεσιν. τοὺς μὲν οὖν 206 C
κίονας οὕτως Αἰγύπτιοι κατασκευάζουσι· καὶ τοὺς τοίχους δὲ
λευκαῖς καὶ μελαίναις διαποικίλλουσι πλινθίσιν, ἐνίοτε δὲ καὶ
20 τοῖς ἀπὸ τῆς ἀλαβαστίτιδος προσαγορευομένης πέτρας. πολλὰ
δὲ καὶ ἕτερα κατὰ μέσον τῆς νεὼς τὸ κύτος ἐν κοίληι καὶ κατὰ
πᾶν αὐτῆς μέρος οἰκήματα ἦν. ὁ δὲ ἱστὸς ἦν αὐτῆς ἑβδομήκοντα
πηχῶν, βύσσινον ἔχων ἱστίον ἁλουργεῖ παρασείωι κεκοσμημέ-
νον>>.

25
                          Δ
   (F 3; 4?)

   2 (2)   ATHEN. 5, 25-35 (36) p. 196 A-197 C(E)·: προσέθηκεν ὁ Μασούριος 196 A
περὶ τῆς ἐν Ἀλεξανδρείαι γεγενημένης ὑπὸ τοῦ πάντα ἀρίστου Πτολεμαίου τοῦ
Φιλαδέλφου βασιλέως πομπῆς Καλλίξεινον τὸν Ῥόδιον ἱστοροῦντα ἐν τῶι
30 τετάρτωι Περὶ Ἀλεξανδρείας, ὅς φησι· <<πρὸ δὲ τοῦ ἄρξασθαι τὴν
κατασκευασθεῖσαν σκηνὴν ἐν τῶι τῆς ἄκρας περιβόλωι χωρὶς τῆς

---

1 τοξοειδῆ Cas -δεῖ A   ἐνετέτατο Cas ἐντέτακτο A   3 τοῦτο Cas τοῦτον A
μέγα δὲ τοῦτο αἴθριον Schwei 'αἴθριον suspectum' Kaibel   8-9 παραλλὰξ τιθεμένων? Kaibel   14 καρποί? Kaibel   17 καταπεπλεγμένοις v -πληγ- A
συγκαταπεπλεγμένοις? Kaibel   21 [ἐν κοίληι] Wil ἔγκοιλα? Kaibel   23 παρασείωι Passow παρασείωι Λ   29 ἄρξασθαι: scil. τῆς πομπῆς (v. 29; p. 167, 30);
den eingang von K.s bericht hat Athenaios für seine übergangsworte (v. 27-30)
verwendet   31 χωρὶς τῆς: χάριν τῆς C

τῶν στρατιωτῶν καὶ τεχνιτῶν καὶ παρεπιδήμων ὑποδοχῆς ἐξη-
γήσομαι· καλὴ γὰρ εἰς ὑπερβολὴν ἀξία τε ἀκοῆς ἐγενήθη. 196 B
τὸ μὲν οὖν μέγεθος αὐτῆς ἑκατὸν τριάκοντα κλίνας ἐπιδεχό-
μενον κύκλωι, διασκευὴν δ' εἶχε τοιαύτην· κίονες διεστάθησαν
5 ξύλινοι πέντε μὲν κατὰ πλευρὰν ἑκάστην τοῦ μήκους, πεντηκοντα-
πήχεις πρὸς ὕψος, ἑνὶ δὲ ἐλάττους κατὰ πλάτος, ἐφ' ὧν ἐπιστύλιον καθηρμόσθη τετράγωνον, ὑπερεῖδον τὴν σύμπασαν τοῦ
συμποσίου στέγην. αὕτη δ' ἐνεπετάσθη κατὰ μέσον οὐρανίσκωι
κοκκινοβαφεῖ περιλεύκωι, καθ' ἑκάτερον δὲ μέρος εἶχε δοκοὺς
10 μεσολεύκοις ἐμπετάσμασι πυργωτοῖς κατειλημμένας, ἐν αἷς 196 C
φατνώματα γραπτὰ κατὰ μέσον ἐτέτατο. τῶν δὲ κιόνων οἱ μὲν
τέσσαρες ὡμοίωντο φοίνιξιν, οἱ δ' ἀνὰ μέσον θύρσων εἶχον
φαντασίαν. τούτων δ' ἐκτὸς περίστυλος ἐπεποίητο σῦριγξ,
ταῖς τρισὶ πλευραῖς καμαρωτὴν ἔχουσα στέγην, ἐν ἧι τὴν τῶν
15 κατακειμένων ἀκολουθίαν ἑστάναι συνέβαινεν· ἧς τὸ μὲν ἐντὸς
αὐλείαις περιείχετο φοινικίναις, ἐπὶ δὲ τῶν ἀνὰ μέσον χωρῶν
δοραὶ θηρίων παράδοξοι καὶ τῆι ποικιλίαι καὶ τοῖς μεγέθεσιν 196 D
ἐκρέμαντο, τὸ δὲ περιέχον αὐτὴν ὕπαιθρον μυρρίναις καὶ δάφ-
ναις ἄλλοις τε ἐπιτηδείοις ἔρνεσιν ἐγεγόνει συνηρεφές, τὸ δ'
20 ἔδαφος πᾶν ἄνθεσι κατεπέπαστο παντοίοις. ἡ γὰρ Αἴγυπτος καὶ
διὰ τὴν τοῦ περιέχοντος ἀέρος εὐκρασίαν καὶ διὰ τοὺς κηπεύ-
οντας τὰ σπανίως καὶ καθ' ὥραν ἐνεστηκυῖαν ἐν ἑτέροις φυόμενα
τόποις ἄφθονα γεννᾶι καὶ διὰ παντός, καὶ οὔτε ῥόδον οὔτε
λευκόιον οὔτ' ἄλλο ῥαιδίως ἄνθος ἐκλιπεῖν οὐθὲν οὐδέποτ'
25 εἴωθεν. διὸ δὴ καὶ κατὰ μέσον χειμῶνα τῆς ὑποδοχῆς τότε
γενηθείσης, παράδοξος ἡ φαντασία [τότε] τοῖς ξένοις κατέστη. 196 E
τὰ γὰρ εἰς μίαν εὑρεθῆναι στεφάνωσιν οὐκ ἂν δυνηθέντα ἐν ἄλληι
πόλει ῥαιδίως, ταῦτα καὶ τῶι πλήθει τῶν κατακειμένων ἐχορη-
γεῖτο εἰς τοὺς στεφάνους ἀφθόνως καὶ εἰς τὸ τῆς σκηνῆς ἔδαφος
30 κατεπέπαστο χύδην, θείου τινὸς ὡς ἀληθῶς ἀποτελοῦντα λει-
μῶνος πρόσοψιν. (26) διέκειτο δὲ ἐπὶ μὲν τῶν τῆς σκηνῆς παρα-
στάδων ζῶια μαρμάρινα τῶν πρώτων τεχνιτῶν ἑκατόν· ἐν δὲ
ταῖς ἀνὰ μέσον χώραις πίνακες τῶν Σικυωνικῶν ζωγράφων,

---

4 δ' εἶχε Schwei δὲ ἔχει A   διεστάθησαν Mus δ' ἐστάθησαν A   6 πρὸς ὕψος A
τὸ ὕψος C   ἐλάττους Mus -τω A   10 κατειλημμένας Schwei -ημμένας (p. 168, 18/9)
A διειλημμένας? Kaibel   11 ἐτέτατο Dalecamp ἐτέτακτο A   16 αὐλείαις (*Syll.*³
736, 35) Studnizka *Abh. Sächs. Ges. d. W.* 30 (1914) αὐλεαις (sic!) A αὐλαίαις ϛν
χωρῶν (v. 33; p. 167, 5) Cas χώρων A   24 ἐκλείπειν C   25 [τότε] W. Otto
26 [τότε] Schwei   28-29 ἐκεχορήγητο Mei   33 σικυωνικῶν C -ιακῶν A

ἐναλλὰξ δ' ἐπίλεκτοι εἰκασίαι παντοῖαι καὶ χιτῶνες χρυσουφεῖς
ἐφαπτίδες τε κάλλισται, τινὲς μὲν εἰκόνας ἔχουσαι τῶν βασιλέων 196 F
ἐνυφασμένας, αἱ δὲ μυθικὰς διαθέσεις· ὑπεράνω δὲ τούτων
θυρεοὶ περιέκειντο ἐναλλὰξ ἀργυροῖ τε καὶ χρυσοῖ· ἐν δὲ ταῖς
5 ἐπάνω τούτων χώραις οὔσαις ὀκταπήχεσιν ἄντρα κατεσκεύαστο
κατὰ μὲν τὸ μῆκος τῆς σκηνῆς ἐξ ἐν ἑκατέραι πλευρᾶι, κατὰ
πλάτος δὲ τέτταρα, συμπόσιά τε ἀντία ἀλλήλων <ἐν> αὐτοῖς
τραγικῶν τε καὶ κωμικῶν καὶ σατυρικῶν ζώιων ἀληθινὸν ἐχόν- 197 A
των ἱματισμόν, οἷς παρέκειτο καὶ ποτήρια χρυσᾶ· κατὰ μέσον
10 δὲ τῶν ἄντρων νυμφαῖα ἐλείφθησαν, ἐν οἷς ἔκειντο Δελφικοὶ
χρυσοῖ τρίποδες ὑποστήματ' ἔχοντες· κατὰ δὲ τὸν ὑψηλότατον
τόπον τῆς ὀροφῆς ἀετοὶ κατὰ πρόσωπον ἦσαν ἀλλήλων χρυσοῖ,
πεντεκαιδεκαπήχεις τὸ μέγεθος. ἔκειντο δὲ κλῖναι χρυσαῖ
σφιγγόποδες ἐν ταῖς δυσὶ πλευραῖς ἑκατόν· ἡ γὰρ κατὰ πρόσω-
15 πον ἀψὶς ἀφεῖτ' ἀναπεπταμένη. ταύταις δ' ἀμφίταποι ἁλουργεῖς 197 B
ὑπέστρωντο τῆς πρώτης ἐρέας, καὶ περιστρώματα ποικίλα δια-
πρεπῆ ταῖς τέχναις ἐπῆν. ψιλαὶ δὲ Περσικαὶ τὴν ἀνὰ μέσον τῶν
ποδῶν χώραν ἐκάλυπτον, ἀκριβῆ τὴν εὐγραμμίαν τῶν ἐνυφασ-
μένων ἔχουσαι ζωιδίων. παρετέθησαν δὲ καὶ τρίποδες τοῖς
20 κατακειμένοις χρυσοῖ διακόσιοι τὸν ἀριθμόν, ὥστ' εἶναι δύο
κατὰ κλίνην, ἐπ' ἀργυρῶν διέδρων. ἐκ δὲ τῶν ὄπισθεν πρὸς τὴν
ἀπό<νι>ψιν ἑκατὸν ἀργυραῖ λεκάναι καὶ καταχύσεις ἴσαι παρέκειντο. ἐπεπήγει δὲ τοῦ συμποσίου καταντικρὺ καὶ ἑτέρα κλί- 197 C
νη(?) πρὸς τὴν τῶν κυλίκων καὶ ποτηρίων τῶν τε λοιπῶν τῶν
25 πρὸς τὴν χρῆσιν ἀνηκόντων [καὶ] κατασκευασμάτων ἔκθεσιν,
ἃ δὴ πάντα χρυσᾶ τε ἦν καὶ διάλιθα, θαυμαστὰ ταῖς τέχναις.
τούτων δὲ τὴν μὲν κατὰ μέρος κατασκευὴν καὶ τὰ γένη μακρὸν
ἐπεφαίνετό μοι δηλοῦν· τὸ δὲ τοῦ σταθμοῦ πλῆθος εἰς μύρια
τάλαντα ἀργυρίου τὴν σύμπασαν εἶχε κατασκευήν.
30 (27) ἡμεῖς δὲ ἐπειδὴ τὰ κατὰ τὴν σκηνὴν διεληλύθαμεν, ποι-
ησόμεθα καὶ τὴν τῆς πομπῆς ἐξήγησιν· ἤγετο γὰρ διὰ τοῦ
κατὰ τὴν πόλιν σταδίου.... (see text in Chapter 2).

---

1 παντοῖαι Schwei -οῖοι A   4 ἀργυροῖ τε καὶ χρυσοῖ Cas ἄργυραι (sic!) τε καὶ
χρυσαί A   7 <ἐν> Cas   8 ζώιων 'figuren' Studnizka προσώπων (p. 169, 23)
Preller   10 νυμφαῖα ἐ. ἐν οἷς Cas νύμφαι ἐ. ἐν αἷς A νύμφαι ἐγλύφθησαν Mei   11
ἔχοντες <ἀργυρᾶ> Mei   13 δὲ καὶ κλῖναι C   14 δυσὶ: τρισὶ Studnizka p. 156 (cf.
v. 23 ff.)   15 ἀψὶς Wil ὄψις A (Studnizka p. 154) ὄψει Br. Keil   21
διέδρων A θένθρων C   22 ἀπόνιψιν C. Döttlicher ἄπουψιν A   23-24 κλίνη. σκηνή
Mei, Studnizka p. 161; 170   24 κυλίκων C -κίων A -κείων Studnizka   25
[καὶ] Cas   28 διεφαίνετο C   29 εἶχε: ἀνῆγε vel συνῆγε? Kaibel

(36) ποία, ἄνδρες δαιτυμόνες, βασιλεία οὕτως γέγονε πολύχρυσος; οὐ γὰρ τὰ ἐκ Περ- 203 B
σῶν καὶ Βαβυλῶνος λαβοῦσα χρήματα, ἢ μέταλλα ἐργασαμένη, ἢ Πακτωλὸν ἔχουσα 203 C
χρυσοῦν ψῆγμα καταφέροντα· μόνος γὰρ ὡς ἀληθῶς ὁ χρυσορόας καλούμενος Νεῖλος
10 μετὰ τροφῶν ἀφθόνων καὶ χρυσὸν ἀκίβδηλον καταφέρει, ἀκινδύνως γεωργούμενον ὡς
πᾶσιν ἐξαρκεῖν ἀνθρώποις, δίκην Τριπτολέμου πεμπόμενον εἰς πᾶσαν γῆν· διόπερ αὐτὸν
καὶ ὁ Βυζάντιος ποιητὴς Παρμένων ἐπικαλούμενος <<Αἰγύπτιε Ζεῦ>> φησί (p. 272 Κnox)
<<Νεῖλε>>. πολλῶν δὲ ὁ Φιλάδελφος βασιλέων πλούτωι διέφερε, καὶ περὶ πάντα ἐσπου-
δάκει τὰ κατακσευάσματα φιλοτίμως, ὥστε καὶ πλοίων πλήθει πάντας ὑπερέβαλλεν· 203 D
15 τὰ γοῦν μέγιστα τῶν πλοίων ἦν παρ' αὐτῶι τριακοντήρεις δύο, εἰκοσήρης μία, τέσσαρες
δὲ τρισκαιδεκήρεις, δωδεκήρεις δύο, ἑνδεκήρεις δεκατέσσαρες, ἐννήρεις λ, ἑπτήρεις λζ,
ἑξήρεις ε̄, πεντήρεις δεκαεπτά, τὰ δ' ἀπὸ τετρήρους μέχρι τριηρημιολίας διπλάσια τούτων·
τὰ δ' εἰς τὰς νήσους πεμπόμενα καὶ τὰς ἄλλας πόλεις, ὧν ἦρχε, καὶ τὴν Λιβύην πλείονα
ἦν τῶν τετρακισχιλίων. περὶ δὲ βιβλίων πλήθους καὶ βιβλιοθηκῶν κατασκευῆς καὶ τῆς 203 E
20 εἰς τὸ Μουσεῖον συναγωγῆς τί δεῖ καὶ λέγειν, πᾶσι τούτων ὄντων κατὰ μνήμην; (Es folgt
F 1).

OHNE BUCHZAHL

3 (3) ATHEN. 11, 49 p. 474 Ε: καρχήσιον· Καλλίξεινος ὁ ῾Ρόδιος
ἐν τοῖς Περὶ ᾽Αλεξανδρείας φησὶν ὅτι ποτήριόν ἐστιν ἐπίμηκες, συνηγ-
25 μένον εἰς μέσον ἐπιεικῶς, ὦτα ἔχον μέχρι τοῦ πυθμένος καθήκοντα.

4 (3) ATHEN. 15, 20 p. 677 CD: ᾽Ισθμιακὸν . . . . στέφανον . . . ., οὗ
μνημονεύει καὶ Καλλίξεινος ὁ ῾Ρόδιος καὶ αὐτὸς γένος ἐν τοῖς Περὶ
᾽Αλεξανδρείας, γράφων οὕτως * *.

OHNE BUCHTITEL

30 **5** (4) PLIN. N.H. 36, 67: *Alexandriae statuit unum* (scil. *obeliscum*)
*Ptolemaeus Philadelphus octoginta cubitorum; exciderat eum Necthebis rex
purum, maiusque opus in devehendo statuendove multo†est quam in exci-
dendo. a Satyro architecto aliqui devectum tradunt rate, C a l l i x e n u s a*

7-20 die fakten (v. 13-19) noch aus Κ.?　7 ποία οὖν C πῶς
οὖν – <ἡ> βασιλεία Wil　οὐ γὰρ <ἡ> τὰ Cas　8 ἐργαζομένη ς　9 χρυσορ-
ρόας C　14 ὥστε: ὡς vel ὃς? Kaibel　ὑπερέβαλε C　16 δὲ om. C
18 πλείω C　31 exciderat cod. Poll. *ceciderat* r *quem* (*h*) *exciderat* v　*Necta-
nebis* Urlichs　32 *statuendoque*?　*multum est* B *inventum est* Detlefsen
33 *satyro* B *na-* r　*aliqui* B *alio qui* r

Jacoby, Fragm. Griech. Hist. III C

Phoenice, fossa perducto usque ad iacentem obeliscum Nilo, (68) *navesque duas in latitudinem patulas, pedalibus ex eodem lapide ad rationem geminati per duplicem mensuram ponderis onerdtas ita ut subirent obeliscum pendentem extremitatibus suis in ripis utrimque; postea egestis laterculis*
5 *allevatas naves excepisse onus; statutum autem in sex talis e monte eodem, et artificem donatum talentis L. hic fuit in Arsinoeo positus a rege supra dicto munus amoris,* [in] *coniuge eademque sorore Arsinoe.*

2. ΖΩΓΡΑΦΩΝ ΚΑΙ ΑΝΔΡΙΑΝΤΟΠΟΙΩΝ ΑΝΑΓΡΑΦΗ

(T 1).

Appendix II

The double cornucopia

Apart from the interpretation of οἱ βασιλεῖς as 'the king and queen', the only piece of evidence in the Grand Procession which may refer to Arsinoe II is the presence of the double cornucopia, or *dikeras*. This object appears in the last section of the text, where items from the Grand Procession are described at random without much perceivable order. Since the textual context of the *dikeras* can only be conjectured, the mere fact of its appearance must be the basis of any argument. A twelve-foot long *dikeras* is carried alone as a ritual object in 202C (line 246) (although the phrase describing it is strikingly truncated), and a second may sit upon the second of the thrones which appear in 202B (line 231). (In the latter case, the manuscripts vary between the readings ἐφ' ἑνός . . . ἐπ' ἄλλου δίκερας (A) and ἐφ' ἑνὸς μέν . . . ἐπ' ἄλλου κέρας (C). Kaibel (ad loc.) suggested ἐφ' ἑνὸς μέν . . . ἐπ' ἄλλου δὲ κέρας as the correct reading (based upon C), but although he and other editors print δίκερας, with A, Kaibel's emendation has greater grammatical merit since δέ is needed here as a correlative with μέν; the necessity of the μέν–δέ construction is indicated by the presence of δέ before the other two objects appearing later in the sentence. However, since the original text could have read ἐφ' ἑνὸς μέν . . . ἐπ' ἄλλου δὲ δίκερας, haplography may have been responsible at some point for transforming δίκερας to κέρας. Since a textually certain κέρας follows upon the fourth throne, it may be that an object other than a *keras* is indeed required for the second throne, but there is no textual or thematic proof that a *dikeras* originally appeared here.) The *dikeras* was the special attribute of Arsinoe II on faience oinochoai and coins, and its later application to royal pairs of the Ptolemaic house is well attested. If the presence of the *dikeras* in the Grand Procession can be construed as a reference to Arsinoe II, the festival must have occurred later than its first known association with the queen, which has important consequences for the date of the Grand Procession, but if the *dikeras* is not the symbol of the queen in the text, its very rarity as an object at that date requires another explanation for its appearance.

It has been assumed from a passage elsewhere in Athenaeus that the *dikeras* was invented by Philadelphus to serve as a fitting attribute for representations of his wife (497B–C):

ἐκαλεῖτο δὲ τὸ ῥυτὸν πρότερον κέρας. δοκεῖ δὲ σκευοποιηθῆναι ὑπὸ πρώτου τοῦ Φιλαδέλφου Πτολεμαίου βασιλέως φόρημα γενέσθαι τῶν Ἀρσινόης εἰκόνων. τῇ γὰρ εὐ-
ωνύμῳ χειρὶ ἐκείνη τοιοῦτον φέρει δημιούργημα πάντων τῶν ὡραίων πλῆρες,
ἐμφαινόντων τῶν δημιουργῶν ὡς καὶ τοῦ τῆς Ἀμαλθείας ἐστὶν ὀλβιώτερον τὸ κέρας
τοῦτο. μημονεύει αὐτοῦ Θεοκλῆς ἐν Ἰθυφάλλοις οὕτως.
> ἐθύσαμεν γὰρ σήμερον Σωτήρια
> πάντες οἱ τεχνῖται.
> μεθ'ὧν πιὼν τὸ δίκερας ὡς τὸν φίλτατον

It is not clear, however, that the opening sentences of this passage refer to the *dikeras*. The rhyton, or horn-shaped drinking cup, was known in Greece from the fifth century BC, when these derivatives from Achaemenid prototypes became popular after the Persian Wars,[1] and the term 'rhyton' was applied in antiquity only to the spouted drinking horns, not to the animal-head vases which are currently called rhyta.[2] Since the rhyton, or *keras*, existed in the Greek world long before Ptolemy Philadelphus, Athenaeus does not refer to its invention in this passage, but to the fact that the vessel was filled to overflowing with natural produce in order to appear richer than the horn of Amaltheia. The latter was always depicted empty in the fifth century, but was filled (although not to overflowing) in the fourth century,[3] following the appearance of the cult of Tyche at the beginning of that century.[4] Tyche's horn is the traditional 'Horn of Plenty', and its adaptation as an attribute of the statues of Arsinoe II should indicate an association of the queen with Tyche.[5] If Athenaeus does indeed refer to a *dikeras* in this passage, it is curious that he does not mention its most salient characteristic, namely its double form. He must have meant instead the *keras* or single horn, which would then have been an earlier attribute of Arsinoe. Although Athenaeus for some reason quotes the lines of Theokles to illustrate his description of the κέρας, and connects the two passages explicitly as the αὐτοῦ shows, nothing concerning the *dikeras* can be extrapolated from the juxtaposition of the *keras* passage and the poem of Theokles. Theokles is otherwise unknown, and the verses may not even refer to Philadelphus.[6] The whole passage cannot, therefore, be invoked as evidence for the *dikeras*, but only for the fact that in her statues Arsinoe was endowed with an attribute richer than the traditional symbol of Tyche. Disregarding the uncertain lines of Theokles, the information provided by Athenaeus concerns the contents of the *keras*, not its shape.

Since the *dikeras* was nevertheless a familiar attribute of the queen, the date and reason for its adoption is relevant since some special connotation made it especially appropriate for Arsinoe. Although a *dikeras* may double the fruitfulness and prosperity of a single cornucopia, this does not explain why it suddenly became desirable to double the shape, since Athenaeus has stated that increased prosperity was indicated by filling the *keras* to overflowing, not by doubling it. A double cornucopia should therefore symbolize the union of two single ones for a specific reason. The *dikeras* is not known as an attribute of Arsinoe until after her death; it appears on the posthumous commemorative coins issued by Philadelphus in her honour[7] and also on the faience oinochoai. Although the chronology and cult function of these vases is not clear, the series in honour of Arsinoe II seems to have run from *c.*270 to 240, wholly after her death.[8] Much of the uncertainty about the chronology of the oinochoai surrounds the inscriptions on the shoulder: ἀγαθῆς τύχης ᾿Αρσινόης Φιλαδέλφου. This may commemorate the personal Tyche (or Agathe Tyche) of the queen

---

[1] H. Hoffmann, *Antike Kunst* iv (1961), 21 ff.

[2] Ibid., 25 and n. 46; id., *Attic Red-Figured Rhyta* (Mainz, 1962), 3.

[3] D. B. Thompson, *Ptolemaic Oinochoai*, 31-2, 54 and n. 5; R. Heidenreich, *Arch. Anz.* (1935), 675.

[4] Heidenreich, 675.   [5] Thompson, 54-5, 83; *Ptol. Alex.* i. 241 ff.

[6] *Ptol. Alex.* i. 232-5, against Thompson, 55.

[7] Thompson, 32 and n. 5; G. Longega, *Arsinoe II* (Rome, 1968), 109 ff.

[8] Thompson, 47.

(which, according to the most natural interpretation, would mean that Arsinoe was still alive), or her assimilation (perhaps posthumously) to the personified deity Tyche.[9] Opinions have varied on this point, and the uncertainty increases the difficulty of using the phrase ἀγαθὴ τύχη as evidence for whether or not Arsinoe was alive when the oinochoai were first created.[10] There is, nevertheless, no proof that the *dikeras* appeared either on the coins or on the vases during Arsinoe's lifetime.

The personified goddess Tyche is a different concept from Agathe Tyche (the personal *tyche* of an individual), but the cornucopia was a standard attribute of both Tyche and Agathe Tyche. Tyche was endowed with the horn of Amaltheia from the beginning of her cult, and the *keras* was also the attribute of a statue of Agathe Tyche at Delos (*ID* 1417 A, II, 26 ff.). Arsinoe may be understood to be somehow associated with both goddesses, and the scenes on the oinochoai may reveal this perhaps partly unconscious fusion.[11] If the worship of a person's Agathe Tyche tends to occur during his or her lifetime, Arsinoe may have received the attribute of the single *keras* while alive. The passage of Athenaeus may indicate that the overflowing *keras* was devised for her statues during her lifetime to signify the worship of her Agathe Tyche. The change in iconography between this overflowing *keras* and the later *dikeras*, which is found only in commemorative representations, still needs to be explained. If the doubling does not necessarily result from increased fruitfulness, neither is it the result of Arsinoe's assimilation to a deity if the deity's attribute was a single cornucopia. The concept of the *dikeras* must signify the union of two separate horns for a specific reason. On the coins of later Ptolemaic kings, the *dikeras* frequently appears in combination with the jugate heads of the deified ruling couple, and the *dikeras* has therefore been understood as the symbol of the joint rule of the king and queen.[12] This symbolism has been extrapolated backwards in time in order to explain the appropriateness of the *dikeras* as an attribute of Arsinoe II, who was the first queen to act as a *de facto* co-regent. However, even if the *dikeras* originally signified Arsinoe's position as constituting one half of the joint rule of the Theoi Adelphoi, this still does not explain why the *dikeras* was an especially appropriate symbol of the joint rule. The *dikeras* obviously emphasizes the role of the monarchs as the joint source of blessings and abundance to the kingdom, but this does not suffice to explain why the Ptolemaic couple adopted the *dikeras* as a symbol;[13] if the *dikeras* did not symbolize a concept other than general fruitfulness, why was it first adopted as a symbol of the ruling pair? If, however, the *dikeras* was taken over as a transferred symbol from some antecedent which had existed before the time of Arsinoe Philadelphus and the joint rule,[14] the association of the former and latter could be made through the *dikeras* precisely because of what it had originally symbolized. The

[9] Ibid., 51 ff.; *Ptol. Alex.* i. 241 ff.

[10] *Ptol. Alex.* i. 241–2; Thompson, 54.   [11] *Ptol. Alex.* i. 241.

[12] Thompson, 33; M. P. Nilsson, *Timbres amphoriques de Lindos* (Expl. Arch. Rhodes V) (Bull. Acad. Copenhagen, 1909), 170–1; J. Charbonneaux, 'Sarapis et Isis et la double corne d'abondance', *Hommages à Waldemar Deonna, Coll. Latomus* xxviii (1957), 135; Ch. Picard, *BCH* lxxxiii (1959), 413 ff.

[13] See particularly Nilsson, *Timbres*, 170–1.   [14] Ibid.

appearance of the *dikeras* in the Grand Procession may illustrate the previous existence of the concept behind the object which was later transferred to the ruling couple.

Although no coherent context can be conjectured for the *dikeras* in the procession, it seems to have a fairly minor role as a ritual object. To consider the possible *dikeras* upon the throne, one of the thrones in the group is dedicated to Ptolemy Soter, but no other 'owners' are specified. It is likely that the other thrones belong to various Olympian deities, not to other members of the royal family (few of whom, in any case, were deified by this date) (see above, p. 117). This *dikeras* appears to be a divine attribute of an unspecified deity, one among many such upon the thrones. The other *dikeras* (the only one which is textually certain) is carried on its own amid other objects which appear to be divine attributes (the herald's staff, the thunderbolt, etc.), but in order to appear at all in the Grand Procession, it must have had some ritual connotation which was clear to the spectators if not to the reader. This *dikeras* has no outstanding importance in comparison with similar objects: for example, its material is not stated and it is twelve feet long, while the *keras* which follows in the same parade of attributes is of solid gold (ὁλόχρυσον) and forty-five feet long.[15] Nothing connects either *dikeras* with Arsinoe II either explicitly or implicitly. If, however, this object *is* intended to be the symbol of Arsinoe alone, various insoluble problems arise. Since there is no evidence that the *dikeras* was used as her attribute before her death, the Grand Procession would, on that sole ground, have had to take place after her death in 270, but this has been shown to be unlikely on other grounds (see pp. 164–5). At the same time, if the procession *did* take place after her death, it becomes even more curious that the *dikeras* appears as such a minor ritual object here, given its prominence on the commemorative coins and oinochoai.

It is easier on all counts to dissociate the *dikeras* in the Grand Procession from Arsinoe II and to regard it as an object which existed before the advent of the queen. If this is correct, the *dikeras* must have been an intermediary symbol which later transferred the connotation of its antecedent to Arsinoe as one of the Theoi Adelphoi, and its explanation may illuminate its eventual association with the royal couples. The answer may lie in the association of Arsinoe II with certain deities. The three-way assimilation of Arsinoe to Agathe Tyche and to Isis (who was herself assimilated to Tyche) is attested beyond doubt on the faience oinochoai since the altars on some which belong to Arsinoe are inscribed ἀγαθῆς τύχης/ Ἀρσινόης/Φιλαδέλφου/Ἴσιος.[16] The three goddesses are also related at Delos.[17] Although their relation may stop short of actual identification at this date, their close association is clear even if it is impossible to unravel the threads of it. The oinochoai may even suggest that they were σύμβωμοι.[18] The *keras* has been shown to be an attribute of Arsinoe, Agathe Tyche/Tyche, and Isis, but if the *dikeras* symbolizes the doubled power of the ruling couple, the other *keras* which makes up the *dikeras* must reflect the other half of the ruling pair. If Arsinoe's *keras* derived from her relation

[15] See Tarn, *JHS* liii (1933), 59.

[16] Cf. Thompson, Catalogue, Nos. 142, 144, 146(?).

[17] *Ptol. Alex.* i. 241.   [18] Ibid., 243; Thompson, 58 ff.

to Agathe Tyche/Tyche and Isis, a divine male counterpart who also was associated with the cornucopia may form the other half of the pair of deities whose symbol was later transferred to the jugate rulers. Sarapis is the male god who has the obvious claim to this role. It is neither possible nor necessary to summarize here the conclusions of the large bibliography of works dealing with the establishment, development, and spread of the cult of this god in Alexandria, but sufficient to point out briefly that Ptolemy I probably introduced the worship of Sarapis, and certainly encouraged it officially.[19] Most of the dedications to Sarapis are made by Greeks of the upper, official, or even court classes, which shows the strong link between the Crown and the cult, and suggests that loyalty to the royal house could be expressed through worship of a god introduced and supported by that house.[20] Sarapis had chthonic, among other, associations, and he was often depicted with the attribute of the cornucopia,[21] which was also a standard attribute of Pluto and shows the connection of these gods with the natural cycles of birth, reproduction, and death.[22] Isis was an Egyptian goddess who had been known to the Greeks for centuries, but she became part of the Greek pantheon as the official wife and consort of Sarapis.[23] The Ptolemaic Isis is also often depicted with a cornucopia (see below) perhaps in order to emphasize her associations with Tyche and Agathe Tyche and their chthonic connotations as well as her own chthonic associations as the wife of Sarapis and as Demeter, the counterpart to Pluto.[24] The union of Isis and Sarapis, and the pairing of their individual cornucopiae into a *dikeras* may be seen in a small ivory sculpture from the Louvre which consists of two intertwined cornucopiae out of which rise (on the left) a male bust and (on the right) a female bust.[25] This piece has been dated to the second half of the second century BC, and the figures have been identified as Isis and Sarapis. The connection of this divine pair

---

[19] Recent studies of Sarapis include *Ptol. Alex.* i. 246 ff.; id., *Op. Ath.* iii (1960), 1 ff.; id., ibid., vii (1967), 23–45; J. E. Stambaugh, *Sarapis Under the Early Ptolemies* (*EPRO* 25) (Leiden, 1972); W. Hornbostel, *Sarapis. Studien zur Überlieferungs- geschichte, den Erscheinungsformen und Wandlungen der Gestalt eines Göttes* (*EPRO* 32) (Leiden, 1973), and review by P. M. Fraser, *JHS* xcvi (1976), 213 ff.; L. Vidman(n), *Sylloge inscriptionum religionis Isiacae et Sarapiacae* (*RVV* 28) (Berlin, 1969).

[20] *Ptol. Alex.* i. 273.

[21] For examples of monuments of all periods depicting Sarapis with a cornucopia see G. J. F. Kater-Sibbes, *Preliminary Catalogue of Sarapis Monuments* (*EPRO* 36) (Leiden, 1973), Nos. 38, 52, 79, 187, 303, 317 (all from Egypt); 449 (Syria), 464 (Paramythia), 468? (Corinth), 530 (Bastaglia), 584? (Syracuse). Stambaugh, 18 ff., has argued that the Hellenistic image of the god at the Serapeum at Memphis held a cornucopia, but see Fraser's review of Hornbostel (n. 19 above) for the difficulty of interpreting the iconography of this statue.

[22] Hornbostel, 350; Stambaugh, 1.

[23] For the importance of the role of Isis as the wife of Sarapis see *Ptol. Alex.* i. 259 ff.; Thompson, 57 ff.

[24] Hdt. ii. 59; *RE* s.v. Isis (1) 2122; Thompson, 32. For representations of Isis and Sarapis together, each holding individual cornucopiae, see Kater-Sibbes, Nos. 512, 483 (a fine bas-relief, probably from Athens; cf. F. Dunand, *Le Culte d'Isis dans le bassin orientale de la Mediterranée* ii (*EPRO* 26) (Leiden, 1973), Pl. lxiv).

[25] Charbonneaux, *Hommages Deonna*, 131 ff.; Pl. xxv, 1 = Kater-Sibbes, No. 248 (cf. Hornbostel, Pl. 361).

and their joined individual cornucopiae with the joint rule of the royal couple is made clear by coins of Ptolemy IV, which show the jugate busts of Sarapis and Isis on the obverse, and the *dikeras* on the reverse (surmounting one or two eagles).[26] The ivory confirms the direct tie of the divine couple to the *dikeras*, and the coins link this association to the reigning couple Ptolemy IV and Arsinoe III. If these associations are not meant to be an actual identification of the royal and divine couples, they at least show their intimate connection: the *dikeras* symbolizes the joint prosperity, power, and divine union of Isis and Sarapis as man and wife, a symbolism which makes the object a fitting attribute for a deified royal couple. If this reasoning can be accepted, the *dikeras* which appears in the Grand Procession of Philadelphus may represent the union of the new divine couple, Isis and Sarapis, and may be the attribute of those deities who existed before the advent of Arsinoe II and the consequent adoption of the object as the symbol of the 'co-regency'. The route whereby the *dikeras* came to be associated with the posthumous commemoration of this joint rule can be traced in a series of stages which embrace the 'marriage' of Isis and Sarapis and their increasing joint importance in a cult initiated and fostered by the royal family, the marriage of Arsinoe and Philadelphus, the connection of Isis, Agathe Tyche/Tyche, and Arsinoe, the deification of the royal couple as the Theoi Adelphoi, and the death of Arsinoe. The fact that the *dikeras* was given to Arsinoe only after her death combines with the strong chthonic aspects of Isis and Sarapis to suggest that the object itself had a definite chthonic connotation. This is supported by later appearances of the object in a context neither divine nor royal, when it has at least a decorative function in specific funerary surroundings. Various East Greek grave reliefs have a single cornucopia as a common funerary emblem, but the *dikeras* also occasionally appears in the same context.[27] It appears also as an emblem on funerary altars from Cos, Rhodes, and Halicarnassus.[28] Since these monuments have been dated to the second century, the use of this emblem probably did not result so much from the close links of the Greek islands with Ptolemaic Egypt as from the generalized funerary connotation of the *dikeras*, which became known and adopted elsewhere in the course of time.[29]

The suggestions that Isis and Sarapis were the original 'owners' of the *dikeras* before it was adopted as an attribute by the deified ruling couple, and that the appearance of the *dikeras* in the Grand Procession reflects this earlier stage of its symbolism, receive some support from a consideration of the importance of the cults of these gods in early third-century Alexandria. Although both Sarapis and Isis in their hellenized form were very recent additions to the Greek pantheon, their importance developed with considerable momentum. The official encouragement given to the cult by the royal family, with the resulting patronage given to it by the supporters of the Crown, is obviously a primary and palpable indication

---

[26] Charbonneaux, 135–6 and Pl. xxvi, 1 = Svoronos III Pl. 36, 14–5.

[27] E. Pfuhl and H. Möbius, *Die Ostgriechischen Grabreliefs* (Mainz, 1977–9), Nos. 156, 158, 170, 405, 852, 2087(?), 2098, 2102 (singe cornucopia); 250, 872 (double cornucopia).

[28] Fraser, *RFM*, Pls. 64 (*d*), 78 (*c*), 79 (*a–c*), 81 (*h*).   [29] Ibid., 110 n. 139.

of this importance, but, in addition, it is significant to note that far-reaching power was sometimes attributed to the divine pair. In the third century, these gods were occasionally called Theoi Soteres, or just Soteres, and in second-century Memphis they were sometimes attributed with an almost universal power.[30] This may have resulted in part from their chthonic associations, since chthonic deities in a sense control nature and life, and this idea of the power emanating from Isis and Sarapis may have made their assimilation to the royal couple particularly desirable.

The *dikeras*, transferred first to Arsinoe II in posthumous commemoration of her 'co-regency', symbolizing, in effect, Arsinoe and Philadelphus as Isis and Sarapis on earth, continued to be used and became the standard symbol of the joint rule in successive reigns. The earliest archaeological evidence for this symbolism at a mature stage of development may be seen in the coins of Philopator, which connect the royal couple with the divine couple and with the *dikeras*, but the association of the rulers with Isis and Sarapis is clear throughout the preceding reign of Euergetes and Berenike II. A group of inscriptions from Canopus records this king and queen as objects of joint dedications with Sarapis and Isis, and the extreme rarity of analogous dedications which associate other deities by name with the sovereigns indicates that Sarapis and Isis had some special, significant relation with the rulers which may even have extended to joint temples where the dedications were made (the Alexandrian Serapeum may have contained one such example of a joint shrine).[31] The *dikeras* in the Grand Procession may therefore have symbolized the joint cult of Sarapis and Isis, to whom some mark of honour might be expected in a festival on such a scale, especially in view of the fact that their cult was being given official, royal encouragement at the time. The (possible) *dikeras* upon the throne would indicate that the throne belonged to those gods, as the other thrones belonged to other gods, and the *dikeras* carried alone, as the attribute of Isis and Sarapis, joins the parade of other divine attributes appearing in this section of the Grand Procession.

[30] *Ptol. Alex.* i. 261.   [31] Ibid., 263.

Appendix III
Kallixeinos the son of Megakles,
Priest of Athena Lindia (*ILindos* 137)

In his edition of the inscriptions of Lindos, Ch. Blinkenberg published a dedication by Kallixeinos, the son of Megakles and the adopted son of Nikasidamos, who held the priesthoods of Athena Lindia, Zeus Polieus, and Artemis Kekoia (*ILindos* 137). The dedication, on a cylindrical base, is dated by the editor to *c.* 210 BC.[1] In his commentary on the inscription, Blinkenberg notes that this man was probably in his later career also a priest of Helios, since his name appears as the eponym on various amphora stamps. His reconstruction of the stemma of this large Lindian priestly family is given in *ILindos* i, p. 36, stemma 9 (Kallixeinos the son of Megakles is labelled *d*). On grounds of chronology (although his suggested date of *c.* 210 can no longer be accepted without further evidence), Blinkenberg also identifies the priest Kallixeinos with Kallixeinos of Rhodes, the author of *About Alexandria*; of further interest is the suggested connection with this Lindian family of the bronze sculptor Callixenus, who is mentioned in Pliny (*HN* xxxiv. 52; see pp. 159 ff.). Since the sculptor is known to have lived during the years 156 to 153 BC, Blinkenberg identifies him as the grandson of Kallixeinos the historian and priest, and labels him as figure *h* on stemma 9.

It is not our concern here to discuss the various hypothetical relationships within this complex Lindian family (which includes several members named Kallixeinos) as they are reconstructed in stemma 9, but only the likelihood of Blinkenberg's tentative identifications of a homonymous grandfather and grandson pair from the family with Kallixeinos of Rhodes and the bronze sculptor Callixenus, respectively. On the one hand, the silence of the sources concerning Kallixeinos of Rhodes does not argue against Blinkenberg, since the author's patronymic and his provenance within Rhodes are alike unknown; Kallixeinos would only have been called a 'Rhodian' outside his fatherland (e.g. by Athenaeus) regardless of whether his city within the island was Rhodes (the city), Lindos, Ialysos, or Kamiros. Since neither the family nor the provenance of the author can be pinned down, his identification with a contemporary, epigraphically attested Rhodian 'Kallixeinos' cannot be ultimately disproved. On the other hand, the paucity of available information concerning Kallixeinos of Rhodes combines with the frequent appearance of the name on the island to lessen

---

[1] Blinkenberg conjectured that Kallixeinos the priest belonged to *c.* 210 BC within the lacuna of the list of priests of Athena Lindia, and he tentatively inserted him under that year in his list of priests in *ILindos* i, p. 115. However, the newer fragment of the list of the priests of Athena Lindia (*Nuov. Suppl. rod.* 16) records successive officials, the first of whose term of office must begin between the years 228 and 216 BC (cf. ibid., adnot. ad loc.). No Kallixeinos appears within the list of priests for the following years, nor indeed do more than a very few other priests who were inserted into the hypothetical list for these years by Blinkenberg before the publication of the new fragment. Consequently, the date of *c.* 210 BC for *ILindos* 137 cannot be accepted on the evidence of Blinkenberg's hypothetical reconstruction of the list.

the probability of any specific identification. The name 'Kallixeinos' is especially prominent in Lindos (over 15 are listed in the Index to *ILindos*, compared with 8 in Rhodes, cf. Index to *IG* XII (1), and 1 in Kamiros, cf. Index to *Tit. Cam.*), which suggests that it was originally a Lindian name; although there may be, therefore, a slightly greater likelihood that the author came from Lindos than from any other Rhodian city, Kallixeinos of Rhodes *may* be the Lindian son of Megakles, but he may equally be any other contemporary Rhodian Kallixeinos who is mentioned in inscriptions, or indeed another who was either unrecorded or who has disappeared without trace. It is simply not possible to know, and Blinkenberg's confidence is unfounded.

The identification of Callixenus, the sculptor recorded in Pliny, with Kallixeinos, the grandson of the Lindian priest, poses greater problems. Although the sculptor and priest are about two generations apart (according to Blinkenberg's dating of the latter), which makes the suggestion that they are grandson and grandfather acceptable in chronological terms, it has been made clear in Chapter 4 that nothing whatsoever is known about Pliny's Callixenus except his occupation and approximate date. In the first place, Pliny does not give the artist's ethnic, and a Rhodian provenance cannot be assumed from him merely from the Latinized form of the name Kallixeinos since the name is attested elsewhere in Greece. (A few examples here will suffice: 6 Boeotians named Kallixenos appear in the Index to *IG* VII, among them inhabitants of Thespiai, Plataia, Hyettus, and Chorsiai; 3 Euboeans with Eretrian demotics are found in *IG* XII (9) 244 A, 26; 245 A, 392; 246 A, 151; an Amphissan Kallixenos appears in *IG* IX (1)^2 (3) 755 b, 17; two others are found in *IG* IX (1)^2 (1) 42, 3 and 25, 39 (from Herakleia probably in Oitaia); for Athenian Kallixenoi, see *PA* 8042–4 (cf. *APF* 9688 VI–VII); *APF* 8041 ff.; *IG* I^2 929, 104). Even if the sculptor was a Rhodian, the prominence of the name at Rhodes has been stressed, along with the resulting difficulty of identifying any two Rhodian Kallixeinoi. Various particular factors seem to preclude the identification of the sculptor with Kallixeinos of Rhodes (these have been discussed above; see pp. 163 ff.), but more general considerations argue against the likelihood of his identification with any other known Rhodian homonym, including the grandson of the priest of Athena Lindia. There is no signature of a Kallixeinos among over 100 known Rhodian sculptors (cf. *ILindos* i, pp. 55 ff.), and although this is not decisive, since his signature may not have been preserved, it is more telling that the name Kallixeinos does not appear within the families of known artists at Rhodes (see, e.g., *ILindos* stemmata 1, 6, 15). The profession tended to be taken up at Rhodes by other family members for generations, and there is no example besides Blinkenberg's stemma 9 in which an isolated member of a family appears as an artist. It is therefore unlikely that the sculptor Callixenus belonged to the large Lindian family whose members included the priest Kallixeinos the son of Megakles. Both of Blinkenberg's suggested identifications should therefore be rejected because of the lack of positive supporting evidence.

Indexes

A. GENERAL INDEX

This index is selective, and does not include references to modern editors.

B. SELECT INDEX OF GREEK WORDS

C. INDEX OF DOCUMENTS AND AUTHORS CITED

C.1. *Inscriptions*

C.2. *Papyri*

C.3. *Passages from Ancient Authors*